The Racing Coopers

The Racing Coopers

By *Arthur Owen*

With a foreword by Stirling Moss
and a preface by Charles and John Cooper

MOTORACES BOOK CLUB
CASSELL
London 1964

This Motoraces Book Club edition was produced in
1964 for sale to its members only by the proprietors,
Readers Union Ltd., at Aldine House, 10-13 Bedford
Street, London, W.C.2, and at Letchworth Garden City,
Herts. Full details of membership may be obtained from
our London address. The book is set in Baskeville type
and has been reprinted by Lowe & Brydone (Printers)
Ltd., London, N.W.10. It was first published by
Cassell & Co. Ltd.

FOREWORD

by STIRLING MOSS

SINCE the end of the Second World War, the increasing interest in cars and motoring in general has reacted on the sport, and in each season greater numbers of enthusiasts travel to the circuits. The racing calendar has become progressively more varied and exciting.

The expansion of motor racing is due in no small measure to the perseverance of such people as Charles and John Cooper, who, since the virtual rebirth of the sport, have worked tirelessly to improve the construction of their racing cars.

Cooper's have always been in the forefront of half-litre, or 500-c.c., car racing, a class that proved an exceedingly useful nursery for drivers, being a practical method of preparing a new works driver. In addition to this the races themselves possess excellent spectator value.

Motor racing successes give a considerable boost to our foreign market, as the latest figures show; in fact, it seems that exports have risen in conjunction with our racing successes.

I started my own racing career by buying a Cooper in 1948. Since then our paths have crossed continually, as I have been a works driver for the Company and have driven the Cooper Formula III, the Cooper-Alta, the Cooper-Climax sports car, and the Cooper Formula I at various times. At the beginning of 1958 I won the Argentine Grand Prix in a Cooper 1·9 Formula I car. In November 1958 I drove the Cooper-Climax 2·2 to victory in the Australian Grand Prix, and later in the New Zealand Grand Prix. I look forward to driving the even more powerful Cooper-Climax 2·5 later in 1959, as well as the Cooper-B.R.M. 2·5, and the Cooper-Borgward 1·9.

PREFACE

WHEN we built our first racing car in 1946, we little imagined that within ten years we would have produced over one thousand cars.

It must be admitted that it has been less worrying reading about it than actually doing it, but this book has recaptured many amusing incidents for us, and we are sure that it will do the same for the reader. In writing it, Arthur Owen has had our entire co-operation, which has been fully justified by our pleasure in reading what is, in effect, the official history of the Cooper Car Company.

The chief aim of any manufacturer of racing cars is to build a vehicle likely to win honour and prestige for the country of origin as well as for the individual constructor. It is for this reason that we use power units of British manufacture in all our works cars.

During our long association with the Coventry firm, they have regularly prepared our engines in seemingly impossibly short periods of time between Grand Prix races. This sort of service is all too often associated with Continental manufacturers, and British enthusiasts owe much to Mr. Lee and his associates who run the Coventry-Climax racing department so reliably.

Now that we have developed a raceworthy Formula I car, which enabled us to gain third place in the World Manufacturers Cup for racing car constructors, we look to the future with renewed enthusiasm and determination.

It has always been our policy to sell our products to private entrants and competitors and to encourage beginners at this, the greatest of all sports. We shall continue to do this, and we feel confident that the British challenge in Grand Prix racing will continue to grow in strength and quality.

CHARLES COOPER
JOHN COOPER

CONTENTS

LIST OF ILLUSTRATIONS

between pages 116 *and* 117

A*

INTRODUCTION

WHEN one has to record the events in the life of the average person, usually there is not very much to write about. In the case of the Coopers, father and son, I found that the reverse was the case; there was so much to write about that my greatest difficulty was to decide what to leave out of the book.

With a father who has been in turn motor-cyclist, inventor, Kay Don's mechanic, racing driver, pilot, and designer of aeroplanes and racing cars, what else could John Cooper be but what he is: probably the most successful racing car designer of this decade.

And with this father and son team, what else could one expect than that the Company created by them should have made more racing cars than any other on this earth?

But then, of course, the Coopers have the 'bug'.

One of the most deadly diseases known to man, or to woman, for that matter, is the 'bug'; deadly because there is no known cure for it. Breaking out in all sorts of odd places, it is one of the strangest phenomena of the twentieth century.

For instance, it is the 'bug' that makes the noble Spanish people go mad with joy when Fangio and Gonzales take the first two places in the Spanish Grand Prix; it is the 'bug' that makes every little village in Italy ring out with the stirring words '*Viva* Ascari', and then prostrates a whole nation at his sad loss. It is the 'bug' that makes Briggs Cunningham spend a million dollars on trying to win one sports car race at Le Mans, and Johnny stay in bed all the week, yet on Saturday wake the neighbours at some godforsaken hour by starting up his blown whatnot, and doing a Le Mans start up to Silverstone.

Why was the film *Genevieve* such a resounding success? Why, because the central characters depicted therein were badly bitten by the 'bug', so all the addicts went along to sympathize.

What made a brilliant young driver give up learning how to run hotels? Why, the 'bug', of course. What made a certain young lady give up discovering new comics for her father's theatre? Once again, the 'bug'.

When bitten by the 'bug', you will travel a thousand miles there and back to Rest and Be Thankful for perhaps two minutes racing, and then your home-made special may blow up on the line, so you won't even get that. But that will not cure you, no sir! You'll be back next time.

Perón, the late President of Argentina, and the present President of Venezuela have one thing in common: they both suffer from the 'bug'; likewise the King of Jordan, Prince Bertil of Sweden, Rubirosa, much-married friend of the stars, and Norman Wisdom are just as much in the grip of the 'bug' as the Finns in Djurgardsloppet or the Sicilian peasants who helped Stirling Moss get his car back on the road in the Targa Florio a year or so back. Two of the saddest cases of the 'bug' I have ever seen are Charles and John Cooper, but of the two, I feel more sorry for Charles. At sixty-three years of age, after a lifetime of suffering from the 'bug', surely now he is entitled to some respite? But oh dear no; only the other week he was up at four o'clock, driving the Cooper racing tender like a demon off to Monte Carlo, to enable one of his racing cars to compete in a Grande Epreuve and show the flag with some success on the Continent. To the Coopers, and to all those countless millions who suffer from it, please accept my sincerest condolences—but what am I saying; I've been bitten by the 'bug' myself!

Hurray for the Bug!

CHARLES COOPER

On 14th October 1893, the Stately Paris Home of Mr. and Mrs. Charles Renard Cooper was rudely shaken by the lusty yells of one Charles Newton Cooper who had seen fit to arrive on that day.

As head of the internationally famous theatrical company known as the Swiss Express Company, Charles Renard (stage name) had been hoping for a boy to carry on the unbroken family tradition dating back to eighteenth-century Drury Lane.

From the earliest possible age it would appear that baby Charles did not agree with the family verdict. When proud mama gave Charles dolls to play with, he threw them away and yelled; when mama showed Charles pretty story books, he yelled; when mama took baby Charles round to the theatre, he yelled. It appears that he only stopped yelling when on the way home he saw the butcher's boy fall off his bicycle; then he laughed so much he fell out of his pram.

To stop him yelling mama was almost ready to hire the butcher's boy for keeps, but Charles forestalled her by discovering *Cars*. For the record, it seems that Charles discovered cars at the same time as Léon-Bollée discovered that he could make a tricycle go with the aid of a horse or so under its bonnet. As far as young Charles was concerned, a visit to the Léon-Bollée was always good enough for a fall out of his pram. Whether these early experiences had any effect on his later life, who can say, but it can most definitely be said that he remained, and for that matter still remains, completely fascinated by anything on wheels.

After some years in Paris, Mrs. Renard moved to her mother-in-law's farm in the Pyrenees, and the Swiss Express Company went on a tour of England. Charles tasted the healthy life of the great outdoors; his greatest ambition was to mechanize a cow, but in this he failed miserably, the stolid cow becoming a most fearsome beast when Charles tried to screw sparking plugs on to its udders. When 'Pop' Renard returned from his tour he gave up trying to get the young Charles interested in the stage and decided that when the boy was old enough to leave school he would be apprenticed to an engineering firm. But shortly after this the family moved to England, and Charles completed his education at Tiffins School, Kingston.

As soon as he was able to sit on a motor-cycle Charles plagued his parents to buy him one, but they, with no little foresight, held out until he was old enough to hold a licence. Overcoming this late start, Charles soon caught up his pals, and within no time at all was the acknowledged Speed Champion of Kingston High Street.

Charles was also remarkably quick in taking his motor-cycle to pieces and putting it back again. (Unfortunately, when finished, he was usually left with several surplus parts, and a defunct engine.)

When he was fifteen, the young hopeful was apprenticed to Napier's of Acton, who were already very famous for their racing cars.

During the time he worked at Napier's, Charles went right through all branches of the factory and finished up in the repair shop. He remembers working on S. F. Edge's record-breaking car.

Charles stayed with Napier's until the outbreak of World War I, when he immediately volunteered for active service, and on 28th August 1914, he was drafted into the Army Service Corps, 3rd M.T. Mechanical Cavalry Division, in which he served with great distinction, going through the heaviest fighting without a scratch, only to be gassed at Valencienne in the 1918 campaign. His narrowest escape was in the Mons area in 1915. Having been on the move all day, the unit was ordered to bivouac in a small village; the men set out to find what shelter they could and Charles bagged for himself a nice dry haystack on the outskirts and was soon in the arms of Morpheus. He awoke with a shock to find it was broad daylight and that strange, guttural sounds were coming from just below the haystack. Fearing the worst, he chanced a quick peep over the top, and then wished he hadn't; he was completely surrounded by German soldiers camping in the field. Doing the only thing possible, Charles lay doggo, without food or water and hardly dared to breathe all that day, through the night and all the next day, until night fell again. By this time Charles was desperate, and was resigning himself to surrender when he had a stroke of good fortune. Some sharp commands came from the encampment, and then the sound of marching feet. The Germans were moving out. Charles wasted no time; he broke the lap record in the opposite direction!

He had completely lost his unit, but was still in one piece, and as luck would have it, he fell smack into the hands of an English infantry unit which was pressing the Germans back through the village. Charles fought with this unit for nearly three months when he caught up with his own unit, only to be nearly put in irons for desertion. It appeared that his platoon had been ordered out of the village shortly after Charles had gone off to find his haystack, and he had not been missed until later. Happily it was all sorted out, but from then onwards Charles made sure that he was banked on all sides by his own men before trusting friend Morpheus again!

When the war finished, Charles was still in the East Suffolk Hospital recovering from the effects of being gassed, and it was not until several months later that he was feeling well enough to think about starting work again. Work for Charles could mean only one thing: cars. Having discharged himself from hospital, he took the next train to London hoping to break into the car business.

After one or two setbacks, Charles talked his way into a small one-man business in Kingston called Derby Motors, and Mr. Derby, the one man in question, was persuaded to put him in charge of the firm's main business of buying Government surplus motor-cycles, reconditioning them, and then reselling them. Although he found the work interesting, Charles had a hankering to start up on his own, so as soon as he was able to get a little cash together he took a lease on a small builder's yard in Ewell Road, Surbiton, parted company with Mr. Derby, converted the yard into a garage, and commenced work under the name of Cooper's Garage.

One of Charles's boyhood chums was our old friend Kay Don; they had done many motor-cycle trials together, and after World War I Don had got a job with the Avon Tyre Company as a traveller, where he built up a fine connexion. In 1921 he bought a Wolseley Viper which he gave to Charles to modify. This car proved a great success and Kay Don won a Gold Star with it. From that time Charles Cooper did all Don's racing work and also acted as his manager. In 1922 Charles married Elsie Paul and in 1923 John was born. When Kay Don went on to Bugatti's, Charles took refresher courses at Molsheim and Strasbourg. Don went from success to success and the Don-Cooper team proved a very hard nut to crack.

Later, Charles got tied up with the Sunbeam Record car which was an experiment that did not quite succeed. Built for attempts on the outright World Speed Record, the car was always catching fire at the crucial moment, and did not achieve its main purpose. On 6th June 1927, Kay Don got his 120 m.p.h. Brooklands Badge with a Sunbeam and on 28th May 1928, his 130 m.p.h. Badge with the same car, tuned by Charles Cooper. He was the first person to gain an award for this speed. Until 1934, the Kay Don-Cooper set-up worked satisfactorily, and the successes gained, particularly at Brooklands, would fill a book. During this period, Charles Cooper drove an M.G. Magnette and raced in a team with George Eyston and Kay Don.

Between the two World Wars, Charles became the first member of the Redhill Flying Club, and learned to fly in under two months. He managed to get passed out as a certified pilot after only thirty hours' flying time, something of a record. Charles bought himself a 'Flying Flea' kit, which was based on a design by a French inventor, Minuet. The complete parts for the plane cost one hundred and fifty pounds, including an Austin 7 engine. Charles was able to fly to Southend quite easily with it, and it used barely two gallons of Pratts (in those days) per hour. The midget plane was able to land on a postage stamp, and was very widely used by amateur flyers all over Europe until the French Government banned its sale owing to the number of fatalities. Charles eventually sold his to a film company. Later he bought a Miles Hawk monoplane with a Gypsy Major engine, and when World War II broke out, it was stored in the Cooper Garage, where it stayed until VE day when it was bought by Dennis Poore.

In 1934, owing to expanding business, Charles decided to get a larger garage, and he managed to get suitable premises down the street at 243 Ewell Road, where the garage is now. In those days it was only a large shed, and Charles employed three people; in 1942 the first extension was added, and two years later the place was rebuilt. Charles himself built most of the extensions, and they have stood the test of time; so, should he be short of cash, he can always get five shillings per hour as a builder! At the present time, further extensive alterations are being made.

JOHN COOPER

DATE—17th July 1923; place—Kingston, London. Born in a heatwave to Charles and Elsie Cooper, one little bundle christened John Newton Cooper, weight normal, hair black, eyes blue, ambitions none, father's ambition—that he should discover motor-cycles and cars very soon.

So soon, in fact, that almost as soon as he could toddle, John Newton was actively assisting his father by removing the grease and oil from the floor of the garage and wiping it off on to his rompers and then licking off the stains: true, he wasn't very sick afterwards, due, as his father put it, to the Castrol base.

John's kindergarten was the garage. Practically his first word was 'glug', which his father swore meant 'car' in baby language. As soon as mother was not looking, father would kidnap John and rush off to the garage to sit him in the latest monstrosity of a car he had created, and with sundry noises off, such as brummp, crunch, zzzz, try to suggest to John in a subtle way that he was out in front in the European G.P. Naturally John appreciated the position, but mother did not appreciate the extra change of nappies.

Wherever father went, John went too: Brooklands, Redhill Flying Club, Trials, everywhere. Mother gave up the fight, she knew she was beaten; she had lost her son to the Speed Bug.

John soon had his first toy car, made by his father. It was most successful, John winning sixty-five Grandes Epreuves with it before writing it off completely in an unholy prang with an Austin 'Chummy' that backed into the garage. Nothing daunted, Charles Cooper began making plans for IT. When John was safely in bed, his father would creep into the garage and work on IT; a tired Charles would turn in early in the morning for a few hours' sleep, after carefully hiding IT away from prying eyes. Mother knew something was up, but if she had guessed what IT was she would have blown her top. Months went by, and even the iron stamina of the older Cooper was feeling the strain; what with racing activities with Kay Don, the garage, and IT, Charles was beginning to look a little green at the gills. And then IT was finished just in time for John's eighth birthday. And wonder of wonders, the secret had not leaked out. What was IT? What else but John's first real car. When it was presented to its new owner, he was delirious with joy, and what boy of eight would not be equally so. To quote John's own words: 'The shock of seeing this beautiful piece of machinery, to be told it was all mine, *and* to be told that within a week or so I would be allowed to race it at Brooklands was too much. I am afraid I wept.' Says Charles Cooper: 'Yes, he wept all right, but only because he wasn't allowed to take it down that very day!'

John's first car had a Francis Barnett motor-cycle engine and gearbox set into a home-made chassis; the engine was in front, chain driven to gearbox, and then chain driven to the back axle, with half-elliptic springs on front and quarter-elliptic springs on back; four-wheel drum brakes, three-speed gearbox, weight about two hundred pounds, and it developed about 9–10 b.h.p., with a maximum speed of about 40 m.p.h.

The next time Charles went to Brooklands, John went too, with *his* car and had a rare old time with it in the paddock. Surely he must have been the youngest racing driver ever to appear at a race-track with a pukka racing car.

John used his Francis Barnett whenever he got the chance for the next three years, and then his father thought it was time to design something faster and more up-to-date for him. He got to work on John's Racing Car Mark II. About this time Charles had a spare 'Flying Flea' engine, so he decided to build the new car round it, and on John's twelfth birthday he was presented with the Mark II.

This was really ingenious; nothing had been spared to make it an up-to-the-minute racer. The engine was the highly modified Austin 7; it had high lift cams, twin carbs, and a special crankshaft, and the car weighed about seven hundred-weight and developed about 35 b.h.p. The most unusual features were the fifteen-inch wheels. When various knowledgeable gents saw them, they shook their heads sadly at the use of such wheels for the first time on a racing car. Little did they realize that within fourteen years, they would be standard on all 500-c.c. racing cars.

The Mark II was highly successful, and had a maximum speed in the region of 90 m.p.h., which in 1935–6 was no mean speed with an Austin 7 based car. John learned a tremendous amount from the Mark II. Although still in his teens, he was gathering experience by constant practice. The car was sturdily built and could stand up to a hammering, which it certainly got when used over grass tracks, and it was not pensioned off by John until he started taking an interest in motor-cycles.

Eric Brandon, who lived down the road, and John, got together with four other lads and formed a club to buy and race motor-cycles. They bought a Rudge and a two-stroke Excelsior. The Rudge cost them four and sixpence and the two-stroke one pound, and after a couple of weeks they bought another two-stroke, this time slightly cheaper—eighteen and ninepence, to be exact. Having hired a field at Thames Ditton, the young stars had some monumental dices, with honours even between Brandon and Cooper. Then John bought a dirt-track Douglas Twin for four pounds, and that was the end of Brandon and Co. But not for long. Brandon retaliated by buying a fairly new Rudge, and from then, we have a slight conflict of opinions; Brandon swears that he saw Cooper off, and Cooper swears he saw Brandon off!

The club members had strict instructions from their parents to push their bikes to the field, as most of them were too young to have licences. These instructions were not carried out to the letter, with the result that one day, they were almost caught in the act. As all the paid-up members were riding down a long avenue towards the field, the leader caught sight of a policeman in the distance. He shouted, 'Copper!' All members immediately dismounted and began pushing. As they came abreast of the policeman, he stopped John and asked if he had been riding his bike. John replied very innocently that he had not, but the policeman was not satisfied and asked why the engine was smoking. John replied that it must be the heat of the day. The policeman gave him a hard look, and waved him on. Needless to say, the club members pushed their bikes to the field from then on.

When John reached the age of fifteen, he left Surbiton County Grammar School and went to work in his father's garage. Having carefully put away half his salary each week, after four months John had saved twelve pounds; plus the three pounds he already had from the sale of his Douglas Twin, there was now fifteen pounds in the kitty. This sum enabled John to branch out into the second-hand car market with the object of buying either a Bugatti or a Bentley. The dealers refused to see eye to eye with him on the value of these marques and, furthermore, took great exception to John's cash offer of fifteen pounds for one of their choice products, so much so that the old adage that the customer is always right went by the board, and John was unceremoniously thrown out.

When a sadder and wiser John returned home, his father came to the rescue. Taking John's fifteen pounds, he went out the next day and purchased a three-wheeled Morgan, which John agreed was quite good value for fifteen pounds. That father had paid another twenty-five pounds on top of John's fifteen was not a thing that Charles thought expedient to mention! John had great fun with the Morgan. With its water-cooled engine working overtime, it could do 90 m.p.h. The time it took from place A to place B was sometimes so quick, that Charles began to wonder whether it would be more prudent to let his offspring charge round the outer circuit at Brooklands, rather than break his neck on the roads. Fortunately, John, being a sensible lad, soon saw the folly of his ways, and slowed down to safer speeds. Oddly enough, this happened after his father said he would break his —— neck if he caught him speeding on the road again!

As John began to show an interest in toolmaking, he was apprenticed to a subsidiary of Hawkers where he learned the trade thoroughly. When he had finished his apprenticeship, John started up on his own in Surbiton and was very successful. Then, as skilled manpower was at a premium, he was directed by the Ministry of Labour to the Admiralty Tool Works where he spent four years working on secret work, including one-man submarines. As he would like to have been a pilot, he tried to get transferred to the Air Force, but the Admiralty would not release him until about two months before the war ended, when he was drafted into the R.A.F. When discharged he went back into the family business, as his father was in hospital following a car accident. The youthful enthusiasm of the son combined with the more mature judgement of the father proved an ideal partnership, and the Cooper Garage prospered accordingly. Charles had built up a first-class business in new cars, and with agencies for Vauxhall and Ford, John spent a fair amount of time on the selling side.

By this time, romance had entered John's life in the form of one Miss Pauline Marie Theresa Elizabeth Brady, who, by some odd coincidence, had been born in the same road as John, Fawcett Road, Kingston. Miss Brady had been keen on ice skating and John had been keen on motor-cycles, so their spheres of interest had differed and they had never met until just before the end of the war, going home on leave, John had been introduced to Pauline, and ice skating and motor-cycles forgotten, the couple spent the week-end on John's 28-foot boat, getting in the way of Captain Charles Cooper.

Needless to say, it was not very long before Captain Charles lost his first mate to the aforesaid Miss Brady, who in turn, lost her title of 'Miss' and became Mrs. J. Cooper, to the great relief of all concerned—John's because he could not live without her, Charles's because he thought she was the nicest girl that John had ever met and, furthermore, because he was fed up with fishing John out of the drink every time he absentmindedly fell over a rope.

THE BIRTH OF THE COOPER '500'

THROUGH all the years Eric Brandon and John had been friendly, quite often Eric would drop into the garage for a chat about racing cars. A subject that was always cropping up was the expense involved in racing, which placed it right out of the reach of the average driver. Both Charles and John were of the opinion that this could be overcome by racing small cars with J.A.P., Vincent H.R.D., or similar motor-cycle engines. This had already been tried by Colin Strang of Harrow with a small Special, built by himself from a Fiat 'Mouse' chassis, with a T.T. Vincent H.R.D. power unit, and also by Clive Lones, using an Austin 7 chassis with a T.T. J.A.P. power unit. Both these designs had been successful, but, of course, the drawback had been the lack of organized races for this type of car.

Nevertheless, the idea appealed to the Coopers, and they decided to build two midget cars to conform to the formula for 500-c.c. racing cars, one for Eric and one for John. At the same time, they would build a sports car for use on the road. The Cooper '500s' were based on a Fiat '500' chassis, using a Speedway J.A.P. engine for the motive power. The two front suspension units were united by a modified frame to give individual springing to each wheel, and the engine was mounted behind the driver and drove a solid axle through a Triumph motor-cycle clutch and gearbox and single chain sprocket. The steering column was centralized, and short driving shafts were provided with universal joints made by Ford's, allowing for independent rear suspension. The wheels were standard Fiat, and the brakes were Lockheed-pattern hydraulic. The engine was air cooled by passing an air vent tube along the chassis. Altogether, it was a most ingenious car, developing approximately 45 b.h.p. at 6,000 revs, and weighing about 550 lb. unladen.

Starting from scratch in June 1946, with the combined brains of the Coopers plus Brandon, the first car was completely built in five weeks and was entered for the Prescott Hill Climb on 28th July. Mark I was surprisingly graceful in line for a one-off job. However, being low on the ground and very light in weight, yet having the powerful J.A.P. engine at the back, it presented many problems. If the revs were not kept up, the engine would stall; secondly, unless the engine was kept clean by steady revving up and down, the plug would oil up; thirdly, when getting away from the line, if the revs were not built up enough and the clutch was not let out quickly, the engine would stall; fourthly, if the revs went up too high, even momentarily, it might result in a bent valve.

The day before the Prescott Hill Climb, Eric and John tried out the new box of tricks on a quiet road near the garage. Needless to say, it did not remain a quiet road for long, but before the confused neighbourhood could organize a riot squad, the gearbox mounting fractured and the car had to be towed back to the garage for repair. However, the boys had learned quite a lot about the handling qualities of the car. Nothing daunted, they repaired the car and took it up to Prescott the following day. Although it was still on the secret list, as soon as the programmes were issued, everybody wanted to see the new '500' perform and John really gave her the gun, braced himself for the fray and let out the clutch. The back wheels turned like mad, the car started to move, and then there was an unhealthy bang and silence. The engine bearers were no longer on speaking terms with the frame. Repairs à la Cooper having been made, the car was ready for practice next morning. This time John got away in a cloud of smoke, and disappeared round the bend in no time at all, only to come unstuck at Pardon where, changing down, he missed a gear and up went the revs; result, one bent valve. Bad luck after such a fine start.

At the next Prescott meeting, John tried again and in practice went quite well, only to come unstuck once more in the competition proper with broken bearer bars and gearbox mountings. Obviously, the J.A.P.'s 45 b.h.p. had too much poke for the rigidly constructed chassis. The answer was a flexible mounting and this proved successful in taking the sudden shock of the terrific on-off acceleration. With this lesson learned, the next move was the famous Brighton Speed Trials, and as the lowest class was the 850-c.c. racing class, the Cooper was entered in that, and showed a clean pair of heels to all and sundry. Time—35·81 seconds. As this was positively the first ever appearance at Brighton of a 500-c.c. car, it is rather interesting to note that on its first appearance at Brighton in 1956, a 250-c.c. Cooper/J.A.P. did the kilometre in 46 seconds, just over ten seconds slower than the first 500-c.c.

To close its first racing season, the Mark I was entered for the West Hants and Dorset M.C.'s West Coast Speed Trials where Brandon showed a sneak preview of his prowess by making the best time of the day in the 1,100-c.c. Class, doing the quarter mile sprint in 24·42 seconds, against an overall best time of the day by Salvadori of 23·32 in a 2-litre Riley. John was only a fraction behind Brandon and did 24·73 to take second place in the 1,100-c.c. Class. These results not only heartened the Cooper entourage, but shook the racing fraternity to the core. It was decided not to enter the last Prescott Hill Climb, but to concentrate on building the second Mark I for Brandon.

That the motoring Press was beginning to sit up and take notice of the little car was evidenced by a whole page layout in the 17th January issue of *The Autocar*, which gave full details of the Cooper Special, together with a very fine illustration of the stripped down chassis, under the heading: 'The Cooper 500—ingenious half-litre racing car, built at low cost with excellent results.'

At the opening of the 1947 Racing Season, right on the front grid were the two Mark I Coopers with their determined jockeys ready to show their big brothers the way home. 'Give us the races and we'll finish the job,' said John, or words to that effect.

The first event entered was the Prescott Hill Climb, and here the Coopers refused to shine, being beaten by Colin Strang, Clive Lones, and Frank Aikens in their respective Specials. This defeat was subsequently avenged at the first ever circuit race for half-litre cars run at Gransden Lodge Aerodrome and in a field of four, Aikens, Strang, Bacon, and Brandon, the last-named proved the most reliable and came home to win by a comfortable margin at 60·21 m.p.h.

On to the Brighton Speed Trials, where the speed committee had now put in a pukka 500-c.c. Class, and here John won the Class in 32·57 seconds.

The next week-end John and Eric went to Poole for the Open Speed Trials and were outstandingly successful, winning every class up to 1,500-c.c., although hard pressed by 'Kitty' Lones in the 500-c.c. and 750-c.c. Classes.

Although the Poole success was in a relatively minor club meeting, it was important in so far as it focused the attention of the motoring world on the '500s'. At the next important Hill Climb at Prescott, in a field of five '500s', Brandon hit the high spots on practice day with a run in under fifty seconds, which shook the boys more than somewhat. Then, as in so many meetings since, it rained on the day and the hill became a skating rink, so Brandon and Cooper received their first baptism of 'Coopering' in the wet. In the ensuing dance up the hill, the Coopers did the 'mambo' in the best Victor Silvester tradition, and finished with a very endearing 'rock and roll' going round the top bend; but get to the top they did in the following times—Brandon 53·46 seconds and Cooper 55·75 seconds. And so they won the 500-c.c. Class split only by F. Aikens in his Special, who made a very fine run in 54·71 seconds. John had an added disadvantage in having to drive with one hand badly burned and in bandages from an accident the previous week.

Another Class win was gained the following week at the Marston Speed Trials with Brandon first and Cooper second, and then to wind up the season, Shelsley Walsh Hill Climb where the officials had kindly put on a special Class for 500-c.c. racing cars. This was a well-attended event and all the budding '500' specialists tried to get their cars on the line, with the result that ten cars turned up. One of the most interesting of the new arrivals in the Class was the Bond Special. Built by Laurie Bond, it was a true miniature car, knee high to a grasshopper, absolutely springless, and with a Rudge engine driving the front wheels by chain. With all this clever and varied machinery about, John and Eric were prepared for a fierce tussle for leadership of the Class, but it was not to be, and the two Cooper cars walked away with the spoils, being over two seconds faster than the third man, Colin Strang (Strang Special). Unhappily, Laurie Bond pranged in his first entry, fortunately without serious damage.

The consistency of the two Cooper cars in their first full racing season had aroused the interest of many people in various parts of the globe, and Coopers were being deluged with orders and enquiries. At a family conference the Coopers decided to form a new company to produce racing cars only, and to put a block of twelve cars into immediate production to be modified and improved in the light of the first season's racing.

The new series Cooper was completely redesigned on the drawing board and emerged lighter and sleeker.

13

COOPER RACING '500' SPECIFICATION

Engine: Unsupercharged single cylinder 497-c.c. J.A.P. racing engine. 80-mm. bore, by 99-mm. stroke. Pushrod operated overhead valves. Producing 45 b.h.p. at 6,000 r.p.m., using dope on a 14 to 1 compression ratio. Highly polished flywheels, connecting rod, and valve gear. The total loss oiling system, pressure fed to the big end and valve gear by a duplex Pilgrim pump supplied from a separate oil tank ensures that the supply of oil to the pump is always fresh and clean. Air cooling by light alloy ducting from the nose of the car on to the exhaust side of the engine. B.T.H. racing magneto. Amal racing carburettor, gravity fed from $1\frac{1}{4}$-gallon tank mounted in the streamlined head fairings.

Transmission: By chain to Burman multi-plate clutch and gearbox, thence by chain to the centre of the rear axle and through universal half-shafts to the rear wheels. Racing type four speed Burman gearbox.

Chassis: Immensely strong and light chassis, with box section side members braced by tubular cross members. Independent suspension, to all four wheels by transverse leaf springs and wishbones, clamped by telescopic double-acting hydraulic shock absorbers. Burman steering| box, three-spoke steering wheel and divided track rod. Cast electron wheels with eight-inch brake drums, cast integrally, and 400 by 15 Dunlop tyres. Lockheed hydraulic brakes on all wheels, with double leading shoes on the front ones.

Body: Single-seater aluminium body, mounted on welded steel framework, rigidly attached to the main frame. Dunlopillo upholstery and racing type perspex windscreen.

Dimensions: Wheelbase—7′ 1″; front track—4′ 1″; rear track—3′ 11″; weight—520 lbs.

The Press had taken a liking to the little motor-cycle cars and on 5th November 1947, *The Motor* gave John Cooper a whole page to himself under the heading, 'Dennis May Introduces John Cooper. All Class and No Betty Martin', and gave a very full description of the single-seater Cooper. This kind of write-up kept popping up in all the leading motoring journals, and in most cases the various scribes went out of their way to heap praise on the minute Cooper organization.

FROM COOPERING IN FUN TO COOPERING IN EARNEST

AMONG the first people to order the series Coopers were Sir Francis Samuelson and Stirling Moss, closely followed by Stan Coldham, 'Curly' Dryden, P. W. K. Page, Spike Rhiando, and G. Saunders. These new recruits, plus John Cooper and Eric Brandon, presented a strong hand against the less organized one-off specials. The 1948 season proved that young Stirling Moss was a 'natural', that all the above drivers had taken to the Cooper driving technique like fish to water, that a Cooper could corner faster and safer than ninety-five per cent of other racing cars, and, most important of all to the average racing enthusiast, that whatever shape you were, be it six foot three or five foot, eighteen stone or seven stone, the sturdy little Cooper would fit you, give of its best and give you a fast and safe ride for your money, a fact more than borne out by such a well-known personality as Bertie Bradnack, weight approximately eighteen stone and height six foot three in recent years.

The season started off with a Class win by John Cooper at the Vintage S.C.C. Luton Hoo Speed Trials. That the series Cooper was an improvement on the Mark I was shown by the times of John and Eric, for John, with the Mark II, had a best time of 89·57 seconds and Eric, driving the Mark I, was second in the Class with 91·20, nearly two seconds slower. Sir Francis Samuelson had not quite settled down with his Mark II Cooper and muffed his run.

On 9th May, Stirling Moss appeared with his cream coloured Cooper for his first meeting at Prescott. He showed a little of the promise that was to come, and finished fourth in the half-litre class, setting up a new class record of 50·01 seconds, only to have this very fine time beaten on the last run up the hill by the old campaigners, Brandon, Strang, and Lones. For the rest of the season, eighteen-year-old Stirling was like a comet going up and up. Out of fifteen events entered, he won eleven, was third once, fourth twice and unplaced once, surely a record that will stand for all time, and made not with the aid of mirrors, but with the aid of the sturdy little Cooper.

The outstanding exploits of Moss did not complete the

Cooper saga for 1948, as John and Eric were also notching up win after win in their own right.

Spike Rhiando had adapted his Cooper to take an 8–80 J.A.P. engine and used it in the B.R.D.C. Manx Cup Race with some success. John, always receptive to a new idea, immediately modified his chassis to take the larger engine. That Spike had stumbled on to something would be an understatement. On 5th June at the Brighton and Hove Stanmer Park Speed Trials, John's win in the 1,100-c.c. Class was nearly three seconds faster than Stirling Moss's win in the 500-c.c. Class.

On 12th June at Shelsley Walsh, John put in one of his finest climbs and won the 1,100-c.c. Class in 40·70 seconds, at the same time breaking the Class record and taking the record for the fastest unsupercharged car. Brandon quietly cleaned up the 500-c.c.s in a time of 44·16 seconds.

On to Prescott on 13th June, and here again John took the Cooper Twin up fast enough to gain a Class win, this time in the 1,500-c.c. Class, Brandon taking the 750-c.c. Class.

Once again, at Prescott on 12th September, John won the 1,100-c.c. Class in 52·67, this time in the wet. Needless to say, Brandon won the 750-c.c. Class in 52·43. During the actual climb, Brandon was able to control the '500' better than John could the 1,100-c.c. with its extra power, and consequently registered a slightly better time. That a wet hill is a great leveller of cars big and small has been proved many times before and since.

While this was going on, other Cooper owners were getting into the act. At Bo'ness on 26th June, S. A. Coldham won the Class from three other competitors.

Spike Rhiando took the 1,100-c.c. Class with his adapted Cooper, time 37·60 seconds, beating such a renowned opponent as D. C. Fry in his Freikaiserwagen.

Stirling Moss cleaned up the opposition at Brough with Coopers second and third. He beat 'Kitty' Lones at the Bouley Bay Hill Climb, Jersey, these two being the only entrants in the 500-c.c. Class, and followed on by winning at Great Auclum from Brandon and Strang.

Now in really great form, Stirling squeezed home to a narrow victory over Hartwell (Monaco Special) and Brandon (Cooper) at the Boscombe Speed Trials.

With this line of four victories in the bag, Stirling could be forgiven for thinking that the Brighton Speed Trials would be another Cooper hand-out, but as it transpired, the reverse was the case. All the Cooper cars were well and truly beaten by one G. R. Hartwell in his Monaco Special. As Charles Cooper put it, 'Just as one marque is running away with all the races, along comes a complete outsider to beat up the favourite and put things back on an even keel again. That's what makes motor racing the great sport it is.'

Brighton was really a turn-up for the book as both Moss and Brandon were beaten by 'Curly' Dryden in a sister Cooper, and the Freikaiserwagen beat up the Coopers in the 1,100-c.c. Class to gain its revenge for Bo'ness.

The first meeting held on the new Goodwood Circuit included a 500-c.c. race, and the Cooper boys were anxious to avenge their defeat at Brighton, and in a field of nine starters, five were Coopers: Dryden, Moss, Brandon, Samuelson and Coldham. These were ranged against Hartwell (Monaco Special), the winner at Brighton, Truman and Strathcarron (Marwyns) and Bacon (F.H.B. Special). In this race, Moss ran away from the field, Brandon stalled on the line, but recovered and gave chase, Strathcarron and Bacon both blew up, leaving only Truman (Marwyn) and Hartwell (Monaco) of the specials, in the chase. Moss went like a bomb and finished on his own with Brandon and Dryden second and third.

A week later at Shelsley Walsh, Stirling Moss made mincemeat of the 500-c.c. Class record and although Colin Strang put in a wonderful climb, he had to give Moss best. In this event all the '500s' ran in the 750-c.c. Class.

The next event was really the most important of the whole season. The R.A.C., having successfully negotiated with the Air Ministry for a lease on Silverstone Aerodrome for a one year experimental period, decided to put on a full-scale 500-c.c. race to precede the Grand Prix race they were running on 2nd October. The race was to be limited to thirty cars, which seemed a bit optimistic at the time, and the chosen thirty would race for fifty miles. Prizes were to be fifty pounds first, thirty pounds second, and twenty pounds third. With all this 'lolly' flying around every '500' that could get to Silverstone was got there in a hurry, and the final entry was twenty-six cars of all shapes and sizes.

The race was started by Earl Howe, and Moss (Cooper) and Strang (Strang) got off to a fine start, followed by Cooper (Cooper), Strathcarron (Marwyn), Coward (Cowlan), Dryden

(Cooper), and Aikens (Aikens Special). Rhiando (Cooper), Fry (Freikaiserwagen), Bosisto (Buzzie II), and Brandon (Cooper) were left at the post and Page (Cooper) broke his final drive chain on the line. Saunders (Cooper) broke a chain in the first lap, Messenger (Messenger Special) was also out after one lap; Bosisto, after his bad start, started pressing and broke his gearbox. Strang seized up on the third lap, and Moss was then firmly in the lead, with Rhiando second, having come through the field, Dryden third, and John Cooper fourth, and Coward close behind. Strathcarron and Gibbs (M.A.C. Special) were soon out and 'Curly' Dryden's Cooper came unstuck with the front engine mounting broken. Moss was still in front by about a second from Rhiando with John Cooper third and Coward, driving very well indeed, fourth.

Then a very common Cooper malady struck out Moss—an engine sprocket nut came off. Spike Rhiando then took the lead with John Cooper second, Coward third, and the rest of the field thinning rapidly, although Page had rejoined the race. Clark (A.S.A.), Flather (Marott), and Smith (Smith) all retired, soon to be followed by C. F. Smith (C.F.S.), Aikens (Aikens), Grose (Grose) and Wharton (Wharton). This left nine cars still running of which six were Coopers. By this time the four leaders were Rhiando first, Cooper second, Samuelson third and Brandon fourth, motoring very well, having passed Coward, who had to pull into the pits for temporary repairs after a very good drive. John Cooper tried very hard to catch the flying Rhiando, but could not quite make it and Spike received the chequered flag at a race average of 60·68 m.p.h. Coopers filled the first four places.

And so on to the last race of the season, a thirty-two-mile race organized by the B.M.C.R.C. and run on Dunholme Airfield. Of the first four placed at Silverstone, only Spike Rhiando turned up, but Moss was present, determined to wipe out the previous week's débâcle. Thirteen cars went to the starting line, six Coopers, one Marwyn, and six one-off specials. The field got away to a good start, Dryden going into the lead, followed by Moss, Strathcarron, and Aikens. The pace became very hot and Strathcarron's Marwyn was the first casualty, the engine seizing solid. Aikens went into a corner too fast and slid right off the road. Moss began pressing Dryden and these two, dicing madly for the lead, were shaken to see Rhiando pass them both. The pace got hotter and hotter and Rhiando's engine began to die out and he was passed by

Moss as though he were standing still. Dryden would not let Moss get away and chased him as hard as he could, but Stirling held him off to win with the magnificent average of 78·56 m.p.h. Coldham (Cooper) filled the minor position.

Back in Surbiton, Charles and John Cooper took stock of the season's successes. Out of sixteen events entered, Cooper cars had won fourteen, their only defeats being the early Prescott meeting and the Brighton Speed Trials. It was a triumphant vindication of their policy of laying down a line of series production racing cars. They had made the racing world sit up, and the lads were not slow in showing their appreciation of a successful marque. Orders began to pour in for Cooper cars, not only from England, but from such places as Ceylon, Finland, Jersey, Belgium, Scandinavia, and many other European countries. The last thing that John wanted to do was to rest on his laurels, and after a chat with his father it was decided to go into full-scale production with the little Cooper cars. As they had also produced a prototype sports car with a four-cylinder Vauxhall engine of 1½-litre capacity, they were prepared to make this to individual specification. In addition, it was decided to modify slightly the Cooper Mark II and call the new model the Mark II

The company also offered the '1,000' Cooper with a choice of two engines, the H.R.D. Black Shadow or the 996-c.c. J.A.P. Sprint engine.

MARK III NEEDS A PASSPORT

During the 1949 season, the extension of half-litre racing both at home and abroad brought many new drivers into the public eye. Here was the ideal training ground for the budding Grand Prix driver, and one teenager particularly impressed Charles and John Cooper. His name was Peter J. Collins, then aged seventeen, and he was duly noted as a probability for high honours later. As judges of motor racing talent the Cooper family have no peer, as can be seen from their record of works drivers: Brandon, Cooper himself, Moss, Leston, Stuart Lewis-Evans, Bueb, Russell, Bill Whitehouse, Salvadori, MacDowell (remember him in the 1955 T.T.?), Ken Carter, Alan Brown, and Brabham. They have never made a mistake in eleven years, a proud record.

April 16th turned out to be a red letter day at the Cooper Garage. John waltzed around like a cat on hot bricks when news reached him that a Cooper car had won its first victory abroad, in Ceylon of all places; the fastest time of the day in the Hill Climb, an excellent start to what proved to be another fine season.

The day before, Eric Brandon had won the Brough Airfield Races at 55 m.p.h. and five days later, another newcomer had his first Cooper win: J. F. Westcott came in first at 62·30 m.p.h. in the Bristol M.C. and L.C.C. Lulsgate Twenty-Mile Race.

May 8th saw the Cooper '500' gain a win in the Helsinki '500' race, this proving to be the forerunner of '500' racing on the Continent. During 1949, races for 500-c.c. cars were held in the following countries: Belgium, Sweden, Italy, Holland, Norway, Switzerland, in that order.

On the home front, the R.A.C. had included a 500-c.c. race in their programme for the Silverstone meeting, and in an exceptionally large field, of which nearly fifty per cent were Coopers, it was notable that Charles Cooper decided to drive and Don Parker (the little man who was to prove such a thorn in the Coopers' side in later years) also entered. In the actual race, Brandon (Cooper) retired early. Moss (Cooper) soon took the lead and stayed in front to win fairly easily from Dryden (Cooper), with Aston (Cooper) third.

MARK III NEEDS A PASSPORT

So far so good, but on 18th May there was to be a sterner test, the Goodwood race meeting. John Cooper attended, although far from well after a bad attack of pneumonia. Definitely against doctor's orders, this, but it did do him good, and when Coldham and Dryden came home first and second in their respective Coopers, he sent the last of the streptococci packing for good and all. Stirling was in great form that afternoon. After retiring in the 500-c.c. race, he made amends in the Second Easter Handicap by winning easily from George Abecassis at the very fast speed of 79·76 m.p.h.—this, of course, with the 1,000-c.c. Cooper. The next six places were also filled by Coopers, with John Cooper seventh and Charles Cooper tenth; so many Coopers, in fact, that one might be forgiven for thinking this was a Cooper meeting, which, indeed, it was.

A week later the name of Cooper was on the lips of the fans in Brussels and the delighted Belgians clapped heartily at the sight of three Cooper cars finishing the 500-c.c. race first, third, and fourth, with W. S. Aston winning in 72·30 m.p.h., Stan Coldham third, and Sir Francis Samuelson fourth. Second place was taken by Don Parker in his Special. Eric Brandon stayed in England to do the Prescott Hill Climb and register his customary win in the 500-c.c. Class and a new Class record in a time of 48·40 seconds.

Stirling Moss was by now looking for fresh fields to conquer, and together with John Cooper and George Abecassis, he made the journey over to the Isle of Man for the Manx Cup. This was a race of sad memories for Charles Cooper, for whilst practising for it fifteen years earlier, Kay Don had crashed badly, killing his mechanic and severely injuring himself. This tragic accident had so overwhelmed Don, that he has never raced again, and consequently England lost one of her greatest drivers.

The three Coopers had Twin J.A.P. engines of 996 c.c. capacity, and Charles Cooper was hoping they would put up a good show against the much heavier machinery entered in the race. His faith was justified very quickly when Stirling put up the fastest lap of the day against a 2-litre Ferrari, driven by D. Folland, Heath's Alta, Fairman's 2-litre Riley, a Cisitalia, and many other blown sports cars. In fact, Stirling would probably have won if the gremlins had not got into his engine causing a mag-drive to shear. George Abecassis had crashed badly in practice the day before, luckily without serious injury, and John did not have the best of luck with his engine, which

B

had oiled a plug and was missing at peak revs. Nevertheless, he finished a very creditable fifth.

The next overseas victory for Coopers was on 28th May in Sweden at the Sharpnack Races, the Cooper marque taking first, third, and fourth places, and on the following day, fourth place in the Swedish Grand Prix.

Stirling Moss, having so nearly won the Manx Cup, decided to 'have a go' in foreign parts and entered for the Italian Lake Garda races, which were for 2-litre and 1,100-c.c. cars, both races being run simultaneously. Stirling did Coopers proud on race day. In a first-class field, including such stars as Villoresi, Count Sterzi, and Tardini, Moss finished well in front of all the 1,100-c.c. cars, and third overall in the race. At this, the first appearance of a Cooper, the Italian racing crowd, usually extremely knowledgeable, did not reckon that such a new-fangled contraption would do well, but after seeing the contraption perform, they were quick to register their approval by giving Moss a wonderful ovation.

On the same day, 10th July, that Moss had shown the flag in Italy, some hundreds of miles north, the '500' Coopers had a field day in a race at Hedemora, Sweden, gaining the first four places. With two international successes in one day, things were looking up. Cooper cars notched up another victory in the 500-c.c. race run at Zandvoort in Holland, three weeks later, filling the first seven places, with Moss taking premier honours.

500-c.c. racing had by now gained tremendous popularity in the Scandinavian countries, and on 28th August a Cooper won at Gardemoen, Oslo; and again, at Kastrup Airfield, Copenhagen, Coopers filled the first three places.

Coming nearer home, on 18th September at Lausanne, Switzerland, Moss entered his Cooper in the 2-litre race and gave them a good run for their money, before blowing up.

The finale for 1949 in the overseas division was a very fine fourth in the Formula Libre Swedish Grand Prix held on 18th September.

On the home front, at Shelsley Walsh on 11th June, Brandon took the 500-c.c. Class in 42·78 seconds, fractionally beating J. (Kaiserwagen) Fry in his Parsenn-Jap, who returned 42·94 seconds. On the whole, Shelsley was a better meeting for the one-off specials in their battle with the production-type cars, and the specials finished second, third, and fourth in this event. Members' Prescott Hill Climb on 12th June saw Coopers in front once again, Brandon winning yet another Prescott in

48·18 seconds, second being J. G. Reece (Cooper) and third C. A. N. May (Cooper).

On 18th June, John Cooper took time off from attempting to keep up with orders for cars, and journeyed to Chester, where he won the 1,100-c.c. sprint. Across the Scottish border, J. Potts, Jnr., in a Cooper, reached the top faster than any other '500', at that so aptly named hill 'Rest and Be Thankful': time—79·30 seconds.

Then all the '500' boys began to work long hours getting their cars ready for the big experiment of the season, the hundred-mile race to be run at Silverstone on 9th July. Seventeen cars faced the starter, and with such drivers as John Cooper, Bill Aston, Don Parker, Peter Collins, and Bill Whitehouse in the field, the pace was expected to be really hot.

From the start it was, in fact, so hot that Braid's Cooper was out in one lap, Sir Francis Samuelson's Cooper out in three, Forbes Clark's Marwyn in four, and Jack Moor's Wasp in five, leaving twelve still running and Saunders (Cooper) fighting for the lead with Aston (Cooper), followed by Whitehouse (Cooper), Collins (Cooper), and Parker (Parker Special), in that order. Further back, John Cooper was taking it easy, no doubt hoping that the pace would crack up the leaders. At Stowe, Saunders overdid it, slid, and Aston, unable to avoid him, smacked him hard, both cars being so bent that they had to retire. Then Whitehouse coasted to the pits and was out, leaving diminutive Don Parker in the lead and going, dare we say it, 'like the clappers'. John Cooper was gaining noticeably on the leaders now and was fast coming into the picture. Collins caught Parker, and they began to dice for the lead, first Parker then Collins, then Parker again; then Parker pulled in to re-fuel, leaving Collins as No 1. boy. The twenty-seventh lap saw two more retirements—Bill Grose in his Special which had been going very well, and Westcott in his Cooper. The order was now Collins, Christie (Cooper), Habin (Cooper), then John Cooper still making up ground and beginning to challenge for third place. Don Parker was some way behind after his pit stop, but was going well and still had a chance. At thirty-five laps, bad luck struck at Christie, who retired with an engine seizure, leaving John Cooper in third place.

It was now a question of whether Peter Collins could hold out against the two Johns, Habin and Cooper, and register his first important win—Habin was still on his tail and John

Cooper was pulling out all the stops. It could now be seen that Don Parker could not make it unless the three leaders packed up. Then, two laps before the finish, John Habin had to retire with a broken oil pump, leaving a straight fight between Peter Collins and John Cooper. Although he tried all he knew to overhaul the leader, John had given himself too much to do and Peter came home a worthy winner of the first hundred-mile race. John Cooper was perhaps a shade unlucky in not winning, his mistake being to allow Collins to get too far ahead initially. Parker threw his chance away by not fitting a long-range tank; nevertheless, he finished third.

Charles Cooper's comment on hearing the result of the race was, 'Didn't I say that young Peter was going places?'

On 17th July, at the Prescott Hill Climb again, Michael Christie had some consolation for his bad luck at the Silverstone meeting by gaining B.T.D. in his Cooper-J.A.P. '1,000'; time—46·76 seconds. The indefatigable Eric Brandon made the 500-c.c. Class his own, beating the Class record; time—48·67 seconds.

The Bouley Bay Hill Climb on 21st July saw Stirling Moss (Cooper 1,000) make third F.T.D. jointly with Dennis Poore; time—56·20 seconds. Syd Logan, the local lad, was very little behind in his Cooper 'Twin' in a time of 57·60 seconds, taking sixth F.T.D. and second place in his Class. Coopers came unstuck in the 500-c.c. Class, C. A. N. May being beaten by Jeremy Fry in his Parsenn Special.

Two more small meetings followed. On 30th July, at Silverstone, three Coopers entered and took the first three places in the 750-c.c. Class, and Eric Winterbottom won two races in the 1,100-c.c. Class with his Cooper-Vincent. And at Hartlepool Promenade Sprints, J. G. Reece took the '500' Class in 16·68 seconds.

The tricky Hants and Berks M.C. Great Auclum Speed Trials were won by the persistent Eric Brandon (Cooper-J.A.P. 1,000) in 22·20 seconds (course record).

The Silverstone B.R.D.C. Race Meeting saw a very good battle between Stirling Moss and Eric Brandon for the 500-c.c. thirty-mile race. Eric got out in front, and although Stirling did his famous slip streaming act behind Eric he did not have the necessary acceleration when the time came to get past and Eric Brandon won the race at a faster speed than the 1,500-c.c. Class. R. M. Dryden was third. The highest placed Special was that driven by Don Parker, who was seventh.

MARK III NEEDS A PASSPORT

On 27th August, at Blandford Camp, Dorset, the Cooper Circus put in some fine racing at a meeting marred by the fatal accident to Gordon Woods in his B.M.W. R. M. Dryden won the 500-c.c. race final in his Cooper-Norton, with two Cooper-J.A.P.s behind. In this race, Major P. K. Braid ran into some trees and in some odd way catapulted his Cooper on to the roof of the Regimental Guard Room. Poor Major Braid was tipped out as the car landed, but luckily escaped with a sprained ankle from surely the most fantastic accident that has ever occurred on a circuit.

The Cooper 'Twins' had things all their own way in the Formula II Blandford Trophy, the big event of the day. Eric Brandon won the first heat at a speed of 82·03 m.p.h., easily beating all the big stuff, and John Cooper repeated the performance in the second heat, this at a speed of 80·27 m.p.h. Unfortunately, the final was stopped after a pile-up involving Jack Fairman (Riley) and G. R. Baird (R.B.L.), with superb avoidance by Eric Winterbottom and Eric Brandon. So although the race was awarded on the basis of where the cars were placed when it was stopped, the Cooper 'Twins' won a moral victory.

On the same day at Craigantlet Hill Climb in Northern Ireland, B. Lee took the 500-c.c. Class in 84·2 seconds.

September opened with the Sunbac Silverstone 500-c.c. race, won by Ken Carter (Cooper). Then followed two hill climbs in quick succession, the first being the Prescott International, where Jackie Reece (Cooper) beat seventeen opponents, including Peter Collins, May, Strang, Lones, Truman, and Ken Carter to take the '500' Class in 48·18 seconds, and in so doing, established a new Class record.

Stirling Moss kept his end up with third F.T.D. and a new 1,100-c.c. Class record into the bargain, with his Cooper 'Twin'; time—44·77 seconds.

In Scotland, on 17th September, J. Potts, Jnr., won the Bo'ness Hill Climb with his Cooper '500', making F.T.D. in 39·70 seconds, a new '500' record.

On the same day as Bo'ness, there was a big meeting at Goodwood and one of the main events was the Madgwick Cup (up to 2 litres U/s). Against Ferrari, H. W. Alta, Veritas, and Riley, the Cooper 'Twins' of Brandon, Moss, and Whitehouse really showed their paces. On the third lap, Aston (Cooper) overdid it at Woodcote and left the road, and Moss moved into the lead, followed by Brandon, with Whitehouse

25

third. In this order they finished, with only Abecassis (H.M. Alta) making a race of it against the flying Coopers. Moss's speed was 82·10 m.p.h.

In the '500' race young Peter Collins proved conclusively that the Cooper 'double knocker' Norton had the legs of the Cooper-J.A.P. by leading the field and winning as he liked from Lex Beels and Stan Coldham. The winner's speed was 74·95 m.p.h., over 4 m.p.h. faster than Stan Coldham when he won the April race in his Cooper-J.A.P.

The season was now drawing to a close, which meant the unpronounceable Rhydynwyn Sprints on 18th September—once again a Jackie Reece field day—B.T.D. and course record with his Cooper-J.A.P. 497-c.c.

To close the fixture list there was the Shelsley Walsh Hill Climb. At this meeting Cooper cars did not have things all their own way, being well and truly trounced in the 750-c.c. Class by G. H. Symonds's blown Austin and notwithstanding a fine run up by Stirling Moss in the Cooper 'Twin'; time— 38·19 seconds. J. Fry in his amazing blown Freikaiserwagen beat him in the 750-c.c.–1,500-c.c. Class and made F.T.D. in 37·40 seconds.

Stirling Moss took fifth F.T.D. and finished third in the R.A.C. Hill Climb Championship. After his extremely successful season, Stirling was invited to drive professionally for H.W. Motors, so he sold the big Cooper which had helped him to plant his feet firmly on the ladder of fame, and ordered a '500' Cooper to drive in the next season's races.

Back at the Cooper Garage, John and his father went over the results of the year, which made excellent reading, better even than the previous year, as the Cooper '500' had been a wonderful success, and in addition, the new Cooper V 'Twin' 1,000 c.c. had already done fine service in the larger classes. The Cooper Car Company could now proudly add to their new brochure the bald statement that '. . . Coopers have won every important 500-c.c. and 1,000-c.c. race in Great Britain and abroad.'

There were only two flies in the proverbial ointment. Firstly, production just could not keep pace with demand, which meant long hours for John in the factory, with consequently less time for him to devote to racing himself. Secondly, by some strange quirk in their characters, the Coopers welcomed competition, which they have always held is the finest thing that can happen to them. At that particular time Coopers were carrying all before them, and quite frankly, they did not like it one little bit.

After the usual yearly family conference, plans were laid down for the Mark IV '500' and in addition, a Mark IV chassis lengthened by one inch to take a 1,097-c.c. V-twin racing J.A.P. engine specially developed for long distance racing. The Coopers were hoping that the '1,100' V-twin would be a worthy contender in Formula II events and with a 14 to 1 compression ratio on dope, 95 b.h.p. at 6,000 r.p.m. and dry weight 600 lb., on paper, it looked terrific. The question was, would it last? Here, John's enthusiasm was countered by sage old Papa Cooper's words, 'Don't bank too much on a motor-cycle engine developing 95 b.h.p. being able to stand up to all the strain involved for too long a period.'

THE F.I.A. SMILES ON FORMULA III

EARLY in 1950, it was confirmed that the International Racing Calendar would include events for 500-c.c. unsupercharged cars which were to be known as Formula III events.

Switzerland, Italy, Great Britain, Holland, Sweden, and France signified that they would like to arrange races for the new formula. The only important stipulations laid down by the F.I.A. were that the races must be at least thirty miles long and that lap distances must be over one mile. The half-litres were growing up.

Before the European racing season started, two overseas wins were gained by Cooper cars. New ground was broken in Australia in January, when a Cooper 1,000-c.c. won the Rob Roy Hill Climb in a new hill record, and in the same month a 500-c.c. was second in Ceylon's first ever road race, this against several blown M.G.s. After one or two false starts, the first International Formula III race was run at Montlhéry, France, on 30th April 1950, and for the first time, also, the British cars faced Continental opposition. Five Coopers went over to France to meet a strong challenge from six front-wheel-drive D.B.s. The British drivers were W. Aston, Ken Carter, S. Coldham, Lionel Leonard, and Sir Francis Samuelson. The Frenchmen were led by Deutsch and Bonnet with D.B.s supported by Eli Bayol.

In the race, the Coopers did not have things all their own way and for the whole of the fifty-mile race, the little D.B. Panhards chased them as hard as they could, but although they were extremely fast on corners, the Panhards lost time on the straight. Two of the D.B.s packed up with gearbox trouble and one of the Coopers with a broken con-rod.

Prior to Montlhéry, on 10th April, the Goodwood races were held and in the 500-c.c. race, John Cooper, putting in one of his rare visits to the track, was extremely lucky to escape serious injury when Peter Collins crashed into his car and ran right up the back of it. Both John and Peter emerged unhurt, but the two Coopers were *hors de combat*, much to John's annoyance, as he had put up the fastest time in practice. The race was eventually won by 'Curly' Dryden in a Cooper-Norton from Stan Coldham (Cooper-J.A.P.). The race had been one of the

most exciting seen for a long time, tightly fought the whole
way and full of incident. It augured well for the season's
Formula III racing, particularly as two new marques had
shown up well in the race, the J.B.S.-Norton, driven by Alf
Bottoms, which had finished third, and the Emeryson 500,
built by Paul Emery and E. Limpus and raced by Emery.

In the five-lap Easter Handicap on the same day, Bill Aston
took the new 1,097-c.c. Cooper-J.A.P. out and registered a win
at an average speed of 73·77 m.p.h.

The next big meeting was at Silverstone, which was notable
for one of the greatest turn-ups for the book, as the saying goes,
in the year's motor racing. The '500' race was run in two five-
lap heats, with a final of ten laps. Among those entered were
Moss, John Cooper, Brandon, K. Carter, A. Brown, W. Aston
(Cooper-J.A.P.s), and Whitehouse, Collins, Dryden, May,
J. Cox, J. P. Fergusson (Cooper-Nortons), plus practically
every well-known '500' exponent, including Alf Bottoms
(J.B.S.), Don Parker (Parker-J.A.P.), Paul Emery (Emeryson-
J.A.P.) and C. Strang (Kieft-H.R.D.). In all, sixty cars were
to run, thirty in each heat. On the face of things, it looked like
another win for the strong Cooper entry and after the results of
the two heats, it seemed that only Don Parker could hold the
flying Coopers.

The Final: The flag fell and a tight bunch of struggling cars
shot into Woodcote Corner. By some strange miracle, there
were no prangs and on they went to Copse Corner, where John
Cooper held the slightest of leads from Parker, Whitehouse,
Brandon, and Moss; then up to Club Corner with Moss in
front of Brandon and Whitehouse, but John Cooper still
leading. On the second lap, Moss overtook Cooper and then it
happened. Up came 'Handlebars' Aikens in his Iota-Triumph
to pass both Moss and John Cooper and go into the lead.
Moss was not having this and by dint of some really fancy
driving, got his nose in front, but almost immediately, Aikens
had his moustache in front once again and the crowd were on
their feet with excitement. Then Don Parker made his effort.
He got in front of John Cooper for a short time but could not
catch the two leaders, and John overhauled him and they both
went at it hammer and tongs, only to be passed by Collins, who
went on to challenge Moss. In this order they came on to the
final lap, Aikens in front, chased by Moss, chased by Collins,
chased by Parker, who was being chased in no uncertain
manner by the rest of the field. Collins somehow got in front

of Moss, but in a do-or-die effort Stirling passed both Collins and the flying Aikens, but this was too much for his sadly misused engine, which blew its top, and Aikens took the chequered flag with 'handlebars' flying, Moss coasting over the line a yard in front of Peter Collins.

One of the first to congratulate Frank Aikens was Charles Cooper, who was highly delighted that he had won such a fine victory and secretly hoped for some red hot competition during the season.

The next day, several of the leading drivers flew over to Belgium for an International 500-c.c. circuit race at Mons, but most of them met trouble. The new Kieft-H.R.D., driven by Ken Gregory, ran out of brakes on the first corner and crashed, Gregory being knocked unconscious, but later recovering without serious harm. Ken Carter and Stirling Moss blew up their Coopers, and it was left to Harry Schell to chalk up a win in his first drive in a Cooper. Second, third, and fourth places were also taken by Cooper cars.

On the same day, at the Hockenheimer Ring, Heidelberg, a '500' Cooper driven by a German driver won the half-litre race.

The next Continental 'do' was organized in picturesque Monte Carlo. Several of the Cooper 'stars' entered and it was a particularly open race as Continental entries included D.B.s, a Simca-Surva with Fiat engine, a Swiss Este-Crosley and a special, built by Lex Beels in Holland. Not surprisingly, Don Parker joined in with his Parker Special. Two heats were run, and the first six in each went forward into the final.

It looked like a straight fight in the final between Moss (Cooper) and Schell (Cooper), and so it turned out. Right from the flag, Harry and Stirling got into the lead and stayed there until the end. Harry drove a very polished race and forced Stirling to pull out everything he had, but cornering on the limit, Moss just held off Schell to win by five seconds, at over a mile per hour faster than his speed in the first heat. The indomitable Parker (Parker) was third, and E. Bayol's D.B. just pipped May (Cooper) for fourth spot.

In England, on the same Saturday, John Cooper took time off to go up to Gloucester for the Prescott Hill Climb and won the 1,100–1,500-c.c. Class. Eric Brandon took the 1,100-c.c. Class. However, 'Kitty' Lones (Tiger-Kitten) had a well deserved victory in the 500-c.c. Class, beating the Class record holder Jack Reece (Cooper-J.A.P.) by over a second.

Encouraged no doubt, by his Class win at Prestcott, John

Cooper joined the Cooper 'Circus' at Goodwood the following week, where a strong '500' cast was assembled, including three Swedish Effyh-J.A.P.s with a claimed maximum speed of 125 m.p.h., and the Cooper shadow, Parker's Special, not forgetting 'Handlebars' Aikens. But this time nothing could shake the Coopers and after Brandon had won the first heat and Dryden the second, Dryden and Peter Collins made mincemeat of the rest of the field, fighting it out alone in their 'double knocker' Nortons. Collins tried his best to get ahead, but Dryden would not yield an inch, and after a wheel to wheel duel for the greater part of the race, Dryden took the chequered flag by about three feet from Collins. John Cooper drove a steady race to finish third, but his Cooper-J.A.P. just could not hold the Nortons. Parker crashed, and the Swedes were never in the picture.

The well-informed *Sunday Times* wrote the next day: 'Britain Wins Midget Cars "Blue Riband" ', and then went on to state: 'British drivers scored a handsome victory in the new '500' International Trophy race. The race, organized by the B.A.R.C., is designed to become a contest for the "Blue Riband" of International 500-c.c. racing. Three well-known Swedish drivers competed yesterday. They included Ake Jonsson, winner of the recent Grand Prix of Finland.'

On the same day, at Aix-les-Bains, Harry Schell, racing his '500' Cooper in American colours, put up yet another fine drive to win the 500-c.c. race. This race was important to Pa Cooper because his very close friend, the great Raymond Sommer, was trying the little Cooper for the first time. But he need not have worried; after the race, Raymond was highly delighted.

Two days later, on 29th May, that consistent performer, Alf Bottoms, came into his own with his J.B.S. 'double knocker' at Blandford. Bottoms really made the Cooper boys sit up, and convincingly won both his heat and the final, and this against both Dryden and Collins in the cars that had walked away with the Goodwood race two days before. There was much scratching of heads by all and sundry.

Shelsley and Prescott Hill Climbs followed in quick succession, Shelsley being notable for a member of the fair sex making F.T.D. in a Cooper, Miss B. Haig getting to the top very swiftly indeed. At Prescott, Peter Collins (Cooper) was fastest in the up to 750-c.c. Class, beating Clive Lones (Tiger-Kitten) by a second.

Over in France, at Angoulême, Raymond Sommer (Cooper) won the 500-c.c. race from Bonnet and Bayol in D.B.s. In Norway, on the same day as Prescott, the Royal Automobile Club of Norway organized a '500' race at the Gardemoen strip near Oslo. The track was very well laid out and the little cars could belt along the two long straights with safety; the two sharp corners were placed so that the cars had to slow right down to take them on the right line. In a field of nine, three Coopers finished first, third, and fourth, the winning car being extremely well driven by Norway's leading driver, Basse Hveem. Ken Carter made the long journey from England to compete, but could only finish third.

At Zandvoort, the annual 500-c.c. race was run on 12th June and once again Coopers had a resounding victory, gaining the first five places, with Ken Wharton taking premier honours to register his first win in half-litre racing. K. Watkins was second and C. D. Headland third.

On 18th June, Harry Schell (Cooper) beat the D.B.s out of sight in an International half-litre race run at Grenoble. At home, on 25th June, the Cooper marque had one of its most successful days of the season. At the Bo'ness Hill Climb in Scotland, it captured F.T.D. and two Class wins, and in addition, in the '500' class, Coopers filled the first three places.

But more important, at an excellently organized race meeting at Brands Hatch, Cooper cars won the Open Challenge Race, the Production Car Race, and the race for the ten fastest cars of the day, and it was Stirling Moss who did the damage, winning all three races.

Just as 25th June was a lucky day for Cooper cars, so 2nd July was exactly the opposite. Ten of the leading Cooper drivers took their cars to France for the Grand Prix of Rheims, preceding which was a sixty-three-mile race for '500s'. The Cooper drivers were Coldham, Moss, May, Aston, Dryden, Carter, Christie, Brown, Whitehouse, and Samuelson. The opposition was led by Leston and Gregory in Kiefts, Parker as always, Bottoms (J.B.S.) from England, and Ake Jonsson (Effyh-J.A.P.), a B.M.W. and several D.B.s leading the Continental challenge. But in motor racing anything can happen, and usually does. The first shaker was the sight of Jonsson's Effyh in the lead after the second lap, then, as all the favourites ran into their various troubles, Alf Bottoms literally flew through the field to take the lead with Jonsson grimly holding on to second place, and only Dryden of the Cooper boys in the picture at all. Aston, May, and Christie retired and lapping at well over 80 m.p.h., Bottoms began to blow up the field. Both Kiefts dropped out, then Coldham and Samuelson (Coopers); Carter pranged, but got the car back on the course and continued. Still lapping steadily at over 80 m.p.h., Bottoms got well in front of the Effyh which, in its turn, was a long way ahead of Dryden. Parker caught up Dryden and Alan Brown made a big effort to pass the two of them, and after a fierce dice with Parker Dryden drew away, and one lap before the finish, Brown passed Parker, only for the engine to seize up. The race had by now become a procession— Bottoms was well ahead of Jonsson who had the edge on Dryden. And so they finished, a wonderful victory for Bottoms; and furthermore the Swedish Effyh-J.A.P. had become a formidable rival to what had been up to now a British monopoly.

Having been very successful with their Formula III race on 12th June, the Royal Dutch Automobile Club organized another to be run at Zandvoort Track on 23rd July. Restricting the number of entries, they hoped for quality, which they certainly obtained. The entries were headed by the two famous Grand Prix drivers, Raymond Sommer and Johnnie Claes, both driving Coopers, Claes for the first time. The others were Parker (Parker Special), Gottgens (B.M.W. Special), J. Flinterman (Kieft), P. Richardson and L. Beels, each driving a Beels Special, R. M. Dryden, C. A. N. May, K. Wharton, A. Rippon, all driving Coopers, and Dillenius, the local driver, also Cooper-mounted. In the race, Raymond Sommer shot into the lead from the start. The field followed in two bunches, Parker, Wharton, Dryden, and Claes fighting it out in the first, and May, Rippon, Gottgens, Flinterman, and Richardson in the second. Beels had a brake lock on his front wheel and catapulted into one of the sand-dunes; although the car somersaulted, Beels was saved by the soft sand and crawled out unhurt. Sommer proceeded to lap the field, but in so doing overstressed his engine and blew up. This left 'Curly' Dryden in front, with Don Parker determined to show him the rear view of the Parker Special, and this battle went on for lap after lap with no quarter asked or given. Behind these two, Wharton had established a clear lead over Johnnie Claes, and all the others were struggling a long way behind. It could now be seen that Parker and Dryden had the legs of the rest of the field, and the burning question was which would hit the finish first. But it was not Parker's day, and on the last lap he ran into trouble with his rear drive-shaft, and 'Curly' flashed over the line to win easily, with Parker second and Wharton third.

Back home at Brands, once again Cooper cars put up an excellent show, winning three finals out of four and also the Championship of the meeting. A pleasing feature of this meeting was the fine win by Paul Emery (Emeryson Special) in the Race I final. As this was Paul's first big win, it must have encouraged him immensely.

The next important half-litre meeting was at Rouen, where Cooper cars added to the season's laurels by taking the first three places against strong Continental opposition, Bill Whitehouse winning from John Cooper and Eric Brandon.

At Brands Hatch, on 5th August, Lex Beels entered his Dutch-built Beels Special, and was joined by Harry Schell, his brother Phillip, and Johnnie Claes, all driving Coopers painted in their various national colours. Leading the home team was Stirling Moss, who was expected to be in his usual winning form. As things turned out, although in the two main races Moss won his heats, in the finals he was well and truly beaten by a comparative newcomer to Formula III racing, George Wicken, who trounced the opposition and won both finals.

The two Schell brothers and Claes did not shine, due, most probably, to being unfamiliar with the very tricky circuit.

A week later, however, the two Schells made no mistake about winning at Gap, in France, Phillip taking the 500-c.c. Class and Harry the 1,100-c.c. Class.

The next day there was an important meeting of '500s' on the Ostend-Middlekerke airstrip attended by nearly all the big names in small car racing. The programme was organized in two heats, a répachage, and then a final. The British contingent consisted of Bottoms, Moss, Whitehouse, Dryden, Coldham, Brandon, Parker, Wharton, Emery, Aston, Wicken, Samuelson, Reece, Moor, Westcott, Rippon, Rogers, Carter, Winterbottom, Truman, Merrick, and Montgomerie-Charrington, twenty-two in all. The Continent was represented by two Beels Specials, several D.B.s, two Coopers driven by Claes and Dillenius, and sundry one-off specials, built by Belgian and French enthusiasts.

The final was run at a cracking pace, and it looked as though Alf Bottoms had the race in hand, being well in front of the field at the half-way mark, but he overdid a corner, spun, and left the race open. Ken Carter took the lead from 'Curly' Dryden and Wharton. Moss and Claes blew up and Whitehouse broke a chain. Bottoms started again and chased after the field to such good purpose that he put up the fastest lap in the process. Carter held off Wharton and Dryden, and Merrick, Parker, and Beels all retired. Brandon and Westcott had a tussle for fourth place, but Brandon's engine was not giving of its best and Westcott got in front. Carter continued in the lead with Dryden second, well in front of Wharton. Bottoms, going like the wind, began to overhaul the field and with three laps to go, he was fifth, but although going faster than the leaders, he had lost far too much ground with his 'gilhoooley' and the best he could do was finish fourth to Carter, Dryden, and Wharton.

On 26th August, at the B.R.D.C. Meeting, Silverstone, Coopers had another successful day, Moss (Cooper) winning the 500-c.c. race from Sommer (Cooper), with Bottoms (J.B.S.) third.

The chief jubilation in the Cooper camp was due to the fact that Moss, in his new Cooper 'double knocker' Norton, had beaten Alf Bottoms fair and square for sheer speed, no mean feat as Alf had proved swifter than the Coopers in several earlier meetings.

Early in September, John Cooper was invited to send a works team to San Sebastian on the Franco-Spanish border for a Formula III race. John eagerly accepted, and took over three Coopers to be driven by Ken Carter, Stan Coldham, and himself. This little party was joined by independents Ted Frost and George Wicken, both with Coopers. The British drivers were faced with formidable opposition from the two Schells and Pagnibon in Coopers, the D.B.s of Bayol and Bonnet, plus Dutchman Lex Beels, Belgian Kahn, Frenchman Henri Otterbein, with their assorted specials.

The event itself was run in two sections, the final winner to be the one with the highest average in both races. Before a wildly enthusiastic crowd, Stan Coldham took the lead in the first heat, but chasing round the houses too fast, he ran off the course and Carter took over to run out an easy winner from George Wicken and John Cooper. The difficult course took a heavy toll of cars—both the Beels Specials and one of the D.B.s pranged badly, the second D.B. blew up, as did Harry Schell's Cooper; Pagnibon lost his gear lever and only Kahn's F.N. of the Continentals showed any fight, finishing fourth.

A considerably depleted field got away to a good start in the second heat. George Wicken took command, hotly chased by the Cooper 'patron' himself; also running strongly were Frost, Coldham, and Carter and the beautifully prepared Belgian F.N. of Kahn's. Both Wicken and Cooper were having a real go and enjoying themselves well in front of the others, when, as often happens in the best regulated families, Wicken's Cooper took a turn and ceased to clatter; probably out of sympathy, John's engine did likewise, leaving a very surprised Ken Carter in the lead, followed at a discreet distance by Frost, then Coldham and Kahn shielding the sunlight from one another, and so they finished. Due to the intricate workings of the 'bods' who judge these things, the results were as follows: 1st, K. Carter (Cooper); 2nd, R. Kahn (F.N. Special); 3rd, J. N. Cooper (Cooper).

At the prizegiving, the 'patron's' lads hit the jackpot with a score of twelve pots and one shield for services rendered, surely an all-time record for one race. When they arrived home, the gang had great difficulty in convincing the Customs that they had not done a job at some foreign duke's joint, and lifted some of his hardware.

On 16th September, at the Lydstep Hill Climb, Ken Wharton entered a Cooper-M.G. This interesting addition to the Cooper range was a sports car built around the standard Cooper Mark IV chassis and propelled by a 1,250-c.c. M.G. engine. Ken took the car up the hill to such good purpose that he smashed the existing class record for 1,100–1,500-c.c. cars. As Ken also made fastest time of the day in his 1,000-c.c. Cooper-J.A.P., and Mrs. Joy Cooke was the fastest lady driver (in a 1,250-c.c. Cooper-M.G.), the Cooper marque cleared the board.

Ken Wharton's F.T.D. beat the existing record by over two and a half seconds. This shattering performance proved the forerunner to a sensational career of hill-climbing successes, made all the more praiseworthy because Ken Wharton used only two Coopers for the next five years, during which time he won the National Hill Climb Championship in 1951, 1952, 1953, 1954, and was level with Tony Marsh in 1955.

The last overseas success of the season was at Perigeux, in France, on 24th September, where Harry Schell captured the lap record.

Meanwhile, at home, on 17th September, the '500' boys were out in force at Brands Hatch. Stirling Moss had flown over specially to be at the Meeting on his twenty-first birthday, and was greeted enthusiastically by the large crowd which had read about his wonderful victory in the T.T. the day before.

The racing itself could only be termed an 'Alf Bottoms benefit', for that worthy won all three of the important finals, giving the Cooper lads a severe headache into the bargain, as he won the Championship of the Meeting race by the length of the straight, easing up. In the first event, Bottoms was second in his heat to Ken Carter and as Stirling Moss won the other heat from Alan Brown and Parker, the final was expected to be 'no holds barred'. Unfortunately, Moss made a very bad start and was left well behind. The race was first led by Ken Carter who was quickly passed by Alf Bottoms and then by Ian Burgess. Carter did not relish this and repassed Burgess to take second spot. Moss, having made up some ground was dicing with Don Parker, Paul Emery, and Alan Brown. Paul's Emeryson Special was lifting its front wheel at least six inches every time it entered Paddock Bend, but this was not worrying Paul a scrap and he carried on regardless. Stirling was really having a go and he simply flew past Brown, Parker, and Emery along the straight and having got Burgess and Carter in his sights, he pressed on for all he was worth, the Cooper-Norton responding magnificently. Neither Carter nor Burgess could hold him off, and only Alf Bottoms stood between him and victory, but friend Bottoms was not the man to let an opponent overhaul him after a bad start and rapidly approached the finishing line, to win by a substantial margin.

In the Brands Hatch Championship, Ian Burgess won the first heat and Bottoms the second, and in the final, Moss was not a serious contender, his Norton motor being very sick after its tremendous effort in the first final. Even if it had been in A.1 condition, it is doubtful whether the flying Moss could have caught the flying Bottoms on 17th September. The latter went into the lead very early in the race and there he remained to the end, to win easily from Ian Burgess and Eric Brandon. The Championship of the Meeting race was another procession with, as already mentioned, the invincible Alf Bottoms winning by a street.

After the meeting, Bottoms announced that he was going to build cars for sale in the following year.

Shortly after Brands came Shelsley, and John Cooper made off with the 500-c.c. Class record—time 42·29 seconds, beating Eric Brandon's old record time by over half a second. As

Cooper cars took both the 1,100-c.c. and 1,500-c.c. Classes, they could go home well pleased with the day's racing.

On 30th September, the last Goodwood meeting of the year was held in pouring rain. The half-litre race was won by 'Curly' Dryden (who had put up fastest time in practice) from Moss and Brandon. Bottoms was strongly fancied, but was left at the post and never in the hunt, three 'double knocker' Cooper-Nortons filling the top places. Coopers had a fine win in the Madgwick Cup race for cars up to 2 litres, being first and third. Bill Aston was never headed and drove an excellent race to take premier honours with G. S. Shillito (1,988-c.c. Riley) second, and Harry Schell, driving his Cooper 1,097-c.c. in American colours, third. Harry was again seen to advantage in the Third September Handicap, which he won against the strongest possible opposition.

The meetings on 7th and 14th October at Castle Combe and Brands brought the season to an end.

At Castle Combe, rain fell during practice, but held off on race day. Cooper cars were interested in six of the nine races, out of which they gained four first, two second, and four third places.

In the first heat for Formula III cars, 'Curly' Dryden led from start to finish, his Cooper being too fast for Clive Lones's Tiger Kitten II. The second heat was a trial of strength between young Peter Collins and Stirling Moss, both Cooper-mounted, and in an exciting race Stirling completed a most spectacular manœuvre. After chasing Collins for three laps, he got on Peter's tail and passed him on lap five. Peter chased for all he was worth and Stirling, seeing he could not hold him off, deliberately led him too fast into Quarry Corner and poor Peter slid on to the grass, losing so much ground in the process that he was no longer a menace to Stirling, who won easily. In the third race for cars between 500 and 1,100-c.c., Ken Wharton demonstrated his virtuosity by winning in his Cooper 1,000-c.c. from O. Poppy (Djinn) and J. H. Webb (M.G.). Ken's beautifully prepared engine did not miss a beat throughout a race notable for the misfiring of the other Cooper 'Twins'.

The race for 1,101–1,500-c.c. racing cars saw Peter Collins very much on his mettle, competing against blown E.R.A.s in his little Cooper 'Twin'. Not a whit overawed, Peter finished a very creditable third to those two fine drivers, Bob Gerard and B. Shawe Taylor, both in E.R.A.s.

In the final for Formula III cars, Moss was unlucky in having piston trouble and the race was fought out by Dryden, Collins, and Burgess, Dryden having to give best to Peter Collins by a bare second, with Ian Burgess bringing up the rear.

The last race of the day was a Formula Libre event, and although three Cooper 'Twins' started, the best they could do against the heavy machinery was Winterbottom's fourth and Wharton's fifth.

Back at Cooper's, a survey of the past season revealed another fine showing for the marque. The overseas successes included notable wins in Spain, Holland, Norway, Belgium, Australia, France, Ceylon, and Monte Carlo. Four famous drivers, namely Sommer, Claes, Wharton, and Harry Schell, had driven the little cars for the first time and each had been delighted. On the home front, the credit side included many fine wins such as Bill Aston's easy victory at Goodwood on Easter Monday with the Cooper 1,100, this, of course, against many Formula I entrants. The debit side included 'David' F. Aikens beating up the 'Goliaths' at Silverstone and Alf Bottoms wonderful wins at Blandford, Rheims and Brands on 17th September.

Looking to the future, although the half-litre movement was spreading rapidly, no longer would Cooper cars be the mainstay of the class. Alf Bottoms was going into full production with the J.B.S., as was Cyril Kieft with the Kieft. At this stage of the game, it was perfectly obvious that the more mature Cooper organization, by using a full season's racing experience under all conditions, was able to improve constantly its '500'. Eventually it overshadowed completely the less efficient one-off specials. Whether, of course, this would ultimately benefit '500' racing, remained to be seen. As the two Coopers started work on the Mark V, true to their policy of bringing out a new model every year, Stirling Moss and Ken Gregory (the Half-Litre Club Secretary), made tracks for Montlhéry Autodrome, where they successfully attacked Class I and J records with the Kieft racing car, thus putting this little car on the map in no uncertain manner.

LIKE THE CURATE'S EGG

For the 1951 season, the Cooper Car Company presented the Mark V with a box section chassis frame, and two $\frac{5}{8}''$ tubes running parallel along the top; the nose and tail were hinged back and front. All the body panels were detachable, and the fuel tanks were placed alongside the driver. The Mark V was also the first '500' to have rack and pinion steering.

During the early part of 1951 the news came through from Australia that Cooper cars had gained three major successes, firstly, a 1,100-c.c. car piloted by J. Crouch had made F.T.D. at the West Australian Hill Climb Championship on 25th February; secondly, the same driver had won the Australian Grand Prix in the same car on 3rd March; thirdly, Les Taylor, driving his 1,100-c.c. Cooper had won a scratch race for cars under 1,500-c.c. at Strathpine, Queensland, on the same day. As Cooper's had further wins at Bathurst on 26th March and the Newcastle Jubilee Hill Climb on 5th May, they completely swept the board in the Australian smaller classes.

Nearer home, the curtain raiser was a race in Northern Ireland won by Charles Headland, Cooper '500' mounted.

So far so good, but the main test of strength between J.B.S. and Cooper had yet to come. Their first meeting of the year was at the Blackburn Welfare M.S.C. 500-c.c. race at Brough and the J.B.S. took the honours, Don Parker coming into his own and winning the final and also putting up the fastest lap.

On the following day, K. Wharton continued his meteoric run of Hill Climb successes by taking F.T.D. at the Lydstep Hill Climb with his 1,100-c.c. Cooper in record time.

March 26th was a very busy day for the little cars with meetings at Gamston (Nottingham), Goodwood, and Pau (France).

At the Nottingham meeting, the Cooper marque won both races in which they entered and, in fact, filled the first three places each time.

At Pau, the Cooper '500' further established its ascendancy over the Continental half-litres and took first, second and third places in the '500' race, Phillip Schell taking the honours with brother Harry second and R. Montgomerie-Charrington third. A fine family victory.

Over to Goodwood, where Coopers did not fare so well, being completely trounced by the J.B.S. in both of the main races. Some consolation for these defeats was gained by Peter Collins and John Cooper as they took the First and Second Handicaps respectively.

So to Castle Combe!

The highlight of the meeting was the J.B.S.-Cooper battle for Formula III supremacy, this time resulting in a win for Cooper. In Heat I Don Parker (J.B.S.) got his nose in front of Ken Wharton (Cooper) and Bill Whitehouse (Cooper) and there it stayed to take the chequered flag by some lengths. (Wharton and Whitehouse could have been forgiven for christening him 'Nosey' Parker!) Heat II saw Ken Carter (Cooper) make most of the running from Peter Collins (Cooper) and Clive Lones (Iota). Bob Gerard was a first-timer in his Cooper in this race, but was not pressing unduly, contenting himself with getting the feel of the car.

The final was terrific. Parker (J.B.S.) shot into the lead from the off, hotly pursued by Wharton, Whitehouse, Carter, and Collins, all driving Coopers. As much as he tried, Parker just could not leave Wharton or Whitehouse, who clung grimly to his tail. From the distance, it looked almost as though Parker was driving a twelve-wheeled car, so close together were the three. Round and round they went with not a hair's breadth between them, but, of course, like all good things, it had to come to an end sometime. Parker, no doubt feeling Wharton's hot breath on his neck, went into Quarry Corner too fast, slid, and Wharton, totally unable to avoid him, hit the rear end of the J.B.S., jumped high in the air, clomped down again and was off, still miraculously in the hunt. Parker's rear suspension was too badly damaged for him to continue and the race crystallized into a fight between Wharton, Whitehouse, and Carter, eventually being won by Wharton after more spinning at Quarry. Whitehouse was second and Carter third.

On the same day at Marrakesh, Morocco, a Formula III race was won by a Cooper, with two others filling the minor places.

On 8th April Brands Hatch opened with a half-litre meeting. The racing was of the highest order and the big crowd assembled was provided with plenty of thrills and hotly contested races.

The J.B.S.-Cooper battle was continued in deadly earnest

and at this stage of the game, J.B.S. had won at Brough and Goodwood and Coopers at Castle Combe, so the Cooper boys, led by works driver Eric Brandon, were intent on levelling matters.

Heat I of the Open Challenge Race saw Cooper works driver Alan Brown trading the lead with Alf Bottoms (J.B.S.-Norton). This went on for five of the seven laps. At one point Bottoms took to the grass, but kept his foot on the floorboards and returned to the track pronto, followed at a discreet distance by Les Leston (J.B.S.) and Bill Whitehouse (Cooper-Norton). It now looked as though Alan Brown had the race in his pocket, but he spun off coming out of Clearways, letting Bottoms through to an easy victory, with Leston second. J.B.S. first and second—now for Heat II.

This time it was John Cooper himself defending the honour of the old firm against 'Curly' Dryden's J.B.S., and a real battle royal it turned out to be, the struggle for the lead taking the two protagonists far ahead of the rest of the field. There must have been some heavy breathing on John's Norton engine that day, for 'Curly' simply could not catch him, and John won by a car's length. One all. Heat III saw the third member of the Cooper works team, Eric Brandon, sail comfortably into the lead with a milling mass of cars bringing up the rear. Coming out of Clearways, it was Brandon well ahead, then Don Parker (J.B.S.), duelling with Ken Carter (Cooper), followed by Jack Leary (Cooper). As the race progressed, it looked a certainty for Brandon, barring trouble, but all eyes were on Carter and Parker who were really having a go for second place. Although faster on the straight, the Cooper was slower round the bends and each of these two masters took his turn to head the other. And so the race progressed—Brandon finishing well ahead with Parker just, but only just, pipping Carter for second place.

On to the fifteen-lap final of the Open Challenge race. This time 'Curly' Dryden shot into the lead, only to be passed on the third lap by Bottoms. Obviously working as a team, Bottoms and Dryden attempted to stave off Brandon, their nearest challenger, which they succeeded in doing for fourteen laps. Every now and then Parker emerged from the pack to challenge the leaders, but on the last lap, by dint of some superb driving, Brandon nosed in front of 'Curly' and managed to split the two J.B.S.s. Then, out of nowhere, Parker appeared to make it a photo finish for third place with Dryden. John

Cooper arrived at about the same time to confuse the issue further. The judges gave the decision to Parker by a tyre's width.

The Brands Hatch Championship was equally exciting. Heat I was won for Cooper's by Ken Carter and heat II by Alf Bottoms for J.B.S., so the final promised to be a thriller. At the start of the fifteen laps, Bottoms took the lead from Brown and Carter (Coopers) and Parker (J.B.S.), but on lap two Bottoms came out of Clearways with clouds of smoke pouring from his cockpit, caused by scavenge pump trouble. Although Alf was being blinded at times by smoke, he stuck it out and kept the lead for six laps until the pressure from Carter caused him to overdo a corner and spin off the course, leaving Carter in the lead. Now Dryden packed up, so it was left to Parker to keep the J.B.S. flag flying, which he did with great gusto, fighting tooth and nail with Alan Brown for second place. Meanwhile, Brandon was creeping into the picture after a bad start and was fast catching Parker and Brown. These three were now going so fast that it looked as if they had a chance of catching the flying Carter. In the final stages of the race, Brown drew clear of Parker and closed up on Carter and almost pipped him on the line. Parker fell back and Brandon swept past him to take third place. A 1–2–3 victory for Cooper's.

For the last race of the day, the Championship of the Meeting race of fifteen laps, there was some difficulty in obtaining enough entries—not surprising after the pasting some of the cars had had in their previous races. But after some considerable delay, the race began. This was not very interesting, however, as Brandon appeared to have the only car running at anything like its peak. Once having taken the lead from Alf Bottoms, he proceeded to win as he liked with Bottoms second and Brown third.

It was now two–all in the J.B.S.-Cooper battle, and after two meetings on 14th April, one in Ireland and one in Sweden, both won by Cooper cars, but in each case driven by a local driver, the battle was continued at Brands Hatch on 21st April. Once again, only fractions separated the rival marques. In the final of the first race, the Open Challenge race, Don Parker (J.B.S.) managed to squeeze that little extra something out of his J.A.P. engine and saw off the 'double knocker' Nortons of Brown and Brandon. The Brands Hatch Championship was won by Alf Bottoms (J.B.S.) after a terrific no-quarter fight with John Cooper (Cooper) and Bill Whitehouse (Cooper). So with two of the main races in the bag, the J.B.S. boys went into the Championship of the Meeting race determined to make a clean sweep, but this time Eric Brandon (Cooper) made the running and showed a clean pair of heels to Bottoms, winning in the very fast time of 66·88 m.p.h., Brown (Cooper) filling third place. Nevertheless, with two wins against one, Alf Bottoms could justly claim a moral victory at this meeting: three to J.B.S., two to Cooper.

On to Luxembourg for the first pukka Grand Prix ever held for half-litre cars and a strong force of competitors, consisting of four J.B.S.s, one Kieft, nine Coopers, one Emeryson, fifteen cars in all, journeyed over for the event. The Continental entries included D.B.s from France, two Giaurs from Italy, several Monopolettas and Scampolos from Germany.

The race was scheduled for 3rd May with practice on the two previous days. This proved extensive, and most of the competitors were working on their cars from early morning until well into the evening trying to suit them to the vagaries of the track, which included a long climb through thickly wooded country leading to a sharp hairpin. Carburation, overheating and suitable gear ratios were the chief worries. The main sufferers from the gear-ratio troubles were the Italian and German cars.

The weather remained fine all through the practice and also for the race itself. After seeing the practice times of the overseas entries, James Richmond, patron of the beautifully turned out Ecurie Richmond Cooper-Norton cars of Brandon and Brown, and Ken Carter with three entries of similar cars driven by John Cooper, Bill Whitehouse, and himself, realized that the main opposition to a Cooper victory would not come from the Continental cars, but the strong J.B.S. team led by Alf Bottoms, ably backed up by Don Parker and 'Curly' Dryden. Bearing this fact in mind, the entire British contingent was in high spirits as the evening wore on, but just before the practice ended, poor Alf Bottoms lost his life in a tragic accident, which may have been caused by his foot getting jammed in the pedals as he was wearing ordinary shoes at the time. The car horrified the spectators by charging through the escape road at full throttle right into a parked car; a sad end to a brilliant and popular designer-driver.

On race day, the half-litres lined up for the two heats and final of the Grand Prix. The first heat caused some confusion amongst the lads as the starter could not make up his mind whether it should be a rolling start or not and finally compromised by making it a bit of each. Two German drivers were caught unawares and started with soft plugs and several other drivers were badly baulked. Not so Alan Brown who immediately gained a big lead which he held for several laps until, overshooting a corner, he let Dryden (J.B.S.) through to a lead that he never lost. John Cooper, overcoming a slow start in excellent style, finished second, and Alan Brown third.

The second heat got away to a much better start and Don Parker (J.B.S.) fairly shot away from the field, the pack in its turn being well ahead of all the foreign cars with the exception of M. Aurnauld (D.B. Panhard); also among the back markers was one Stirling Moss (Kieft), an odd role for him. Parker kept up the pressure and finished an easy winner 16 seconds in front of his nearest rival, Eric Brandon (Cooper), Bill Whitehouse was third in a Cooper, and Aurnauld's little D-P in sixth position was the highest placed Continental car.

For the twenty-five-lap final, Dryden and Parker were on the front row with John Cooper in the middle, but at the fall of the flag it was Alan Brown who took the lead by shooting round Don Parker who had stalled on the line. Dryden also got away well, and chased Alan Brown as hard as he could with John Cooper trying to pass Dryden and Carter clinging to his heels. But determined to catch the lot was Don Parker and before the first lap was over, he was actually in third place. However, his J.A.P. engine could not stand such inhuman usage for long, and very soon a valve fell in and Parker was out. John Cooper overshot a corner and dropped back but continued to motor brilliantly and was soon back in the picture. At eight laps it was Brown, Dryden, Carter, with John Cooper eighth; at eleven laps Dryden was out with engine trouble, leaving Carter in second place with John Cooper now fourth. Brown came in on the fourteenth lap to refuel, losing 19 seconds, which allowed Carter to take the lead from him. John Cooper was third. Carter's lead was short-lived, as three laps later, he came in with a broken chain, leaving John Cooper in second place and fast catching Alan Brown. Thereupon John's chain broke also and he was out, after a fine drive. Brown now kept the lead undisturbed until the end. Alan Rippon (Cooper-J.A.P.) and Sir Francis Samuelson (Cooper-J.A.P.) were second and third. Both of the placed men had driven a carefully planned race rather on the style of the tortoise and the hare and fully deserved their final placings. This victory gave Great Britain her first G.P. success since Henry Segrave won the Spanish G.P. in 1924.

Two days later, the main contestants at Luxembourg were back home at Silverstone for the big meeting sponsored by the *Daily Express*, and even Papa Cooper turned up for this race.

The 500-c.c. event was run over thirty-five miles, and proved that the Ecurie Richmond had the answer to getting that little extra out of a Norton engine by meticulous tuning, as shown only two days before at Luxembourg. At the fall of the flag, C. D. Headland (Cooper-Norton) went into the lead closely followed by Clive Lones (Iota-J.A.P.). However, this lead was short-lived, for Eric Brandon (Cooper-Norton) and Alan Brown (Cooper-Norton) soon took over, and although Lones kept his Iota moving as fast as he could, Brandon and Brown got well clear of the field. The only other cars anywhere near them were Lones, C. Headland, and Peter Collins (Cooper-Norton). The last-named gave her the gun, determined to be in at the kill, but unfortunately overdid Woodcote and rolled his Cooper over twice. He was removed on a stretcher, but declined to stay and rose from his bed, so to speak, to drive his Dyna-Panhard later at the meeting. In the meantime, Brandon kept his lead from Alan Brown, and these two ran out a fairly easy first and second, although Clive Lones drove an excellent race and finished a worthy third, only 18 seconds behind Eric Brandon. Papa Cooper was not going to let the youngsters get away with anything—no sir! Charles had a tough battle with none other than Spike Rhiando (Flather Steel Special), which went on for quite a few laps, until he got in front and stayed there.

On the same day, the Australian Newcastle Jubilee Hill Climb was won by a Cooper-Vincent driven by John Crouch. On the following day, Phillip Schell, also Cooper-mounted, won a half-litre race at Orléans in France, and over in Northern Ireland, the Carncastle Hill Climb was won in record time by H. Graham in a Cooper.

On 12th May, at Brands Hatch, a large Whit-Saturday crowd saw the first of the 1951 International Formula III races. Among the international drivers competing were Pierro Taruffi, driving Papa Cooper's Cooper-Norton, Lex Beels and Richardson, both driving Beels-J.A.P.s, K. Ericsson and Pepperson, driving Swedish Effyhs, Liagre from France with his D.B., and Harry Schell with his Cooper. The two races were the Open Challenge Race of four ten-lap heats and a fifteen-lap final, and the *Daily Telegraph* Trophy Race of four ten-lap heats and a forty-lap final.

The biggest surprise in the Open Challenge Race heats was Ecclestone's win in heat 1 with a Cooper-J.A.P. in a faster heat time than the Cooper-Nortons, and the crowd was well behind him in his efforts to win the final. Alas, after leading the field for several laps, poor Ecclestone had to retire with engine trouble, leaving the way clear once more for Eric Brandon (Cooper-Norton) to win from Gray and Brake with the rest nowhere. In this race, Don Gray's Cooper-J.A.P. was outstanding and held its own with the 'double knocker' boys.

Once again, B. E. Ecclestone was expected to figure in the first three as his heat time was the second fastest, but it was not to be, and furthermore the strong Brown-Brandon combination was decisively beaten by Don Gray (driving his meticulously prepared Cooper-J.A.P.), who led home Alan Brown (hampered by a damaged rear suspension) and that great-hearted tryer, Paul Emery (Emeryson-Norton) who had three wheels on the deck most of the way. André Loens, driving his usual dashing race, was well up with the leaders with the J.B.S.-Norton, but had the misfortune to break a stub-axle and shed a wheel; he shot through the paling fence at Paddock, luckily without injury. Brandon, with his engine sounding very rough, retired about half-way through the race to join Ecclestone in the paddock with a similar engine malaise.

During this period, a strong team of Cooper boys, headed by John Cooper, Ken Carter, and Bill Whitehouse, had made the journey to Monza for the Grand Prix on Whit-Sunday. John Cooper was eminently successful in lifting the main hardware, although B. Taraschi made a fine race of it with his clever little four-cylinder Giaur, beating Ken Carter, Whitehouse, and Philip Schell, all in Coopers, in the process.

The same Cooper team travelled to Genoa, where they completely swept the board, filling the first four places. This time, Taraschi could do no better than fifth, Ken Carter taking the premier honours with Whitehouse second and John Cooper fourth.

Back home, on Whit-Monday at Goodwood, a Kieft-Norton in the hands of Stirling Moss put paid to any thought that the Cooper supremacy was going to go unchallenged, for in the final of the '500' International Trophy, Moss ran away from the rest of the field, and in driving one of the finest races of his young career, broke the half-litre lap record at 84·50 m.p.h. In the race itself, Moss got away third behind Brandon and Brown (both Cooper-Nortons), but on lap two he fairly steamed past Brown, and a few moments later passed Brandon on the inside at Woodcote, a difficult manœuvre at the best of times. He then built up a big lead, absolutely throwing the Kieft through the corners. Behind him, Brown passed Brandon but could do nothing about the flying Moss, and on the penultimate lap Gerard, in sixth place, was lapped by Moss. The only other change in the leaders was when D. A. Clarke (Cooper-Norton) passed Brandon to take third place.

During Whitsun week there were four other meetings of various degrees of importance in each of which Coopers registered successes. On the Monday, in Jersey, both the 1,100-c.c. and 1,500-c.c. classes were taken at the Bouley Bay Hill Climb; on the following Saturday at Prescott Hill Climb, H. C. L. Williams set up a new class record for '500s', climbing in 47·54 seconds with C. D. Headland second. On the following day at the same venue, Coopers captured three classes, 1,100-c.c. Sports Cars: first, B. H. Lister (Cooper-M.G.); 500-c.c. Racing Cars: first, C. D. Headland; 1,100-c.c. Racing Cars: first, C. N. Heath, and F.T.D.

Up in Scotland, on 20th May, they held a small meeting, in which a name that was destined to appear as a winner of one of the world's most important races figured in the results for the first time, to wit, Ninian Sanderson, who was second in his Cooper '500' to A. McGlashen (Cooper).

It might also be mentioned, as the name will crop up at various intervals later, that a certain dark gentleman, A. C. B. Chapman, took premier honours at Castle Combe (12th May) in a 750-c.c. Club race in a car of his own design, christened *The Lotus*. On 26th May, a big crowd watched the West Essex C.C. Boreham meeting and after the big stuff had had its way, Eric Brandon took the 'tiddler's' class prize to register a win for Coopers at the expense, this time, of Collins (J.B.S.-Norton) and McAlpine (J.B.S.-Norton).

The same day, at Silverstone, an Independent beat the factory-made cars in the five lap races for Formula III cars: E. J. Moor (Wasp) won from C. D. Headland (Cooper) and C. Arengo (Arengo).

With so many events clashing at this time, it was not surprising that the five lap Scratch Race for Formula III cars at

Dundrod, Northern Ireland, attracted only seven entries, and Peter Collins (J.B.S.-Norton) had no great difficulty in holding off the challenge of Gallagher (Leprechaun) and N. Pugh (Cooper) although Pugh did, in fact, make the fastest lap time.

On 3rd June at Eifelrennen on the Nurburgring, the British Cooper cars and drivers gave a perfect demonstration. Ken Wharton (Cooper-Norton) took the lead early in the race and held the other Coopers off until quite near the end, when Ian Burgess (works Cooper-Norton) managed to get by him to take the flag by a nose. The other two works cars of W. White-house and Ken Carter finished third and fourth respectively.

On 24th June, at Draguignan, once more Coopers gained all the honours, this time the Ecurie Richmond Cooper-Nortons driven by Brown and Brandon being first and second, and Phillip Schell third.

Home in England, all was set for the International Meeting at Brands Hatch, but prior to this Jackie Reece, in his Cooper-M.G., had put up a fine performance in the I.O.M. British Empire Trophy Race by finishing third to Moss and Gerard.

At Brands Hatch, on 23rd June, Coopers faced a strong challenge from the J.B.S.s of Don Parker, Dryden, and West-cott, and as it turned out the honours were even. J.B.S. won the final of the Open Challenge Race and Coopers won the final of the International Trophy Race. Although Kieft, D.B., and Beels Special were all represented at the meeting, none of them could hold either J.B.S. or Cooper in the final races. The order in the Open Challenge Race was: first, R. M. Dryden (J.B.S.-Norton); second, H. L. Daniell (Emeryson); and third, D. H. Gray (Cooper-J.A.P.); and in the International Trophy Race: first, D. H. Gray (Cooper-J.A.P.); second, J. N. Cooper (Cooper-Norton); and third, D. Parker (J.B.S.-J.A.P.).

At Shelsley on the same day, Ken Wharton broke the record for the Hill in 37·27 seconds in his 1,100-c.c. Cooper-J.A.P., and Peter Collins won the 1,500-c.c. Class in his Cooper. Next day, at near-by Prescott, Peter broke the 1,100-c.c. Class record again with his Cooper in the excellent time of 47·17 seconds.

There was much activity on 30th June, with three separate meetings, the Midland M.E.C. Silverstone Racing Handicap (which was won by Charles Headland with his Cooper '500'), and at the Boreham West Essex C.C. event the J.B.S. versus Cooper show went on again, Peter Collins scoring for J.B.S. in Heat I and Alan Brown (Cooper-Norton) in Heat II, but in the fifteen-lap final, it proved a clean sweep for Coopers, with Brandon winning from Brown and Ecclestone.

At the third fixture, the Bo'ness Hill Climb, Coopers also made a clean sweep. Ken Wharton won both the 500-c.c. class and the 1,100-c.c. Class and made F.T.D. into the bargain.

The season was by now getting well under way and with some very important '500' races organized on the Continent, the Ecurie Richmond and the Cooper works teams made several successful forays abroad. The full programme on the Continent was Avus, Rouen, Zandvoort, Nurburgring, Grenzlandring and Madrid. As these were the most important for prestige purposes, we will deal with them first.

On 1st July, at Avus, Germany, there were none of the well known British drivers present, but several British-made cars were entered in the names of their German owners. In this case, P. Richardson, driving Lex Beels's brain-child, the Beels-J.A.P., showed all the Effyhs, D.B.s, and Kieft-Nortons a clean pair of heels, and waltzed home a worthy winner at a speed of 87·85 m.p.h., which represented the fastest time ever put up in winning a Formula III race, an encouraging success for the popular Lex.

A week later the Cooper works team was at Rouen, where in an exciting race, John Cooper pulled out all the stops on the last two laps and left the field to win by a street from his nearest challengers, the D.B.s of Chaussat and Liagre, with Ken Carter fourth. Bill Whitehouse, the third works driver, retired with a very *mal-de-tête* engine.

Following this race, on 22nd July at Zandvoort, Stirling Moss gave Cyril Kieft's Formula III aspirations another boost by gaining a clear-cut victory over Les Leston (J.B.S.-J.A.P.) and J. Habin (J.B.S.-Norton).

In the meantime, the Cooper works team, the Ecurie Richmond, and several independent drivers had made preparations to go down to Nurburgring for what promised to be one of the big events of the year. In all, there were forty-nine starters for the Formula III race run over six laps each of fourteen and a half miles of this nightmare circuit, which consists of every kind of bend from slow hairpins to flat-out curves, a steep plunge down the Fuchsrohre, quickly followed by two right-left-right curves, then a long climb to the famous Karussel curve, with its one car's width of banking, then more and still more bends until after Brunnchen the cars come to the double Schwalben Schwanz (Swallow-tail), and from there a long, bumpy straight from Dottinger Hohe brings them back to the start. Several of the British boys had a sinking feeling in their stomachs on seeing the course for the first time.

The entry consisted of eight British driven cars, two Dutch Beels-J.A.P.s, three French D.B.s, three Swedish Effyhs, which were to do battle with the large German contingent of Monopolettas, Scampolos and other German specials.

On race day the forty-nine starters lined up on the grid in eleven rows, and as the flag fell, the first five, Moss, Carter, Whitehouse, Schluter, and Brandon got away in fine style. Within seconds Alan Brown had joined them from the second row, and then a solid mass of cars passed with an ear-splitting noise that could be heard for miles. Deutz (Scampolo) and Komossa (Scampolo) were left at the post and Glutz (Scampolo) drove back to his pit, then changed his mind and shot off to join the rest of the pack. Lex Beels (Beels-J.A.P.) also drove slowly back to his pit and retired. By now the leaders had reached Schwedenkreutz, and Moss was in the lead by a fraction from Brandon, then about forty yards behind came Carter, Whitehouse, and Brown. Some distance farther back was Schluter's Monopoletta leading another pack composed of John Cooper (Cooper), Svensson (Effyh), Ted Frost (Emeryson) and then the rest of the field already beginning to straggle. At Breidscheid, Moss had increased his lead considerably and as he came past the stands several minutes later, he was well ahead of second man Eric Brandon, with Brown, Carter, and Whitehouse nearly thirty seconds behind.

By now several cars had retired and others sounded very rough. As the last car went by, the spectators craned their necks expecting the leaders to come round once again, but on this long course, it was some time before the staccato note of the Kieft's exhaust announced that once more Stirling was on the way. This time, Brandon had decreased the lead slightly, but Stirling was still way out in front. Brown had closed up on Brandon, but Carter had dropped back, leaving Whitehouse in fourth place, Schluter in fifth place and going very well, then John Cooper, Ted Frost, Svensson, Hansen (Effyh) and Richardson (Beels-J.A.P.). Then a murmur from the crowd denoted that something was afoot, and those of the British contingent who could understand German hastened to spread the news that Moss, when 39 seconds in the lead, had retired with a broken steering arm. This meant that, barring accidents, it should be a straight fight between Ecurie Richmond and

51

Cooper works. And so it proved. The Brandon/Brown Coopers seemed to have a slight edge on the Whitehouse/John Cooper cars, and although he tried his best, Whitehouse could not catch second man Brown. As for Eric Brandon, it was certainly his day and he won the race after a wonderful drive with five seconds in hand. John Cooper chased Schluter hard, and on the fifth lap passed him for fourth place, as did R. Montgomerie-Charrington (Cooper-J.A.P.) whose fine effort enabled him to finish fifth. Thus five British Coopers took the top places, and the highest placed foreign car could do no better than sixth. As John Cooper disappeared under an overwhelming mass of people, he might have been forgiven if he had emerged with a larger size in hats, but not John; his only comment was, 'If only we could do the same with Formula I.'

Six weeks later the Ecurie Richmond reappeared in Germany, this time at Grenzlandring, and after their devastating performance at Nurburgring, they were considered hot favourites for the Formula III race. They proved this to be correct by gaining an easy 1–2 victory on this very fast course of 5·7 miles. Brown led Brandon in this case, and both G. W. Patterson (Cooper) and R. Montgomerie-Charrington (Cooper) drove very well to finish third and fourth, to make it another Cooper demonstration of strength. W. Komossa (Scampolo-B.M.W.) was the highest finishing foreign entry, in fifth place.

The last Continental '500' race was in sunny Madrid on 21st October and was run in the usual style, two heats (twenty-two laps) and a final of thirty-one laps. Ecurie Richmond was there with its brace of fast cars, as was Ken Carter (Cooper), J. Coombs (J.B.S.-Norton), A. D. Gill (Cooper-Norton), Montgomerie-Charrington (Cooper-J.A.P.) and R. Frost (J.B.S.-Norton). These, with the mixture as before in Continental cars, made up the entry. On paper it seemed to be a continuation of the J.B.S. versus Cooper duel that was taking place at most meetings in England. In heat I Eric Brandon was flagged in front of J. Coombs, who drove a very neat race in the J.B.S.-Norton. In heat II Ken Carter took the chequered flag in front of R. Frost, but in the final, Eric Brandon had things all his own way, after Carter had blown up his engine, the Ecurie Richmond Cooper coming home an easy winner from J. Coombs and A. D. Gill, with the steady Montgomerie-Charrington fourth.

Whilst all this had been going on abroad, the boys at home were keeping busy with meetings every few days and sometimes two or three on the same day. On 7th July at the Rest And Be Thankful Hill Climb, Ken Wharton received a slight setback to his Hill Climb Championship aspirations (*only*) making 2nd F.T.D., although he won the 1,100-c.c. class for supercharged cars. In the 500-c.c. class, H. L. Williams (Cooper) was first and Ninian Sanderson was second. F.T.D. was put up by Dennis Poore driving the awe-inspiring Alfa-Romeo in absolutely fearless style, to set up a new record for the hill in 56·32 seconds. The sight of the Alfa's tyres smoking all the way up the hill had to be seen to be believed.

It was clear at this point that Dennis Poore, the 1950 Hill Climb Champion, was going to have his work cut out to hold the championship against his chief contender, Ken Wharton, in the Cooper 'Twin', and with two wins to Wharton at Bo'ness and Shelsley and one win to Poore at the 'Rest', the next stage would be at Bouley Bay on 26th July. Prior to this meeting, the B.R.D.C. held a meeting at Silverstone on 14th July and put on a twenty-lap race for '500s'.

This was a serious débâcle for the Cooper marque, for Stirling Moss, driving the Ray Martin Kieft-Norton, not only broke the 500-c.c. record for the track in practice, doing a lap in 1 minute 59·6 seconds, just under 87·00 m.p.h., but in the race itself got so far ahead of the field, including works and Ecurie Richmond Coopers, that at the end of the first lap as he passed the stands, the rest of the field had not yet come round Abbey Curve, over two hundred and twenty yards away. Moss continued to motor round with such ease that he was able to wave to friends and even to take a look at a plane circling overhead. He eventually won one of the easiest races of his career, slowing up but, nevertheless still a minute ahead of his nearest challenger, Wharton (Cooper-Norton), with Moor (Wasp-Norton) third.

Two more Club meetings followed with varied fortunes for Coopers. On 21st July at Gamston, Sheffield, a twenty-eight-lap race was won by H. L. Williams (Emeryson-Norton) from J. Coombs (J.B.S.), with A. M. Beardshaw (Cooper-J.A.P.) third. At Winfield, Scotland, the result was: first, Peter Collins (J.B.S.-Norton); second, C. Hunter (J.P.-J.A.P.); third, A. McGlashen (Cooper-J.A.P.).

On 26th July, at Bouley Bay, the stage was set for the next round in the Hill Climb Championship. Here Ken made F.T.D. and also established a new course record in his 1,100-c.c. Cooper 'Twin'. Dennis Poore made two of the finest climbs ever

c

seen on the hill, taking the unwieldy blown Alfa round the tricky corners at what seemed an impossible speed, but on this narrow course it was a hopeless task, and he was well beaten by the little Cooper by two seconds exactly. This win virtually sealed the fate of the Championship, for even if Poore won both of the remaining International Hill Climbs, he could only draw with Wharton, the rules stating that a driver should nominate four Hill Climb results out of the six allowed. Wharton, with three wins and one second had to win only one more Climb to win the Championship outright.

Croft, on 28th July, and Ibsley, on 4th August, were the curtain raisers for the big International meeting at Brands Hatch on 6th August. At Croft a one-off Special put it across the J.B.S.s and Coopers, for Jack Moor (Wasp Special) carried off the hundred pounds first prize in the final of the Formula III race, cutting through the field in grand style to win after 'Curly' Dryden (J.B.S.-Norton) had seemed to have the race in hand. Two laps before the end, for no apparent reason, he had gone into a spin and finished second, limping in with a buckled rear wheel. A. M. Beardshaw (Cooper-J.A.P.) gained third place. Incidentally, this superb win put Moor into third place in the *Autosport* two hundred pounds Championship.

The West Hants and Dorset C.C. Meeting at Ibsley was keenly fought, but Peter Collins (J.B.S.-Norton) emerged the victor, leading in André Loens in a similar car by a small margin, with Eric Brandon (Cooper-Norton) a far from disgraced third.

Then all hands on deck for Brands, but what promised to be an excellent day's sport was practically washed out by some atrocious weather, causing the meeting to be cancelled when only three parts finished. The Cooper chassis stood up very well to the terrible conditions, and one of the works cars registered a popular win in the hands of Bill Whitehouse in the final of the *Daily Telegraph* International Challenge Trophy Race.

The fifth heat and the final of the Open Challenge Race were abandoned.

As is often the case, the Nottingham S.C.C. Formula III Race at Gamston on the same day was graced with quite good weather and Collins (J.B.S.-Norton) made off with the '500' race, with Gerard (Cooper-Norton) second and Reece (Cooper-J.A.P.) third. In the Handicap Race Webb (Cooper-J.A.P.) won from Swan (J.P.-Norton) and Kearon (Cooper-J.A.P.).

Alan Brown scored another win for Ecurie Richmond at the Boreham Race Meeting on 11th August and L. Leonard scored with his Cooper-M.G. in the Sports Car Class up to 1,500-c.c. Just to make it cosy, Ray Merrick carried off the Formula II Racing Car Class with his Cooper-J.A.P. 1,100 c.c.

At Craigantlet, Ulster, the fifth International Hill Climb was won by Sidney Allard (Allard) on 11th August, and as neither Dennis Poore nor Ken Wharton competed, it meant that Ken had won the Hill Climb Championship for Cooper's —a great honour for this tiny concern.

For Silverstone on Saturday, 18th August, the Half-Litre Club put on two one-hundred-mile races, and received a remarkable entry of eighty-nine cars, of which sixty-nine participated. Alan Brown won the first hundred-miler for Ecurie Richmond after a most spectacular race when the leaders both stopped four laps from the end. But back to the start. Thirty-one cars lined up for the first race, and with a terrific roar, they all got away except B. Wheeler (Cooper) who stalled on the line. Alan Brown (Cooper) got in front of a mixed bunch comprising J. Coombs (J.B.S.-Norton), J. K. Brise (Cooper-J.A.P.), Charles Cooper (Cooper-Norton), Peter Collins (J.B.S.-Norton), C. Headland (Cooper-Norton), and J. D. Habin (J.B.S.-Norton). As the race settled down, the three leaders in turn were Coombs, Brown, and Headland, who were passing and re-passing in rapid succession. Peter Collins then moved up with the leaders. At eleven laps Brown was in the lead, followed by Headland, Coombs, Collins, Brise, J. D. Habin, Aston (Cooper-Norton), Charles Cooper, and Dryden, in that order. Frost (J.B.S.-Norton) was now out with a broken chain and Brown increased his lead over Headland who also drew away from Collins (now in third place) and Coombs. On lap seventeen Headland's race was run, and he coasted back to the pits. Brown was now about 16 seconds ahead with Collins in second place but dropping back slightly.

At half distance, the order was still Brown, by 20 seconds, Collins, Coombs, Habin, J. K. Brise, Dryden, Papa Cooper (really going well), Patterson (Cooper-J.A.P.), coming into the picture for the first time. Alan Rippon (Cooper-Norton) was out and Ken Smith (Smith-J.A.P.) rejoined the race after a lengthy halt. At thirty laps Aston retired whilst in sixth place. The first six were now Brown, still over 20 seconds in front of Collins, then Habin, Coombs, Papa Cooper, Patterson. On lap thirty-six Collins stopped just in front of the pits as his carburettor had come adrift; Allan Moore (J.B.S.-Triumph) was in clutch trouble, and poor 'Papa' then packed up when lying fifth with the same trouble as Collins. Lap thirty-nine, and Brown pulled into his pit to refuel; bad organization there cost him many valuable seconds, and when he finally got away, Habin was about 55 seconds in front. Then came the moment of drama. The two leaders, Habin and Coombs, both stopped dead on the circuit, letting Brown through into the lead again. Patterson had been making up time all through the race and was now in second spot, both first and second being well in front of the field. But still more drama. On the last lap, on the run in to the finish, Brown's engine cut right out. Fortunately for him, he had sufficient momentum to carry through to the finish, otherwise it would have been Patterson's race. 'Curly' Dryden was a good third, and there were thirteen finishers.

The second hundred-miler was also tremendously exciting. Right through the long race, the issue was in doubt. Thirty-nine cars assembled at the starting line and they all got away to a perfect start. There was a real humdinger of a scrap for the lead, and with Ken Carter (Cooper-Norton), André Loens (J.B.S.-Norton), John Cooper (Cooper-Norton), Les Leston (J.B.S.-Norton), Norman Pugh (Cooper-J.A.P.), Bob Gerard (Cooper-Norton), and J. F. Annable (Cooper-J.A.P.), all contriving to pass each other about every other yard, it was not until lap four that Norman Pugh emerged from the pack with anything like a lead. On his tail were Gerard and Carter, followed by John Cooper. Eric Brandon (Cooper-Norton) seemed to be taking it easy, no doubt with the length of the race in mind. On lap five Ken Carter got his nose in front of Pugh, Gerard dropped back with a bent tail clipped by Gregory's Kieft, Loens, grimly determined, fought his way in front of Pugh, and Brandon was now seen to be making up ground. At eleven laps the order was Carter, Loens, Pugh, Leston, Cooper, and Annable; Brandon was tenth. Then came four retirements, Loens and Don Parker with engine trouble, Spike Rhiando (Flather Steel Special) crashed, causing him to shed a wheel, and Jack Moor (Wasp-Norton) with a broken chain. On lap twenty-two, Carter's engine began to sound woolly and John Cooper passed him to take the lead, with Leston, Brandon (now well in the hunt), Pugh, Annable, and Gregory behind him in that order.

On lap twenty-three John Cooper's clutch smashed to pieces and seconds later Pugh's engine blew up in a big way. This left Carter once again in the lead, but with an engine fast losing its edge. Brandon and Leston were neck and neck for second place and gaining on Carter, and on the next lap they both passed him. Carter was now being passed by car after car, and on the thirty-second lap his engine seized and he was out. In the meantime, Leston was leading Brandon by a nose and Ken Gregory had pulled his finger out and was going like the clappers with the Kieft, so much so that he caught Brandon on the thirty-ninth lap and then set about doing likewise to Les, but the latter put his clog down and widened the gap. In response to 'faster' signals from the Ecurie Richmond pit, Eric Brandon tried his best to close up on the flying Leston, but to no avail. Alfred Moss in Ken Gregory's pit also hung out the leaden boot sign to the Kieft driver, but it was no use, Leston would not be caught, and he finished the race over five seconds in front of Gregory, with Brandon 28 seconds behind in third place.

After all this excitement things were quiet until 1st September when there were two meetings on the same day. At the Brighton Speed Trials that genial giant Bertie Bradnack purloined the 1,100-c.c. Racing Car Class with his 'blown' Cooper, and L. Leonard gained another success with his Cooper-M.G. in the 1,100–1,500-c.c. Class for Sports Cars. At Silverstone, Collins (J.B.S.-Norton) won from Brandon (Cooper-Norton) and Leston (J.B.S.-Norton) in the Final of the S.U.N.B.A.C. Meeting. Next day, by an odd coincidence, the S.C. and N.B.A.C. meeting at the same track was won by Peter, with Brandon and Leston as before, and at the same average speed, 75·43 m.p.h.

Ken Wharton, the new Hill Climb Champion, took F.T.D. in his stride at Lydstep on 2nd September, with his Cooper-'Twin', and in Scotland up-and-coming Ninian Sanderson won the 750-c.c. Racing Car Class at Turnberry with his Cooper '500'.

September 9th, at Prescott, saw Wharton (Cooper 1,000-c.c.) make F.T.D. and a new Hill record at 43·81 seconds, to win his fourth International Hill Climb of the year. C. A. N. May (Cooper-J.A.P.) was beaten in the 500-c.c. class by 'Kitty' Lones, who set up a new record of 45·66 seconds.

On the same day, at Croft, Charles Headland (Cooper-Norton) gained a victory in the 500-c.c. race at the expense of Don Parker (J.B.S.) and Jack Reece (Cooper-J.A.P.). Peter Reece had a Cooper-M.G. win in the Sports Car Race up to 1,500-c.c.

Fortunes varied in the J.B.S. versus Cooper battle at Brands, for on 9th September, Cooper's won 2–1 with the Open Challenge Race and the Junior Brands Hatch Championship going to Cooper's and the Brands Hatch Championship going to J.B.S. But at Brands on 23rd September the position was reversed, for J.B.S. won 2–1, taking the Open Challenge Race and the Junior Brands Hatch Championship against the Cooper win in the Brands Hatch Championship, so both sides were keen to fight it out in the last 'Brands' of the season on 21st October.

Because of the great interest aroused by the '500' meetings, an 'extra' was run on 22nd September at Silverstone by the Peterborough M.C. In the final of the half-litre event, Brandon had a terrific dice with C. D. Headland for the whole of the ten laps, and, in fact, Brandon won by just over one second, after averaging 75·16 m.p.h. for the race. Les Leston, in the very fast J.B.S.-Norton, could do no better than third.

Ken Wharton lowered the record at Shelsley to 36·62 seconds on the same day with his blown Cooper.

The end of the season was fast approaching and racing moved over to Castle Combe for its last meeting of 1951. This turned out to be a most unfortunate meeting for in one of the Formula III qualifying heats, R. M. 'Curly' Dryden lost his life when his J.B.S. overturned at Camp Corner, and in the final of the Formula III race, J. D. Habin came unstuck in the gulley at Paddock Bend and suffered severe injury. The race was won by Headland (Kieft-Norton) from Gerard (Cooper-Norton) and Parker (J.B.S.-J.A.P.).

A six-lap race for '500s' was included in the Gamston (Nottingham) Meeting, on 6th October, and this was won by Collins (J.B.S.-Norton) from Brown (Cooper) and Reece (Cooper).

The Scratch Race at Brough on 7th October resulted in a win for Reece (Cooper) from Brandon (Cooper) and Parker (J.B.S.), and the Winfield fifteen-lap race, perhaps a little overshadowed by the recent tragedy involving poor 'Curly' Dryden, provided the most exciting racing of the day. Gerard, Reece, and Parker really went to town and as one scribe put it, 'for nine-tenths of the race, the leading three could have been covered by the proverbial blanket.' Nearing the end, Gerard pulled just that little extra out of the bag and won a most thrilling race at a speed nearly as fast as Stirling Moss in the H.W.M. in the Formula II race. Parker was second and Reece third.

And so to the last event of the season at Brands. This was to be the continuation of the Cooper versus J.B.S. battle, spiked by the strong Kieft entry, and most of the big stars were there with the exception of the Cooper works team and the Ecurie Richmond, both of which were in Madrid as previously mentioned. In the Open Challenge Race, out of the four heats, Stirling Moss (Kieft-Norton), put up fastest time in winning heat III at 65·86 m.p.h., but he split his gearbox in the process and had to miss the final. The other three heat winners were— heat I: D. Gray (Cooper-Norton); heat II: J. Brise (Cooper-J.A.P.); heat IV: S. Lewis-Evans (Cooper-Norton). In the final, Stuart Lewis-Evans made all the running and won fairly easily from D. Gray (Cooper-Norton) and Don Parker (J.B.S.-J.A.P.).

Stuart Lewis-Evans showed that the first final was no fluke by winning the final of the Junior Brands Hatch Championship as well, and, together with his wins in the heats, this made four 'firsts' for the brilliant young driver. As to the Brands Hatch Championship, it was completely dominated by Moss in the Ray Martin Kieft, who, having borrowed a gearbox from a disabled friend, won both his heat and the final in the easiest possible fashion. Only N. J. Gray (Cooper-J.A.P.) finished on the same lap as Moss, with Don Parker a bad third. The meeting was marred by a tragic accident which cost the life of H. Parker, who overturned his Cooper at the top corner.

For the manufacturers, Cooper had won two finals, Kieft one, and J.B.S. none, so at this last meeting, it could be said that Cooper's gained the honours.

Summing up, out of eighty-five major events involving Cooper's, the cars had won fifty-six, including four International Hill Climbs, which gave Wharton the Championship; also two big wins by John Cooper at the Monza G.P. and Rouen, with other foreign wins at Luxembourg, Genoa, Eifelrennen (first five cars), Dragnuignan, Madrid, Grenzlanring (first four cars) and Nurburgring (first five cars), one hundred-miler, and the largest proportion of the big home events.

Against this, J.B.S. had eighteen wins, including one hundred-miler, and Kieft had five wins, four with Moss up and one with Headland. All these successes, however, had been important ones, such as Zandvoort and the Brands Hatch twenty-five-lap final on 21st October. The Independents had not fared too well, only one Continental car winning a major event and out of the five wins by independent cars, the most important were the Beels-J.A.P. victory at Avus and Moor's Wasp win at Croft.

As to '500' racing as such, there is not much doubt that the years 1951-3 were the peak years, and that gradually, as the Cooper overcame its rivals one by one, and particularly as the Continental cars had to take a back seat in '500' events, interest in these wonderful small cars tended to decrease. And as John Cooper was the first to admit, the sad demise of Alf Bottoms had a great effect on '500' racing. I take leave of the B.R.D.C. *Silver Jubilee Book* to quote from the chapter devoted to '500' racing by John Cooper in which he said, 'This chapter would not be complete without special mention of that grand sportsman whom we all greatly miss, the late Alf Bottoms, designer and driver of the very successful J.B.S. "500" and I feel sure that all enthusiasts and followers of the 500-c.c. movement will agree with me when I say that, had he lived, competition in this field would have been keener than it is to-day.'

At the annual family conference, the Coopers, father and son, could look back on the 1951 season with some satisfaction, but far from resting on their laurels, they were already planning a larger capacity racing car based on the valuable knowledge and experience they had obtained in racing to date. Also on the drawing board was a completely redesigned Cooper '500'.

THE ADVENT OF THE COOPER-BRISTOL

FOR 1952 the Cooper Car Company presented the Mark VI '500' with multi-tubular chassis, magnesium rear uprights, triangular magnesium housing for the final drive. Fuel system —two front side tanks with filler caps connected by balancer pipe and (optional) two rear tanks connected to those in front; the whole car was lowered one inch, the saving in weight being 65 lb. The Cooper works team was announced as the 'Ecurie Richmond' pilots, Brown and Brandon, together with John Cooper. In February some advance publicity in the motoring press made it clear that Cooper's had a pukka Formula II car (up to 2 litres) on the stocks, which they intended to produce in small quantities, the idea being to build ten of them for 1952. This new venture from the tiny Cooper factory was coming at a very opportune moment, as there had been an announcement from the Continent that there was to be a general switch-over from Formula I to Formula II which would give Britain a chance with the already well tried H.W.M., Alta, Connaught, Frazer-Nash, and now the new Cooper, against the all-conquering might of Italy and France.

Another item of interest to the racing fraternity was the $1\frac{1}{2}$-litre Cooper-M.G. conceived by Lionel Leonard. This was a basic Cooper chassis with an M.G. modded 1,500-c.c. TC/TD M.G. power unit and a Leonard/Davis designed body. This pretty little car created quite a furore at the opening Goodwood meeting. The Cooper-M.G. scaled 11 hundredweight and amazed everybody by giving a P.W.R. of about 150 b.h.p. Progress in a few short years has been so fast that to-day nobody is surprised that the Cooper-Climax 'double knocker' for 1958 developed nearly 450 b.h.p. per ton, with 190 b.h.p. for the power unit, but that is another story.

Having successfully tested their Formula II car, Charles and John Cooper submitted it officially to the public. It was designed and built around the well tested B.M.W.-based Bristol 1,971-c.c. engine.

Specification of the Cooper-Bristol Formula II Single Seater (as given in the *Cooper Year Book*):

Engine Dimensions: Cylinders: 6; bore 66 mm.; stroke

96 mm.; piston area—31·8 sq. in.; valves—inclined pushrod O.H.V. in hemispherical heads; compression ratio—8·5:1.

Engine performance: Max. b.h.p.—127 at 5,800 r.p.m. Max. b.m.e.p. 152½ lb/sq. in. at 3,500 r.p.m. B.h.p. per sq. in. piston area—3·78; peak piston speed, ft. min.—3,460.

Engine details: Carburettor—3 Solex 32 BI down-draught; ignition—coil or vertical magneto; plugs—K.L.G. L.80; fuel pump—A/C mechanical; fuel capacity—24 galls.; oil filter—Vokes full-flow; oil capacity—10 pints; cooling system—pump assisted.

Transmission: Clutch—Borg and Beck; gear ratios—(top) 3·46; (3rd) 4·47; (2nd) 6·31; (1st) 10·1. Rev. 10·0; prop. shaft—open; final drive—bevel gear on frame.

Chassis details: Brakes—Lockheed hydraulic, 2 I.s front and rear; brake drum diameter—10 ins.; friction lining area—134·4 sq. ins.; suspension—(front) transverse leaf and wishbone I.F.S.; (rear) transverse and leaf wishbone I.R.S.; shock absorbers—telescopic hydraulic; wheel type—cast alloy, incorporating brake drum; tyre size—front 500 × 15; rear 550 × 15; steering gear—rack and pinion; steering wheel—light alloy.

Dimensions: Wheelbase—7' 6"; track (front and rear)—4' 2"; overall length—11'; overall height—3' 2"; ground clearance—5"; dry weight—9 cwt. 3 qr. 12 lbs.

Maximum speed: 137 m.p.h.

Body: 18 gauge alloy fitted with Dzus fasteners.

Young Michael Hawthorn, having heard about the new Cooper-Bristol, talked the matter over with his father, Leslie Hawthorn, and Bob Chase, an old family friend, who wished to buy a car for Michael to race for him, and they decided that this would be the ideal car for Mike's entry into big racing. So they both went down to Surbiton to see 'Papa' about it. Charles welcomed them with open arms, as, having seen some of Mike's drives with out-of-date Rileys tuned by his father the previous year, he was sure that this twenty-three-year-old enthusiast was a natural. It was therefore arranged that as soon as the works cars were finished, Mike would have the next car off the line.

By now the racing programme had begun in earnest and all eyes were focused on Goodwood's Easter Monday meeting which is usually considered the showplace and general try-out base for the bigger cars after their winter hibernation. The Cooper works team with John Cooper at the helm had decided to make this International meeting the occasion of the debut of the Cooper-Bristol, and both Leslie Hawthorn and Charles Cooper concurred. What happened is now history, for against very strong opposition, the Cooper-Bristol won every race in which it appeared and was only beaten by the 4½-litre Ferrari in the Formula I race. It won the Lavant Cup, made the fastest lap and filled the first three places; also it won the Chichester Cup. The effect on the daily press was electrifying, and overnight Mike Hawthorn became famous and banner headlines proclaimed the arrival of a new super racing car.

The Lavant Cup: with a most terrific turn of speed, Mike Hawthorn tore away from the field, with George Abecassis (H.W.M.) rather slow off the line, but picking up well and moving into second place. Bill Aston (Aston-Butterworth) and Eric Brandon (Cooper-Bristol) were racing neck and neck for third place, and Alan Brown (Cooper-Bristol), headed the rest of the field. Coming round to the chicane, Hawthorn got through cleanly, but Abecassis overdid it and crashed into the barrier. Brown and Brandon both passed Aston and piled on the speed in an effort to catch the 'Farnham Flyer', but Mike, driving very calmly, more than held them off. Aston's Aston-Butterworth began to run out of brakes and slowed, and none of the other cars could keep up with the Cooper-Bristols, so Mike led the team in to a great 1–2–3 victory, to the obvious delight of the crowd.

The Chichester Cup: World Champion Juan Fangio accepted the offer of a ride in the Cooper-Bristol from John Cooper, and besides Hawthorn (Cooper-Bristol), there were Richardson ('Thin-Wall' Special), Wharton (2-litre E.R.A.), Rolt (Delage-E.R.A.), Poore (3·8 Alfa), Fotheringham-Parker (Lago-Talbot) plus sundry other Maseratis and the like.

On form, the 'Thin-Wall' looked an obvious winner, but not to Mike; he got another flyer from the gate and with Fangio back-marker on the fourth row of the grid getting boxed in by slower cars, he made tracks round the 'Thin-Wall' and got well ahead of the field. Tony Rolt's blown Delage, a good second, was going really well in the hands of its experienced pilot, and Fotheringham-Parker's Talbot was fighting it out with Poore's veteran Alfa behind the two leaders. Fangio battled through the field, but the Cooper-Bristol sounded sick and refused to give of its best for the 'Maestro'—perhaps it was overawed by the occasion. Meanwhile, Hawthorn was holding a 10-second lead on Rolt and going like a bomb, but Tony is not easily discouraged and chased Mike as hard as his grand old banger would carry him. Fotheringham-Parker had by now got the better of Poore, and so the race ran its course with Mike the winner by 10 seconds from Rolt, and Fotheringham-Parker 19 seconds behind in third place. For the record, Fangio finished sixth, his Cooper-Bristol suffering from carburettor trouble. Nevertheless, the urbane Juan Manuel pronounced himself very satisfied with the road-holding qualities of the car.

Alan Brown overcame his handicap to win the Second Easter Handicap, and then the question on everybody's lips was whether the all-conquering Cooper-Bristol would gain another success against 'Pépé' Gonzales who was to take over the 'Thin-Wall' Special in the Richmond Trophy (Formula I) race.

Once again Mike Hawthorn got away to a fine start, but he had a tough customer in 'Pépé' who has been known to make some sensational starts himself. They raced neck and neck up the straight, but from the stands it could be seen that Gonzales began to draw away going towards Fordwater, and coming into St. Mary's he held a lead of about thirty yards—hardly surprising with $4\frac{1}{2}$ litres against 2 litres. But as the race progressed, the large crowd was amazed by the skill and daring of the twenty-three-year-old driver from Farnham; not only was he keeping in front of Duncan-Hamilton (4·5 Talbot) and George Abecassis (H.W.M.) both of whom are no slouches, but he was hot on the trail of Gonzales, acknowledged as one of the world's finest drivers, who was having to press the 'Thin Wall' to its maximum to hold him off. 'Pépé', always a joy to watch, was at the peak of his form and going through the corners in absolutely fantastic slides, broke the lap record at 90·00 m.p.h. And where was Mike? Why, hanging on with supreme courage and still in sight of the Ferrari. But even he could not give $2\frac{1}{2}$-litres to Gonzales, and gradually the gap between the two cars began to widen, yet at the finish, only the length of the straight separated the two drivers. Need anything more be said? Charles Cooper, normally a quiet and self-effacing man, was observed to have a bright glint in his eye and to walk with a jaunty gait on his way back to the pits.

The following week at Ibsley Mike Hawthorn continued his winning run with the Cooper-Bristol by taking both the Formula II and Formula Libre races, and in doing so defeated the official H.W.M. team of Duncan Hamilton and George Abecassis. He also set up a new circuit record.

However, H.W.M. got their own back at Silverstone on 10th May at a most successful meeting watched by a record crowd of 125,000.

The big event of the day was the International Trophy Race run in two heats and a final of thirty-five laps. The entry contained some very strong Continental opposition, including two of the latest Ferraris, a Gordini 'Six', three Gordini $1\frac{1}{2}$-litres, two Maseratis, three of the large 12-cylinder Ferraris, and two Veritas-Meteors.

Heat I: Hawthorn shot into the lead from the start, with Behra (Gordini), Collins (H.W.M.), and Macklin (H.W.M.) on his heels; next came Schell (Maserati) and Wharton (Frazer-Nash) bunched together with Bira (Gordini) looking for an opening. Aston (Aston-Butterworth) was in trouble with plugs, and Richards (H.A.R.) was outclassed. Hawthorn's Cooper-Bristol had opened up a small gap on Behra, but try as he may, he could not shake off the forceful Frenchman. The two leaders, in their battle for supremacy, were drawing away from the H.W.M.s. Schell began to drop back and Bira mastered Wharton for fifth place. Dowling (Connaught) suddenly unearthed some more horses and shot past Wharton and Bira, lapping in 2 minutes 2 seconds consistently. Collins took over third place from his team-mate, but both were losing ground to the two leaders. Behra put his clog down and began lapping in 2 minutes dead in an effort to get on terms with Hawthorn. Dowling's Connaught gave up the ghost and Whitehead passed Schell. Behra continued to press but Hawthorn had the measure of him and also put in a final lap of 2 minutes, to take the flag 2·4 seconds in front of the Gordini. Collins was third some distance away, Macklin fourth and Bira fifth.

Heat II: At the fall of the flag, Hamilton (H.W.M.) and Fischer (Ferrari) shot away together. Manzon (Gordini) gave her too much gun and was slow away in consequence. Fischer led the field through Hangar Straight, but Manzon made up ground very well and coming into Woodcote Corner, had taken the lead. Fischer and Hamilton were locked in combat striving for second place, followed by a pack comprising Abecassis (H.W.M.), de Graffenried (Maserati), Parnell (Cooper-Bristol)—driving very well indeed—Rolt (H.W.M.), Baird (Ferrari), and Brown (Cooper-Bristol). McAlpine (Connaught) and Watson (Alta) both pulled into the pits for a plug change. Manzon still kept his lead. Hamilton strove to get on terms and this went on for six laps until Hamilton retired with a smashed differential, leaving Fischer in second place. Parnell climbed up the ranking and was now in fourth position. It seemed obvious now that, barring accidents, Manzon was not going to be caught, and the rest of the field settled down to fight for the minor positions. However, after a fine drive, Parnell retired, and on the ninth lap Fotheringham-Parker (Connaught) slid coming out of Becketts and crashed into the crowd, injuring three spectators and damaging his wrist. At ten laps, the order was Manzon, Fischer, Rolt, Baird, and this was kept up until the end. Gerard (Frazer-Nash) retired and Watson (Alta) finished last after many pit stops.

Final: Amidst great excitement, the twenty-six cars got away without incident. Once again Mike Hawthorn shot into the lead, closely followed by Fischer (Ferrari) and Behra (Gordini). Manzon (Gordini) repeated his performance in heat II and spun his rear wheels which slowed him off the line. Coming round for the first time, Hawthorn's Cooper-Bristol was leading from Behra and Fischer; Rolt (H.W.M.) was slip streaming Fischer, but had the misfortune to drive into a stone thrown up by Fischer which smashed his goggles, causing a splinter to enter his eye. Pluckily, he carried on, although in considerable pain. Behind Rolt were Brown (Cooper-Bristol), de Graffenried (Maserati), Baird (Ferrari), and Macklin (H.W.M.), the last-named now making an effort to pass the other three. At this stage Manzon coasted in to the pits, out with transmission trouble. Now Hawthorn and Behra were going at it hammer and tongs, with barely a bonnet's length between them. The third time round, Behra had snatched the lead from Hawthorn, but very close behind were Rolt and Macklin, followed by de Graffenried and Fischer, who appeared to be biding his time. Then came drama. Next time round, Hawthorn was in third place, having been passed by the two H.W.M.s, and as he pulled into his pit, pointed to his gearbox. And where was Behra? Not in sight, but through the glasses he could be made out pushing the Gordini pitwards, out with transmission failure.

Macklin and Rolt now began to circulate in 1–2 formation, about ten seconds ahead of their nearest challenger, Fischer. The position at eight laps was: Macklin, Rolt, Fischer, Baird, de Graffenried. Brown was in trouble with a sick engine, Hamilton had retired, and Collins (H.W.M.) had stopped at the pits for a temporary repair and was now trying desperately to get back into the race. On lap eighteen, Schell retired with broken steering. With twenty-two laps behind him, Macklin was securely in the lead with Rolt still second. The crowd was on its feet every time the H.W.M.s passed the stands, and at twenty-four laps the position was, first, Macklin; second, Rolt; third, Fischer; fourth, de Graffenried; fifth, Baird; sixth, Whitehead; seventh, Bira; eighth, Wharton. Three laps later Hawthorn returned to the race after having his gear lever repaired and recorded a lap in 1 minute 59 seconds, the fastest lap in the race so far, but he was over five laps in arrears, so could not now figure in the main results. At this stage, the only change in the leading six was Whitehead, whose Ferrari had replaced Baird's similar car in fifth place. Baird's car began spraying the course with oil, with Crook's Frazer-Nash the first to hit it, resulting in Crook sliding right off the course, damaging his undertray and causing him to be black flagged. The oil flag slowed other cars before any more damage could be done. Macklin had now increased his lead on Rolt to about ten seconds and driving like a veteran, he looked a sure winner. Fischer made his first mistake and slid, letting his compatriot, de Graffenried, through into third place. The race ran its course in this fashion. The two H.W.M. drivers drove in to a thunderous ovation, as did Mike Hawthorn for his gallantry in carrying on in a hopeless position. As to the Cooper equipe, they had the satisfaction of seeing Mike Hawthorn win the first heat and make the fastest lap time in the final, which might have had a different result if Mike's gear lever had not snapped off. But that is motor racing.

At Boreham, on 17th May, Mike Hawthorn put in a late entry for the Cooper-Bristol which was accepted. He once again demonstrated his supreme skill with the Formula II car by winning the Formula Libre race and putting up a new track record at 92·02 m.p.h.

In the meantime, the Écurie Richmond team was having a crack at bigger game, i.e. the Swiss Grand Prix at Berne. This was a real test of strength, as Ferrari had sent a team of four cars, driven by Farina, Taruffi, Simon, and Fischer. Gordini had sent three cars driven by Behra, Manzon, and Bira; H.W.M. had Moss, Collins, Abecassis, and Macklin; de Graffenried and Schell had entered Maserati-Plates, Wharton had a Frazer-Nash, Ulmen a Veritas, Hirt and Rosier private Ferraris, de Terra a Gordini 1,500, and Stuck an A.F.M.V.8. These, with the two Cooper-Bristols, made up the complete entry of twenty-one cars.

In the race Farina (Ferrari) took an early lead from his team-mates Taruffi (Ferrari) and Simon (Ferrari). The batch following were led by Behra (Gordini), Moss (H.W.M.), Manzon (Gordini), Collins (H.W.M.), and Brown (Cooper-Bristol). After two laps, Moss moved up and passed both Behra and Simon to take third place behind Taruffi. This effort was shortlived, as on the third lap Moss came in for a change of plugs, a costly delay that put him back to seventeenth place. Rosier (Ferrari) crashed badly and was nearly run over by Macklin (H.W.M.). The order was now Farina, Taruffi, Simon, Behra, and Abecassis (H.W.M.), who had moved up swiftly from the rank and file. Collins lost a wheel due to a broken rear axle, and with considerable skill, he managed to fight the car to a standstill at the side of the track. A few moments later, the same thing happened to Abecassis, who was not so lucky. The H.W.M. climbed a bank and threw the driver out. He was diagnosed to be suffering from bruises and shock: it was a miracle that he escaped alive. John Heath then flagged his remaining cars in, much to the drivers' relief. Farina blew up on lap seventeen, leaving the lead to Taruffi, followed by Simon, Behra, Fischer, and Wharton (Frazer-Nash). Simon was called in at twenty-two laps to enable Farina to take over, and at thirty laps Taruffi led Behra by 17 seconds, with Farina 20 seconds behind Behra. On lap thirty-six Farina passed Behra, who was having trouble with a loose exhaust pipe, and held second place until his engine lost its tune and he retired. Taruffi was by now so far ahead that he could afford to ease off a little. Behind him Fischer was secure in second place with Behra third, well ahead of Bira's Gordini; Wharton was fifth and Brown was sixth, but the Bristol engine sounded very rough. On the sixty-first lap, Bira retired after a fine run; this left Wharton in fourth place and Brown fifth. They took the chequered flag in that order. Brandon was eighth and last as there were only eight finishers in this gruelling race. With two starters and two finishers, Coopers could feel well pleased with their new Formula II car in its first Continental foray.

On Whit Saturday, Mike Hawthorn journeyed north to Charterhall, where he succeeded in lifting the swag from under the noses of Dennis Poore and Joe Kelly in the shape of the twenty-lap Formula Libre race. The race was notable for two things; one, that Leslie Hawthorn's expert tuning plus Mike's expert driving were becoming an irresistible combination in home events, and also on the strength of his performance with the E.R.A. without rear brakes, Ron Flockhart was an 'up-and-coming' driver.

The Whit Monday Meeting at Goodwood was next visited by the Hawthorns, and the Sussex International Trophy became Mike's property in fairly easy fashion, as, having taken the lead on the second lap, he stayed in front right up to the flag on the fifteenth lap. Bob Gerard (E.R.A.) harried him throughout the race but did not have the speed to get in a decisive blow; Dennis Poore (Alfa-Romeo) was third, some distance back.

The eyes of the motoring world were now focused on Dundrod for the Ulster Trophy on 7th June. Rumour had it that B.R.M. had nominated Fangio and Moss to handle their cars, and the entry list included Osca, Ferrari, and Talbot, so, of course, Hawthorn had to be in with them. It is worth going into details about this race because in it, Mike put up one of the greatest performances of his career. It is said that largely on account of this episode, Enzo Ferrari invited him to join the Ferrari Grand Prix team, with Ascari, Farina, and Villoresi at the end of the season, a great honour and one that startled the whole of the racing world. Entries were: Fangio (B.R.M.), Moss (B.R.M.), Giraud-Cabantous (Talbot), Etancelin (Talbot), Taruffi ('Thin-Wall') Ferrari, Rosier (Ferrari), Hawthorn (Cooper-Bristol), Kelly (Alta), Baird (Maserati), Moore (H.W.M. Jaguar), Flockhart (E.R.A.), Bira (Osca). At the beginning of the race, Hawthorn got the Cooper-Bristol away very smartly, whereas Moss and Taruffi were stuck on the line. With most of the bigger machinery rather slow to get into its stride, Hawthorn began to make hay while the sun shone and was soon well ahead of the field on this tricky circuit. Soon after the start of the race, Bira crashed, but crawled out unhurt, and after the first lap of 7·4 miles, Hawthorn came past the stands exactly 19 seconds in front of Kelly, with Baird third, and Rosier, Giraud-Cabantous, Etancelin, and Moss following in that order. Fangio had spun but was now getting up steam, and Taruffi had some ground to make up but was going very fast.

The quite fantastic Hawthorn led the field for five laps; this with a 2-litre unblown engine against the biggest and most powerful machinery in racing. While this was in progress, Fangio began to overtake car after car and on lap three, was behind Kelly and in third place. Moss was having serious

69

trouble as his B.R.M. had a badly slipping clutch, the top of the gear lever was missing and finally, he began to get chronic over-heating which caused him to retire on lap five. Fangio's B.R.M. was going better and passed Kelly and was now in second place. But Taruffi came up in a rush to pass Fangio who was having great difficulty in holding the B.R.M. on the narrow circuit. At this point Hawthorn had a lead of 32 seconds, but Taruffi, with a very much more powerful car, began to close with him at the rate of fifteen seconds a lap and soon the inevitable happened. Taruffi passed Hawthorn going into the eighth lap. At quarter distance the Italian driver led by 30 seconds from Hawthorn and Fangio was 4 minutes behind. Flockhart was driving very calmly and quickly and was a good fourth. At the half way stage, Taruffi was 1 minute 6 seconds in front of Hawthorn; Fangio, Flockhart, Rosier, Kelly, Baird, Etancelin, and Moore followed in that order. Shortly after, Flockhart had the misfortune to run out of fuel and retired, but not before he had shown that his run at Charterhall was no fluke. Hawthorn recaptured the lead when Taruffi came in for a change of wheels and a refuel and led by four seconds. British hopes soared when the little green car held on to its lead by a hairsbreadth for lap after lap. Hawthorn was sensational, but after holding the lead for five laps, Mike had to pull in for fuel, oil, and water, which let Taruffi through again. Fangio was getting fuel starvation and made a pit stop to see what could be done, but as it could not be cured, he carried on. He made several more pit stops and after a fifteen minute rest for a work-over, the car was pushed to the dead car park. In the closing stages, Taruffi increased his lead over the Cooper-Bristol and was flagged a very worthy winner. Two green cars followed him over the line, Hawthorn's Cooper and Kelly's Alta. Only six cars finished.

On the following day in the Monza Grand Prix the Ecurie Richmond team put up a fine show in finishing fifth and sixth to four Ferraris driven by Farina, Simon, Fischer, and Walker, in that order. In this race, Fangio crashed and received serious injury whilst driving a new six-cylinder Maserati.

The important Grand Prix of Europe was run at Spa, Belgium, on 22nd June, and as Mike Hawthorn had decided to join the Ecurie Richmond on the Continent, the complete team was represented in the race. With Fangio in hospital, the three works Ferraris looked set for an easy race. Moss was driving a new two seater G-Type E.R.A. with a Bristol engine.

The entry was made up of five H.W.M.s (Macklin, Frere, Collins, Laurent, Gaze), Aston (Aston-Butterworth), Wharton (Frazer-Nash), Manzon and Behra driving the works Gordinis, Legat (Veritas), O'Brian (Gordini), de Tornaco (Ferrari), Bira (Gordini), Claes (Gordini) and Ascari, Taruffi, and Farina were down to drive the works four-cylinder Ferrari.

The race was run in heavy rain which resulted in several accidents, happily none serious. On the first line of the grid, Taruffi stalled, and Behra led from the start from Ascari, with Farina third a few yards behind. Ascari passed into the lead after the first lap and Farina passed Behra and immediately got to grips with Ascari. The pair raced neck and neck for the second lap, then Ascari began to pull away. Taruffi had by now shot through the field and was in fourth place. Ascari was lapping at 104 m.p.h. and drawing away from Farina at about three seconds per lap. On lap twelve Taruffi got past Behra, and this made Ferraris 1–2–3. The race was being run under the most treacherous conditions which caused Taruffi to skid at Malmédy Corner, and Behra, close behind, shunted him, both cars being badly bent, the drivers not at all. This left the way clear for Manzon (Gordini) to take third place. Wharton and Hawthorn were having a terrific dice for fourth place, and Wharton, in a 'do or die' effort, passed Mike, but seconds later over-did a corner and went off the road backwards right into a wire fence. Had he not had the presence of mind to duck at the crucial moment he would have been decapitated by the wire. Moss had an engine seizure on the first lap which caused him to crash, so he was out but quite unhurt. Frere was driving very well and was fifth, with Brown (Cooper-Bristol) sixth; the other British cars were well back. At fifteen laps Ascari was 38 seconds in front of Farina, with Manzon and Hawthorn about three minutes behind Farina. At twenty laps the positions were the same, but Farina was 56 seconds behind Ascari, and Manzon was leading Hawthorn; thirty laps, Ascari 1 minute 33 seconds in front of Farina, who was three-quarters of a lap ahead of Manzon, with Hawthorn as steady as a rock in his first Continental race, content to stay in fourth place. After thirty-six laps, Ascari toured over the line with no one in sight; Hawthorn, Frere, and Brown in that order, followed Farina and Manzon.

The Rheims G.P., a week later, was not a very good day for the Cooper-Bristols—they had trouble in varying degrees. Hawthorn's seemed to have lost its tune, Brown's went well for a few laps and then began to use up oil so fast that he used all the oil in the pits to prevent it from seizing; Brandon had carburation trouble, and after several pit stops, Hawthorn finished highest of the Coopers in seventh place. Brandon finished eleventh and Brown retired. The sensation of the race was the defeat of the all-conquering Ferraris driven by Farina and Ascari/Villoresi by Behra's Gordini, a well deserved win for one of the greatest tryers in the game—Gordini *Le Sorcier*.

Mike Hawthorn entered for the G.P. of the A.C.F. Rouen, but once again had engine trouble and did not finish in the first ten, the race being won by Ascari with Taruffi second and Farina third; 1, 2, and 3 for Enzo Ferrari.

Now the scene moved back to England for the British G.P. at Silverstone on 19th July, where a hundred thousand spectators saw some of the finest racing of the season.

At eleven forty-five a.m. precisely, the large field got away to a perfect start; within seconds it had vanished round Copse. After the thunder, everything seemed strangely hushed, then almost before one realized it, two red cars appeared round Woodcote, Ascari and Farina in their Ferraris. But where were the green cars . . . yes . . . a splash of green, Poore (Connaught), Dowling (Connaught), Parnell (Cooper-Bristol), Thompson (Connaught), then a touch of blue—excited French voices— Manzon (Gordini)—green—shouts of 'Come on, Mike!' as Hawthorn went by, looking very confident with red Taruffi (Ferrari), barely a yard behind. Then a pause, and a bunch of mixed-up colours as the rest of the field flashed by, leaving Brown (Cooper-Bristol) to motor to the pits with a slipping fan belt. Peter Hirt (Ferrari) lost his anchors and retired; Ascari came round again with a sizeable lead on Farina, who was being pressed by Poore, with Dowling not far behind. Hawthorn passed Thompson, and Manzon was in trouble with clutch slip and retired shortly afterwards.

At five laps, Ascari piled on the pace and led Farina by 12 seconds; Poore was only 8 seconds behind Farina, Dowling 3 seconds behind Poore. People were asking what had happened to the Connaught, where had this new-found speed come from. Taruffi pressed on and had passed Hawthorn, who was driving a perfectly balanced race and intended to go the whole distance non-stop. At twenty laps a lot had happened; Taruffi, after being given the 'speed it up' sign from his pits, succeeded in squeezing past Dowling, but had not been able to catch Poore until Dennis spun on some oil dropped on the course, which gave the Ferrari driver a chance to get through, which he gladly took. The position was now Ascari 19 seconds ahead of Farina; Taruffi was third, a bare four seconds in front of Poore who had recovered from his spin and was driving an inspired race. Brown had stopped again, still with fan-belt trouble. Murray (Cooper-Bristol) had stopped for fresh plugs. Gaze's H.W.M. had an ignition fault. At forty laps, Ascari was running away with the race, but the Ferrari pits were worried. Farina had pulled in for a magneto check-up and a complete plug change, losing three minutes, and Taruffi simply could not shake off Poore. Hawthorn was beginning to move up and lay in fourth place after taking Dowling and Thompson in turn.

At sixty laps, Ascari had lapped the entire field and was going even faster than before. Taruffi was still second, but Poore made a pit stop which cost him a minute, and Hawthorn's tactics paid off as he now occupied third place. Poore was 47 seconds behind Mike, with Farina fifth and Thompson sixth. That completed the leader board. Moss (E.R.A) had retired with an overheated engine. Murray's Cooper-Bristol was in the dead car park with Gaze's H.W.M. and the Ferrari pits were getting more and more relieved as it was perfectly clear that, barring trouble, Ascari could not be caught. Poore was in trouble (later diagnosed as swallowing some toxin in the orange juice he swallowed during a pit stop), and Taruffi breathed a little easier. Nevertheless, Hawthorn was still in third place and within striking distance of the second Ferrari.

At eighty laps the three leaders remained as before, but the dauntless Thompson again passed 'Doc' Farina whose engine sounded as though it could do with an examination! Poore held on despite the pain of a badly swollen tongue and the race ran its course in this fashion: first, Ascari (Ferrari); second, Taruffi (Ferrari); third, Hawthorn (Cooper-Bristol). Credits . . . four Connaughts started and four finished, fourth, fifth, ninth, and sixteenth, and another superb drive by Mike Hawthorn in the Cooper-Bristol.

The result of the British G.P. brought Mike Hawthorn into prominence in the World Championships. He was now joint fifth with Robert Manzon, with seven points. Above were Alberto Ascari, first, with twenty-seven points, Pierro Taruffi, second, with nineteen points, Guiseppe Farina, third, with sixteen points and fourth place was taken by Troy Ruttman with eight points gained at Indianapolis. It had been a long time since a British driver and a British car had figured so high in these placings, but this was only the beginning of a golden era for British drivers.

Over to Boreham where the main attraction was a two hundred-mile race for Formula I and II, run together, although the results would be separated for the two classes. The entry comprised all the important drivers and cars in G.P. racing, the only exception being the Ferrari and Gordini Formula II teams which were due to appear at the Nurburgring the following day. Gonzales and Wharton were down to drive the B.R.M.s. Facing them in the big class were Villoresi, Rosier, and the Brazilian, Francisco Landi, all in 4·5 Ferraris. The team of four 4·5 Talbots were driven by Philippe Etancelin ('Phi-phi' of the cloth cap), Pierre Levegh, Alberto Crespo, and Yves Giraud-Cabantous. Joe Kelly (Alta), Roy Salvadori (Maserati), de Graffenried (Maserati), Graham Whitehead (E.R.A), and Eugène Chaboud (Talbot) made up the balance. In the Formula II section, Ecurie Richmond had their two Cooper-Bristols entered, to be driven by Brown and Brandon. Mike Hawthorn was in with his Cooper-Bristol; Stirling Moss (E.R.A), Bobbie Baird, Franco Cortese, Bill Dobson, and Peter Whitehead were all Ferrari mounted. Two Connaughts were in the hands of Dennis Poore and Ken Dowling. The single entries of Spencer King (Rover), O. E. Simpson (Alta), and Ron Willis (B.M.W.), were joined by four privately entered Cooper-Bristols, driven by André Loens, John Barber, Archie Bryde, and Ninian Sanderson.

Half an hour before the start of the big race, the overcast sky really let rip and the torrents began to wash the smiles off the faces of the assembled drivers. One thing was certain, the B.R.M. would take some holding. Wharton looked a trifle worried, Gonzales not at all. Then they were off, eight lines of cars got away in an incredible rush with Villoresi at the head, closely followed by Landi and Rosier. Gonzales and Wharton were literally fighting to get their cars off the line, the B.R.M.s sliding all over the place with colossal wheel spin. Going into Hangar Bend, Villoresi led from Landi. Then Rosier, and Gonzales, whose leaden foot soon made up for the B.R.M.s' slow start. Following them was Hawthorn, leading the 2-litres, and then came Etancelin, Salvadori, Moss, Brown, Wharton, Crespo, and de Graffenried in quick succession. Villoresi kept his lead the second time round, but Gonzales was determined to get to the front, and correcting enormous slides as a matter of course, he forced the car in the right direction and hurled it past Landi, who looked a trifle surprised, as well he might, and got behind Rosier, who was now lying second. On lap three, it was Rosier's turn to look surprised as the noisy B.R.M. slid past him in a cloud of spray. This awesome exhibition of fearless driving in the wet came to an untimely end when Gonzales attempted Hangar Bend at a fantastic pace and came unstuck in a backwards slide which took him off the course into the straw and a parked car, from all of which Pépé emerged unhurt, but saying some nasty things in his own language as he wended his way back to the pits.

Hawthorn was now in fourth position and made up a good deal of leeway every time he went through Hangar Bend. Moss in the E.R.A. figured on the big Shell-Mex board in sixth place. Wharton was having an awful time with the second B.R.M. and found it difficult to keep on the road. Brown and Loens were remarkably steady and well placed should anything happen to the leaders. Poore (Connaught) was also moving up and was behind Moss. Landi had been trying to take Rosier for some time but the Frenchman had kept him at bay so far. Villoresi was still leading, but a fresh downpour slowed him down slightly. The leading green car was not affected and, if anything, went faster and was on Landi's tail. The four leaders now lapped the remaining B.R.M. in which Wharton was driving the race of his life just to keep it on the road, and now it was clear that the red Ferrari, the blue Ferrari and the yellow Ferrari were *not* going as fast as the green Cooper-Bristol. At Tower Bend Mike passed Landi and then shot past a shocked Rosier at Orchard Corner, to take second place behind Villoresi. How the crowd loved it as the green car came past the stands in second place overall. The débâcle of the B.R.M. was forgotten. On lap twenty-four Villoresi was but 20 seconds in front of Mike and in the most appalling weather conditions, the 'Farnham Flyer' was giving away $2\frac{1}{2}$-litres to one of the world's finest drivers and making a race of it. Making a race of it! An understatement. On lap thirty Mike passed Villoresi and led the race overall—absolutely incredible! Landi blew a tyre and pulled in for a quick change and Loens retired with engine trouble. The position was now Hawthorn, Villoresi, Rosier, Etancelin (Talbot), Brown, who was driving perfectly, and Landi.

By now the rain had stopped, but nobody seemed to have noticed as all eyes were glued to that little green car which was leaving the red Ferrari by five seconds a lap. The peak was reached on lap forty-two where Hawthorn was 40 seconds in front of the field. Landi passed Brown and Etancelin and was now third. The B.R.M. had been lapped a second time and by now Wharton had had nearly enough. But the tide turned as the track began to dry so that the powerful Ferraris began to grip the road surface and nothing the little Cooper could do could stop Villoresi and Landi from catching up. Gobbling up four or five seconds each lap, Villoresi was but the length of the straight behind, and two laps later he passed the Cooper. But that was nothing to Mike. He repassed and the crowd went mad. Going into Tower Bend, the Italian passed again and Mike got up beside him, but the Ferrari's superior power told and it drew away. The track was drying very quickly and Landi was fast making up ground. Brown was still second in the Formula II Class and Moss third. Brandon was also coming into the picture and was ninth overall. Landi really put on the pressure and lapped in a shade under 90 m.p.h. Hawthorn was trying too hard and his engine was losing its edge. On lap sixty, Landi passed him and chased after Villoresi, but Mike was secure in third place and led the Formula II Class by over a minute.

In the closing stages of the race the sun shone brilliantly and Landi did his best to catch his No. 1, but failed by ten seconds. Hawthorn came in to terrific cheers, having won the Formula II race. His motor was far from sound and it seemed as though water had penetrated into the magneto. Brown and Moss came in to more cheers, only ·4 of a second separating them after sixty-six laps. Brandon was fifth and Ninian Sanderson's Cooper-Bristol seventh. All of these, of course, were in the Formula II Class. Credits . . . once more the Cooper-Bristol had proved itself, finishing first, second, fifth, and seventh in this important race. The order in the Formula II race was: first, M. Hawthorn (Cooper-Bristol); second, A. Brown (Cooper-Bristol); third, S. Moss (E.R.A.). In the Formula I race: first, L. Villoresi (4·5 Ferrari); second, F. Landi (4·5 Ferrari); third, P. Etancelin (4·5 Talbot).

On 23rd August, a club meeting at Turnberry, in Scotland, was attended by fifty thousand people, who were pleased to see the B.R.M. win a race in the hands of Reg Parnell. The other surprise was that Mike Hawthorn had forsaken his Cooper-Bristol for this meeting, and was driving a Connaught in the Formula II race. The main opposition came from André

Loens, Ninian Sanderson and John Barber who were driving Cooper-Bristols. Dennis Poore (Connaught) was most unfortunate, for at the start of the race he was rammed by Skelly's Frazer-Nash, and had to retire with a bent back wheel. The others had a fine dice, with Hawthorn showing his skill this time with the Connaught and proving a good winner. André Loens was driving with almost non-existent brakes, but that to André was a detail, and he was well up with the leaders until the last lap when he blew up, leaving Barber and Sanderson to chase Hawthorn home.

Six days earlier, Mike Hawthorn had put up another magnificent show with his Cooper-Bristol in the Dutch Grand Prix at Zandvoort, and taking on the complete might of the Ferrari and Gordini works teams, he had finished fourth, behind Ascari (Ferrari), Farina (Ferrari), and Villoresi (Ferrari). The H.W.M. team could do no better than seventh (Hamilton) and eighth (Macklin). Moss (E.R.A.) retired. This gave Hawthorn some more points in the World Championship in which he was now joint fourth behind the three Ferrari works drivers. To gain such a high position in the World Table at the age of twenty-three and with a newly designed car was a most amazing performance and one which may never be emulated.

September 7th was the date of the Italian G.P. and although Cooper-Bristols were there in strength (Hawthorn, Brown, Brandon, and Wharton), Monza posed a question that the Cooper-Bristols could not solve. A car designed with a 137 m.p.h. maximum could not compete with cars that could exceed 160 m.p.h. on this extremely fast circuit. All the Cooper-Bristols finished, but the highest placed was Wharton in ninth position.

The next appearance of the Cooper-Bristol was at Snetterton, but unhappily Mike Hawthorn had a nasty accident whilst practising at Modena after the Italian G.P. and was in the London Clinic having injured his ribs. In his absence, John Barber (Cooper-Bristol) more than kept the Cooper flag flying by winning the fifteen-lap Formula Libre race from Eric Thompson (Delage S.) and Ken Watkins (Allard).

The International Meeting at Goodwood the following week attracted a very big entry, and Cooper-Bristols were entered in the Woodcote Cup, the Goodwood Trophy, and the Madgwick Cup, and although poor Mike Hawthorn still lay ill in London, Alan Brown saw to it that the team was not disgraced. Far from it, for his driving was wonderful to watch and was one of the 'hits' of the meeting. Duncan Hamilton took over Mike Hawthorn's Cooper, but unfortunately the power unit blew up in practice.

The Madgwick Cup was won by K. H. Dowling in a Connaught, with Dennis Poore (Connaught) second and Alan Brown (Cooper-Bristol) third. Brown led for the first two laps and then had master-cylinder trouble which slowed him down and enabled the two Connaughts to get through and lead until the end.

In the Woodcote Cup, Formula Libre, against three B.R.M.s, the 'Thin-Wall' Special, Ferraris, Connaughts, and Moss's E.R.A., Alan Brown refused to be awed in the slightest degree and was away from the start with the B.R.M.s of Gonzales and Parnell and ahead of Farina (Ferrari). Although passed by the latter half way round, he refused to be browbeaten by Rosier in the 4½-litre Ferrari and held fourth place from first to last, to the astonishment of such performers as Salvadori (Ferrari), Dowling (Connaught), Moss (E.R.A.), etc., and at the end of the race he was only 13 seconds behind Gonzales in the winning B.R.M., who was followed in by Farina and Parnell.

In the Goodwood Trophy, Brown went one better, and shot into the lead from B.R.M.s, Maseratis, Ferraris, Connaughts, and Altas, and not until they were coming out of Madgwick Corner did Gonzales (B.R.M.) wrest the lead from him with a deafening blare that almost pushed Brown off the road. To make matters worse, Parnell (B.R.M.) followed a length behind, adding his yowl to the din. Brown held off the third B.R.M. of Wharton's for a whole lap, but then had to give it best (maybe he could not stand the noise), and settled down in fourth place overall and at the head of the 2-litre Class. He held this position until the fourth lap when Poore (Connaught) began to dice with him. Moss (E.R.A.) was also chasing him up and these three were having a private battle of their own, until Poore squeezed past Brown whose car seemed to be losing its edge. Brown kept on Poore's tail with Moss close behind for four more laps and then his engine blew up, leaving Poore comfortably in the lead to take the 2-litre prize, with Moss second in the Class, the larger class being dominated by the B.R.M.s of Gonzales, Parnell, and Wharton.

As Pépé Gonzales said (in Spanish) after his victory, 'Had the car gone so well in the past it would have had many successes.' And he was dead right.

THE ADVENT OF THE COOPER-BRISTOL

The final meetings of the year for the Cooper-Bristols were Castle Combe, on 4th October, and Charterhall on 11th October. They were both Club meetings and with Hawthorn still unwell, the Ecurie Richmond carried the main Cooper hopes, but at Castle Combe in the twenty-lap Formula II race there was considerable drama when J. Barber (Cooper-Bristol) slid across the field at Old Paddock Bend. Alan Brown (Cooper-Bristol) shunted him and knocked him into Peter Whitehead (Alta). Luckily the three drivers escaped with slight grazes, but the cars were badly damaged and took no further part in the day's racing. The race was won by the up-and-coming Roy Salvadori (Ferrari), with Ken Wharton second in his Cooper-Bristol and Ninian Sanderson, similarly mounted, third.

At Charterhall the Coopers appeared to be suffering from a hard season's racing (which was not surprising) and did not show to advantage, although the Cooper-E.R.A. had its most successful day to date, finishing fourth in the forty-lap Formula Libre race. This interesting combination promised great things on paper; with the standard Cooper 2-litre chassis added to the very potent blown 2-litre E.R.A. engine, it could have been great, but never achieved the success it deserved and eventually faded from the scene. As to the Cooper-Bristols, in the Formula II race Ken Wharton's car made a good show at the beginning and led from Poore's Connaught which passed him on the second lap, only to be repassed by Wharton who led until lap eight when Poore once again took the lead. On lap ten Wharton retired, leaving Brown (Cooper-Bristol) in third place, which he was unable to hold, being passed by Moss (G. Type E.R.A.) and then McAlpine (Connaught). The order stayed Connaught, E.R.A., Connaught, Cooper-Bristol, but Brown's car was sick and he fell back behind Oliver (Connaught) and gradually slipped out of the picture, retiring on lap thirty-three with timing chain trouble. With the Coopers out of the race, the three Connaughts set about Moss's E.R.A. which they vanquished to make the race a 1–2–3 triumph for Connaught and a pleasant thought for sponsor Ken McAlpine to hibernate with during the winter.

Whilst all this Formula II activity had been in progress and Ken Wharton had won the Hill Climb Championship with his Cooper for the second time, the Cooper Formula III cars were having unparalleled success all over the world, their total of major wins for 1952 being fifty-seven, including a clean sweep of all the foreign races with the exception of the race at Draguignan, France, won by André Loens for Kieft. They had also won the hundred-mile race at Silverstone and eight 500-c.c. Hill Climbs. Against this, J.B.S. had slipped from the scene with one win at Brands Hatch, against eighteen wins the previous year. The Independents had recorded the same number of wins as 1951—one to Revis, two to Leston-Special, two to Arnott, making five in all, but Kieft had replaced J.B.S. as the chief challenger to Cooper's with twenty-four wins in 1952 against five in 1951. At one time during the year, it looked as though Cyril Kieft would have an even stronger hand with the diminutive but quite fantastic Don Parker, almost unbeatable at home, and Stirling Moss a director and works driver at home and abroad. However, a long series of misadventures starting at Brussels with a completely written off Kieft and culminating in the front of his Kieft collapsing at Namur on 20th July when leading the field, decided Moss to resign from the Board and go back to his first love at Surbiton. That this move was right was more than proved when the midget Cooper helped Moss to win his third Gold Star, for in it, out of his last seven races, he gained four firsts, one second, and two thirds. Cooper Formula III cars won in Brussels, Finland, Luxembourg, Nurburgring, Chimay, Orléans, Rouen, Switzerland, Namur, Amiens, Zandvoort, Grenzlandring, Stockholm, Australia, and Singapore. They swept aside all the Continental opposition, which could not win a single race, and showed that Britain was unsurpassed in the manufacture of half-litre cars.

John Cooper's superb win at Grenzlandringrennen, Germany, deserves special mention because, driving the record breaking streamlined Cooper with a Norton engine in place of the J.A.P. used at Montlhéry, he won the race by the proverbial length of a street and set up a remarkable average of 102·64 m.p.h. In so doing he was the first British driver with a British car to win a post-war race at over 100 m.p.h. His fastest lap was 106·62 m.p.h. which beat the 500-c.c. course record by a substantial margin. Moss and Brandon in standard Cooper-Nortons fought out the minor positions, with Brandon gaining second place by the skin of his nose.

The expected tremendous three-cornered contest for Formula III superiority between Cooper, Kieft, and J.B.S. did not materialize. After the tragic death of Alf Bottoms, all the drive went out of the J.B.S. organization. Cooper's successfully vanquished Kieft mainly on the score of better preparation and a more efficient chassis design. Although at certain stages of the season Kieft cars appeared to be swifter, they were nothing like as reliable as the Coopers.

With this solid record of success in both Formula II and III, the Coopers, father and son, set to work to improve the Cooper-Bristol for 1953.

CORONATION YEAR

CORONATION YEAR will be remembered by all for some great British achievements in the field of motor racing, such as the glorious victory at Le Mans by the team of British Jaguars, the fine win by a Franco-British team in a hundred per cent British car in the Monte-Carlo Rally, and young Michael Hawthorn's epic win in the French Grand Prix. And this was the year that 'Papa' Cooper could have been forgiven for hoping that the Cooper-Bristol would win Britain's first Grande Epreuve since Segrave's Spanish G.P. victory with the Sunbeam in 1924. These high hopes were quickly dashed when it was seen that the almost standard Bristol engine could not possibly develop the b.h.p. needed to compete with Ferrari and Maserati, not to mention Gordini. This heartbreaking experience was also shared by H.W.M. and Connaught, and although the British chassis design was proving first-class, only one word could describe the engine position—'outclassed'. Some readers might perhaps mention the B.R.M., but the cold hard facts remain five years hence, as they were then, it is still virtually unproven. For 1953, the Cooper-Bristol was presented with the compression ratio altered from $8 \cdot 5:1$ to $10:1$, and this, together with careful tuning, was giving 150 b.h.p. with a maximum speed of 145 m.p.h., a welcome increase, but unfortunately nothing like enough. The 500-c.c. Cooper Mark VII was identical to the Mark VI except that it was planned to give a softer ride by the substitution of Armstrong four-inch shock absorbers (front and rear) in place of the Newton & Bennett, as used hitherto. The Cooper works team consisted of Eric Brandon and Stirling Moss, a strong hand in any language. The Cooper Company had been honoured by an invitation to send a works team of Cooper-Bristols to the Argentine to race at the new 'October 17 Autodromo Municipal' of Buenos Aires. This invitation was taken up by Alan Brown and John Barber with the Frazer-Hartwell Cooper-Bristol. Charles Cooper decided to go along as team manager, and thoroughly enjoyed himself.

The Argentine G.P. took place on 18th January, and President Perón and the beautiful Eva were interested spectators, along with over half a million racing fans. The Cooper-

Bristols were faced with the strongest possible opposition, including works teams from Ferrari, Gordini, and Maserati. The race itself was another demonstration of the overwhelming superiority of the Ferrari 'four' with 1952 World Champion Alberto Ascari winning from Luigi Villoresi, Froilan Gonzales (Maserati) third, and Mike Hawthorn, in his first race under the Ferrari wing, fourth. Fangio (Maserati) showed fight and was second for over thirty laps, then retired with rear drive failure. The crowd was badly controlled and in the excitement of the race, gradually encroached on the course and on the thirty-sixth lap, Farina (Ferrari) skidded on a sharp turn and crashed into the crowd with disastrous consequences, ten being killed and many injured. Farina sustained injuries to his foot. The two Cooper-Bristols were models of reliability, but were lacking in the necessary power to keep up with the Italian cars and finished eighth and ninth.

A repeat performance of the above was staged a fortnight later under the rather grandiose title of the Ninth Grand Prix of the City of Buenos Aires, and Ferrari filled the first three places with Farina winning from Villoresi, and Mike Hawthorn improving to third place, over thirty seconds in front of Gonzales. Brown (Cooper-Bristol) blew up his engine, and John Barber (Cooper-Bristol) finished twelfth.

After their rather disappointing show in the Argentine, the motoring press was inclined to question the point of sending the Cooper-Bristols abroad to show the flag at the first European G.P. of the year at Syracuse, but once again, the uncertainty of motor racing was demonstrated when three Cooper-Bristols started and two finished, not way down the field, but third and fourth, and fifth place went to the Cooper-Alta.

In the Syracuse G.P. the entries comprised the entire Scuderia Ferrari team: Hawthorn, Ascari, Villoresi, and Farina; two of the new six-cylinder Maseratis with Baron de Graffenried as No. 1 driver; Louis Chiron with the very fast 2-litre Osca; Rodney Nuckey, Eric Brandon, and Tom Cole with Cooper-Bristols, Peter Whitehead (Cooper-Alta), and de Tornaco (Ferrari). From the start three of the works Ferraris shot into the lead, very shortly to be joined by the fourth. Then lap by lap they began to draw away from the field, the order being Ascari, Farina, Villoresi, Hawthorn, with de Graffenried (Maserati Plate) fifth and Chiron sixth. On lap five Villoresi retired with valve trouble, leaving the other three Ferraris still comfortably in the lead. As lap followed lap, Ascari built up a substantial lead over second man Farina, with Hawthorn very relaxed a short distance away in third place. The Ferrari mechanics sat back complacently, only to be rudely shaken by the great Alberto's appearance at the pit with a broken hub on one wheel. Many minutes elapsed before the sweating mechanics could put the matter right and Ascari rejoined the race some distance behind the leaders, only to retire shortly after with a blown-up engine. Having flagged Hawthorn in, Ascari took off once again and in a tremendous burst of acceleration, put up the fastest lap of the day, but the Ferrari could not stand the pace and a couple of laps later, the Hawthorn car blew up too. This left Farina well in the lead from de Graffenried with Chiron third and Nuckey (Cooper-Bristol) coming into the race with a chance of minor honours. With three cars out of the race, the Ferrari pit was far from happy, but Farina kept circulating steadily well away from the others. At half way the order was the same, and the Ferrari boys had their fingers crossed, but this was not the day for superstition, and at three-quarter distance a puff of smoke from Farina's exhaust heralded the end and the last of the Mohicans joined its fellows. A startled 'Baron', having seen yet another red blob at the side of the circuit, made tracks for the wide open spaces and ran out a worthy winner, at an average speed of over five m.p.h. faster than the previous year's race time. He was followed home by Chiron's Osca and then the three green cars of Nuckey, Brandon, and Whitehead, in that order. Tom Cole (Cooper-Bristol) had the misfortune to have a tyre burst, which caused him to crash, the car overturning and catching fire, but Tom crawled out unhurt, although the car was a complete write-off.

This welcome success decided the plan of campaign of the Cooper camp for 1953. Come what may, the cars would be entered for all the major G.P. and International races, and together with the strong challenge of the '500s', it was hoped that Cooper green would be to the forefront in Continental racing. A brief resumé of seventeen of the most important events follows.

Goodwood Meeting, 6th April

The Earl of March Trophy, Formula III. Alan Brown (Cooper) won this race comfortably after leading all the way, and also set up a new half-litre lap record. Moss (Cooper) and Reg Bicknell (Erskine-Staride) fought a no-quarter battle throughout the race for second place. Bicknell claimed that position for four laps, only to be deposed on the final lap by Stirling who became an astonished Stirling when Bicknell repassed him at the chicane, and with both drivers with their feet through the boards, Bicknell got the Staride over the line by exactly 0·4 second. Ken Tyrell (Cooper) suffered severe facial injuries when his car charged a sandbank.

The Lavant Cup, Formula II. This race was something of a disappointment from the Cooper point of view. The Cooper-Alfa-Romeo was on show for the first time with Paul Emery driving. The Cooper-Alta had the wrong kind of springs, and none of the six Cooper-Bristols showed to advantage. The race should have been won by Roy Salvadori (Connaught), but when leading easily, he had the sheer bad luck of having the connecting rod from his accelerator pedal snap, within sight of the finishing line; his initial speed carried him over the line in second place to Baron de Graffenried (Maserati). Tony Rolt (Connaught) was third and Peter Whitehead's Cooper-Alta was fifth, the highest placed Cooper.

Second Easter Handicap, Racing Cars. Ron Flockhart (E.R.A.) drove brilliantly to win from the 35 second mark, and held off Whitehead (Cooper-Alta)—30 seconds, and Wharton (Cooper-Bristol)—22 seconds. De Graffenried put up the fastest lap in an effort to make good his handicap of seven seconds, but was penalized for jumping the start.

Third Easter Handicap, Racing Cars. This looked a set-up for G. H. F. Dunham (Alvis), as he made full use of his 38 seconds start and had a clear lead from the backmarkers, until he met the same fate as Salvadori in the Lavant Cup, blowing up within sight of the chequered flag. This allowed through into first place the brand new Ecurie Ecosse pilot, Jimmy Stewart (Cooper-Bristol), with Leslie Marr (Connaught), following close behind, second, and the anguished Dunham just staggered to the line before Sparrow (Cooper-Bristol) came thundering through.

The Richmond Trophy, Formula Libre. In this race, the Coopers were up against the very heavy stuff and could not cope with an 'on form' B.R.M. driven by Wharton, which ran away with the race, second spot going to Taruffi (Ferrari), and third to de Graffenried (Maserati). The only Cooper-Bristol in the field finished sixth, Bob Gerard up. Peter Whitehead drove the Cooper-Alta, but retired after six laps with engine trouble.

THE RACING COOPERS

This meeting was one of the highlights of the home season, and a crowd of over a hundred thousand watched a day's racing that the French might describe as *formidable*. Faced with a strong challenge from the Continental Formula II cars, the various British marques showed terrific fight, but they were powerless against an inspired Michael Hawthorn, driving the 'Flying Horse' Ferrari for the first time in England. The practice period had been somewhat marred by an accident to Stirling Moss who had flipped his Jaguar C at Abbey Curve on the rather slippery surface and been pinned underneath the heavy car. He was extracted safely, and although very shaken he pluckily turned up for racing the following day.

The curtain raiser was the 500-c.c. race, and with Moss a non-starter, the favourites were Brandon (Cooper), Parker (Kieft), and Bicknell (Staride) with only fractions between their practice times. It was delightful to see three entirely different makes of cars on the front line, the fourth being Truman (Cooper). Second row protagonists were Leston (Leston Special), Brown (Cooper), and Clark (Cooper), and behind them were twenty-four of Britain's foremost '500' exponents. The hors d'œuvre was, in fact, the main course, and the race had the enormous crowd on its toes from the off.

The flurry of cars into Woodcote had to be seen to be believed! It was amazing that a multiple pile-up was avoided (well, who says the age of miracles is past?)—a split second and the agonizing moment was over. The little yellow Staride of Bicknell was leading by a narrow margin from Parker's Kieft, but coming into Stowe it was Parker and not Bicknell in the lead, Brandon battled with Clark for third place, and Wicken (Cooper), Stuart Lewis-Evans (Cooper), Sanderson (Cooper), Headland (Kieft), and Leston (Leston-Special) just battled. Brandon made up some ground on Bicknell who was grimly hanging on to Parker. Clark stopped to fix a plug lead, Lones (Tiger Kitten) oiled a plug. Bicknell, Parker and Brandon were playing catch-as-catch-can and fast drawing away from the rank and file. Nurse (Cooper) retired on lap three with no compression. On laps seven and eight Bicknell had forced his way into the lead only for Parker to snatch it back on lap nine; Loens (Kieft) and McGlashan (Cooper) both retired on lap nine, Loens with a broken gearbox and McGlashan with a broken fuel pipe. On lap ten, Brown was out with engine trouble, and on the same lap Parker was repassed by the indomitable Bicknell, whereas Brandon, in a desperate attempt to cut the two leaders off at Stowe, went into a spin (a rare occurrence for him) and lost much valuable time. Leston had also dropped back with plug trouble, leaving Truman, Lewis-Evans, and Headland to chase Brandon in case he made another mistake. The exciting duel for supremacy was still going on at the head of the table, with many of the crowd yelling their heads off and Mike Erskine just as excited as the rest as his protégé looked like making off with the swag. On the last two laps it seemed as though Parker was driving an eight-wheeled car, the two combatants were so close together, but Don unearthed the little bit extra that some others have not got and took the flag one whole second before Bicknell, to record a wonderful win from a gallant second. Brandon was placed third some 18 seconds behind the two top placed men, and Don Truman battled out of the pack to take fourth place.

With Kieft, Staride, and Cooper in the first three places, 500-c.c. racing in England was becoming very open once again.

On to the larger stuff. In heat I of the International Trophy, Baron de Graffenried (Maserati Plate) won a fine race from a far from fit Moss (Cooper-Alta) with B. Bira (Maserati) third. Moss and de Graffenried shared the fastest lap of 1 minute 54 seconds (92·43 m.p.h.).

Heat II was Ferrari versus Cooper-Bristol all the way, with Hawthorn snatching a precarious lead from Wharton, which he held until the end, to win by one second in the very fast time of 28 minutes 23 seconds (92·81 m.p.h.), with Roy Salvadori (Connaught) third. Fastest lap—M. Hawthorn—1 minute 51 seconds (94·93 m.p.h.).

Twenty-eight cars qualified for the final and front line grid occupiers were Hawthorn (Ferrari), Wharton (Cooper-Bristol), Moss (Cooper-Alta), and de Graffenried (Maserati). The race was somewhat spoiled by de Graffenried incurring a penalty of one minute through jumping the start, which more or less put him out of the running. Hawthorn (Ferrari) came through behind de Graffenried the first time round, with Trintignant (Gordini), Moss, Wharton, and Bira (Maserati) following. The chart on lap five showed Hawthorn in the lead with de Graffenried second one second behind (plus one minute penalty). Wharton had displaced Trintignant in third place, Moss and Bira had dropped back and Salvadori (Connaught) and Rolt (Connaught) had moved up. On lap eight, Trintignant came to grief losing a wheel in front of the Guests' Enclosure which, unfortunately, injured a spectator. The Frenchman held the car magnificently and brought it to rest on the grass out of the way. Moss's extremely fast Cooper-Alta went by sounding very ropey. At ten laps the position was Hawthorn, de Graffenried, Wharton, Salvadori, Rolt and Bira, the last-named cornering *au* Bira *suprême*, but lacking the speed on the straight. However, with his one minute penalty de Graffenried was not really in the first six, which meant that Wharton was second to Hawthorn. Chiron (Osca) retired with a split fuel tank and Wharton began to put on the pressure in an all-out effort to catch Hawthorn. After sixteen laps, de Graffenried gave up trying to catch the 'Farnham Flyer' and give him a one minute start in the bargain, and drove to his pit to retire.

British hopes began to rest too heavily on Wharton's Cooper-Bristol, for it began to misfire and drop back, but another green car soon took its place when Salvadori seized his chance to pass the ailing Cooper. At twenty laps Hawthorn was leading from Salvadori, then Wharton, Rolt, Bira, and Moss in that order. Shortly after, a brace of Connaughts were second and third when Rolt passed Wharton. Hawthorn was trying his best to leave the green cars, but still only a few seconds separated the three leaders. With five laps to go, Hawthorn led by 12 seconds from Salvadori, with the rest of the cars spreading out a little; third Rolt, fourth Wharton, fifth Bira, sixth Whitehead (Cooper-Alta), who had displaced Moss (pulled in for a quick check and refuel). Wharton's car had valve trouble and Bira set out to catch him, which he did on the penultimate lap, and Hawthorn zoomed over the last laps to win by 12 seconds from Salvadori, who handled the fuel injection Connaught very competently. Rolt brought the sister car into third place. Bryde's Cooper-Bristol caught fire and its pilot baled out with slight burns.

On the following day, many hundreds of miles away in Helsinki, the annual G.P. was held in Djurgard Park, and before a 'Silverstone' crowd of about ninety thousand extremely courteous and pro-British Finns, the Coopers put up a fine show, with Rodney Nuckey (Cooper-Bristol) winning the Formula Libre race by ·6 second from Roger Laurent (Ferrari) and Kurt Lincoln (Cooper-Norton). The Finnish champion, Lincoln, gained a popular win in the '500' race, from P. Loivaranta (Elhoo Special) and John Cooper (Cooper-Norton). Three days later at Tampere, Finland, Nuckey repeated his win in the Formula Libre race with the Cooper-Bristol, and the Formula III race was won by P. Loivaranta (Cooper) from John Cooper (Cooper) and Kurt Lincoln (Cooper), so 'Patron' John arrived home very pleased with himself.

May 16th was an important day in Northern Ireland for the Ulster G.P. Once again it proved a straight fight between the red and the green: Hawthorn (Ferrari) against Wharton (Cooper-Bristol). The race was run in two heats of ten laps each and a final of fourteen laps, the general rule being that the first three in each heat should qualify for the final, plus fourteen of the fastest finishers. In actual fact, only eighteen cars were fit for the final. The first heat was won by Hamilton (H.M.W.) and the second was won by Hawthorn (Ferrari). With de Graffenried (Maserati), Bira (Maserati), Collins (H.W.M.) and Swaters (Ferrari) all out of the final with various ailments, it looked as though the main excitement would come from Hawthorn, Wharton, and Moss, but the crowd was disappointed to hear over the Tannoy that Moss was a non-starter owing to gearbox trouble.

With rain falling, on the first lap of the final Wharton (Cooper-Bristol) took an early lead from Baird (Ferrari), with Kelly (Alta-Bristol) and G. Whitehead (Cooper-Bristol) close behind, but by the fourth corner, Hawthorn had passed Baird and was hard after Wharton, whom he passed going into Quarry Corner. Baird was really motoring and passed a rather surprised Wharton on lap three; Whitehead, Chiron (Osca), Hamilton, Salvadori (Connaught) and McAlpine (Connaught) were doing their level best to keep up, in that order. Hawthorn pulled out all the stops and began drawing away slightly from Baird and Wharton who seemed intent on their own private battle which was proving a proper 'do'. The three leaders were by now well away from the field, where P. Whitehead (Cooper-Alta) began to move up, taking Scott Douglas (Connaught), Lawrence (Cooper-Bristol), McAlpine, and Salvadori in turn. On lap ten Wharton breathtakingly slid past Baird on the narrow circuit and began to pile on the pace in a frantic effort to catch 'Golden Boy', but although he brought his lap times down with a rush, Hawthorn replied with a five-minute lap which clinched the issue, and won him his second race at Dundrod. It was rather ironical that Hawthorn should be the one to beat the Cooper-Bristol with a Ferrari, as casting one's mind back to Dundrod 1952, Mike had battled so heroically in his Cooper-Bristol against Taruffi's Ferrari. Still, who could complain at being beaten by modest young Mike; certainly not Ken or John Cooper who both held him in high regard. The result was: first, J. M. Hawthorn (Ferrari); second, K. Wharton, (Cooper-Bristol); third, W. R. Baird (Ferrari).

Sunday, 31st May, was a busy day for the International drivers, two meetings being held, one at Albi, in Southern France, and the other at the Eifelrennen, Germany. The main Formula I and II teams went to Albi and the Formula III giants went to Germany along with the H.W.M. team.

The Albi G.P. Final. After two heats the two Cooper entries, driven by Cole and P. Whitehead, had managed to get into the final and were faced with the full might of B.R.M. led by Fangio, assisted by Gonzales and Wharton; also Rosier (Ferrari), Bayol (Osca), Trintignant (Gordini), Mières (Gordini), de Tornaco (Ferrari), Giraud-Cabantous (Talbot) and Claes (Connaught). During the race, the B.R.M.s gradually shattered the opposition and at about the half way stage, the three cars were 1–2–3, but then tyre troubles almost completely eliminated them, a factor that caused Wharton nearly to lose his life when the B.R.M. threw a tread at about 120 m.p.h., went out of control, crashed into a telegraph pole and overturned. Wharton was miraculously thrown clear and escaped with severe shock. Previous to this, Fangio had thrown a tread on lap ten, causing the car to charge a bank, breaking the B.R.M.'s rear hub, and Gonzales with the surviving car had stopped to change a tyre stripped to ribbons. So this left Rosier (Ferrari) in the lead, Gonzales second, Trintignant (2·5 Gordini) third, Mières (2·0 Gordini) fourth and leading the Formula II cars, and Whitehead (Cooper-Alta) fifth and second in the class. Although Gonzales tried his best to catch the Rosier Ferrari, the minute it had gained by his pit stop was too much of a handicap and Rosier was a popular victor by 31 seconds from Gonzales with Trintignant third; two Frenchmen in the first three.

At the Eifelrennen in the Formula III race, the Cooper cars gained an overwhelming victory, taking the first five places. Moss (Cooper) and Brandon (Cooper) diced it out for three-quarters of the race, and then the Moss mastery began to tell and he drew away from Brandon and won by over three minutes. Two German drivers, A. Lang (Cooper) and O. Kolan (Cooper), had a race-long duel for the minor position, which went to Lang by a nose. The highest finishing car other than a Cooper was the Weeke Special, sixth. John Coombs retired early on with one of Erskine's Starides. The race was run in heavy rain.

The Formula II race gave Baron de Graffenried (Maserati) a well-earned win, although he was pressed all the way by the H.W.M.s of Frere and Collins, who finished second and third. Moss's Cooper-Alta seemed somewhat off-form but he managed to finish sixth. No other Coopers took part in the race.

In the Rouen G.P. on 28th June, Formula I and II were run together. Moss entered with his Cooper-Alta and Gerard with his Cooper-Bristol. Neither did particularly well, Moss losing first gear early on, which placed him at a great disadvantage on the tricky circuit. However, both cars finished, Gerard eighth overall and second in the 2-litre Class and Moss tenth overall and fourth in the 2-litre Class.

On to Rheims for the G.P. on the following Sunday, where Wharton and Gerard entered Cooper-Bristols and Moss the Cooper-Alta. The British cars, including the H.W.M.s and Connaughts, were completely overshadowed by the Ferrari-Maserati duel which ended in a victory for Hawthorn (Ferrari) by one second from Fangio (Maserati), who was ·4 second in front of Gonzales (Maserati), who was 3 seconds in front of Ascari (Ferrari), who was 3 seconds in front of Farina (Ferrari), so with 7 seconds covering the first five cars after over two and a half hours of racing, at an average speed of 113 m.p.h., need anything more be said?, except that Mike became the fourth Englishman ever to win a grande epreuve. For the record, dependable Gerard (Cooper-Bristol) finished eleventh, highest of the British-made cars.

On to Avus, where, on 12th July, the International meeting contained both Formula II and III races and in view of the long, fast straight, John Cooper entered with the Cooper streamliner for the 500-c.c. race. Although John eventually won as he liked, the race contained plenty of drama, for on the very first lap there was a multiple pile-up involving Loens (Kieft) who was shunted and pushed into the back of Brandon (Cooper), causing a German driver in a Cooper to take evasive action and overturn. Keller (Gilera Special) also avoided these cars, but blocked Cooper (Cooper) who swerved, hit the high banking, then bounced off and hit Keller's car. Out of this mêlée, Brandon retired, Loens got away again, the German driver who overturned emerged unhurt, but the car was a write-off, Keller was also out and John Cooper's car was virtually undamaged, but had stalled. John used his strong arm to good purpose and began pushing the car really hard in the hope that he could get it going again. The temperamental Norton had other ideas and it was fully three minutes before a very hot and perspiring John could jump in and chase after the field like a scalded earwig, returning a lap of 3 minutes 2 seconds in so doing. By attaining speeds of around 130 m.p.h. down the straight, John soon had the leading cars of Nuckey (Cooper) and Kuhnke (Cooper) in his sights, and six laps from the end, he passed both to win at a speed of 93·58 m.p.h.

The Formula II race promised well for the Cooper-Bristols of Brown and Nuckey, particularly as they shared the second best practice time, but they flattered only to deceive, for Brown crashed on the first lap and Nuckey held Swaters (Ferrari) for a while, a broken wish-bone ending his challenge. The race was won easily by Swaters from Kling (Veritas) and Helfrich (Veritas).

At home the scene was set for the British G.P. and British hopes for the race centred on a strong entry of Cooper-Bristols, Cooper-Altas, Connaughts and H.W.M.s, but Ferrari and Maserati were far too strong and most of the British cars retired leaving Bira (Connaught) seventh and Wharton (Cooper-Bristol) eighth, as the highest green finishers. Ascari (Ferrari) won from Fangio (Maserati) and Farina (Ferrari). Mike Hawthorn (Ferrari) finished fifth after one of the most fantastic spins ever seen on a track in which the car went backwards at at least 100 m.p.h. right through the grass at Woodcote Corner. How Mike kept the engine running through all the gyrations remains one of the miracles of motor racing. However, the fifteen-lap Formula III race was a great consolation for the disappointment that the vast crowd received in the G.P., for no foreign cars could hope to compete with the all-conquering '500s' of Merrie England and in point of fact, none turned up to try, so the sole remaining question was which marque of the home teams was going to prove successful. Moss (Cooper) soon settled this by leading all the way and winning by 16 seconds from Brandon (Cooper) and Stuart Lewis-Evans (Cooper). The Starides of Coombs and Fenning went very well indeed and Coombs finished fourth and Fenning fifth.

On August Bank Holiday Sunday all the big stuff was at the Nurburgring for the Sixteenth German G.P., the Cooper marque being represented by Moss (Cooper-Alta) and Brown and Nuckey both Cooper-Bristol mounted. All the Coopers were reliable on this most difficult circuit, but lacked the speed to hold the Italian cars. Moss (Cooper-Alta) drove a beautiful race under great difficulty, experiencing gearbox trouble for several laps before the end, but surviving and finishing sixth. Nuckey finished eleventh, after having shock absorber troubles and Brown unluckily spoilt a hundred per cent demonstration of reliability by breaking down a mere half-lap from the finish, after driving for three laps with his rear suspension flapping about in a most disconcerting manner. It might be pointed out by the uninitiated that the above does not sound like a demonstration of reliability at all, but to counter this it can be added that out of thirty-three starters in the G.P., only sixteen finished, with Farina (Ferrari) winning from Fangio (Maserati) and Hawthorn (Ferrari).

A week later at one of the minor G.P.s at Sables d'Olonne, Moss managed to gain a place in the two races which were bracketed together to make the Final General Classification. He was fourth with the Cooper-Alta in the first heat and fifth in the second and due to his consistency, was placed third overall to Rosier (Ferrari) and Chiron (Osca) in the results list. Once again he drove really well, but was let down by a faulty gearbox.

At home, at Charterhall, Coopers had a day out winning the up to 1,500-c.c. sports car race (Davis–Cooper-M.G.), the up to 2,500-c.c. sports car race (Walton–Cooper-Bristol), the Formula III race (Moss–Cooper-Norton), and most important of all, the Formula II race (Wharton–Cooper-Bristol). This left only the unlimited sports car and the Formula Libre races in both of which Cooper-Bristols finished fourth in the hands of Walton and Sanderson respectively, truly a red-letter day for Surbiton.

Over the sea again for the Swiss G.P. and with only one Cooper entered in the hands of Wharton, the best that could be hoped for was a high placing. The dependable Ken finished seventh, the race being another Ferrari benefit, Ascari leading in Farina and Hawthorn, only nine cars finishing out of twenty, and Wharton's Cooper-Bristol was the highest placed British car.

Another minor G.P. at the end of August was at Cadours, and the cars passed the memorial plaque which remains a poignant reminder that the great Raymond Sommer lost his life whilst racing on this rather hazardous track. Without the

Ferrari works team to contend with, Amedée Gordini's boys gave short shrift to the private Italian entries and thrilled their fellow-countrymen with a 1–2–3 victory—Trintignant, Schell, Behra. Wharton, in the singleton Cooper, took sixth place in the final.

With the Italian G.P. the last grande epreuve of the season, there was a full line-up of works teams, including Ferrari, Maserati, Gordini, Connaught, and H.W.M., the semi-works Cooper-Bristols of Wharton and Brown, together with two Oscas, Moss's Cooper-Alta, and one or two other private entries, making a field of thirty cars. As in 1952, the extremely fast Monza circuit showed up the power deficiency of the British units, and the highest finisher was Alan Brown in twelfth place. The race was exciting from the Italian point of view inasmuch as the struggle between the Maserati-Ferrari teams attracted all eyes, the race-long duel being eventually won by none other than Juan Manuel Fangio (Maserati) from three Ferraris, with Farina, Villoresi and Hawthorn up, the first Maserati victory in a 1953 grande epreuve.

Eric Brandon led the usual strong British challenge in the International '500' race at Agen, France, on 27th September. He was joined by father and son Lewis-Evans (Coopers), Bradnack (with Cooper tucked underneath his arm), Bueb— a new name in '500s', but destined to leave his mark—(Arnott), Loens (Kieft), and Brise (Arnott). The international flavour in the mix was led by Beels, now Cooper-mounted, Lang (Cooper), Hanson (Effyh), Gilomen (Cooper), Chazalet (Volpini) and Audibert (Acero Special), plus Davis and Fitzau with early Cooper-J.A.P.s. With twenty-four entries, the race was won in three heats with three cars from each heat going into the final. Heat I was won by Lewis-Evans, snr. (Cooper), Heat II by Brandon (Cooper) and Heat III by Loens. Bradnack, Brise, and young Lewis-Evans all retired with various mechanical troubles. In the final, Brandon, Bueb (Arnott), and Loens (Kieft) diced for the lead, followed by Papa Lewis-Evans and Davis, but after one lap Loens had the misfortune to have a rear tyre slowly deflating, causing the car to steer very badly. Brandon soon got ahead of Bueb, whose car seemed to be losing its sting. With Loens in trouble and Bueb's car not spot-on, Brandon took complete command of the race and ran out an easy winner from steady Lewis-Evans, snr., with Gilomen taking third position, after Davis's old Cooper looked certain of a place, but it shed a chain on the last lap.

From Agen back to Goodwood, run the day before and one of the closing highlights of the 1953 season in England, where the Surbiton firm's cars had an off day, being defeated by home products in the Formula II and III races. In the Madgwick Cup (Formula II), Salvadori found some fantastic revs under the bonnet of his Connaught, and not even Moss (Cooper-Alta) at peak form could shake him from the lead once he got in front. With the polished Rolt (Connaught) clinging like glue to Moss's heels, the race proved very exciting indeed, as apart from the three leaders, Wharton (Cooper-Bristol) and Gerard (Cooper-Bristol) had a grand dice, with the mastery going to Ken. With Moss unable to catch Salvadori, he had to pull his finger out to hold off Rolt, a feat accomplished by a mere two-fifths of a second.

In the Woodcote Cup (Formula Libre) the Coopers were up against Hawthorn, the eventual winner, in the 'Thin-Wall' Special and the B.R.M.s of Fangio and Wharton, and against such opposition Moss (Cooper-Alta) did extremely well to finish fourth in front of all of the smaller capacity cars.

The 'tiddlers' race was one of the best of the day, and the full staff of '500' boys was present, the principal cast being well assorted, i.e. Moss, Nuckey and S. Lewis-Evans (Cooper), Bicknell (Staride), Parker (Kieft), Thornton (Arnott), Emery (Emeryson), Leston (Leston). The five-lap race soon crystallized into a Parker–Lewis-Evans–Bicknell battle, which had the spectators biting their nails. For four of the five laps, Parker kept a narrow lead over his two rivals, and having succeeded in holding them off for so long he was horror-struck to see the sleek Cooper of Lewis-Evans get its nose in front at Lavant on the last lap, leaving Parker precious little time to get on terms, but he slipstreamed young Stuart right into the chicane. The Cooper driver had lamentable luck as he missed a gear coming out and left the way clear for Don to win. Bicknell finished third only lengths away.

The Goodwood Trophy (Formula Libre) was pretty nearly a repeat of the Woodcote Cup, Hawthorn ('Thin-Wall' Special) winning from Wharton (B.R.M.), except that Gerard got his Cooper-Bristol up to third place after Fangio retired with his B.R.M. Hawthorn broke his own lap record.

A few more minor meetings followed, and down came the curtain on 1953 racing. Summing up, Formula II looked a clear case of Coopers being always the bridesmaid and never the blushing bride; Formula III remained more or less as before. Coopers had swept the board on the Continent with the exception of Chimay, Belgium, and Agen, both of which were won by André Loens (Kieft). They had won on fresh ground, such as Morocco, Nairobi, Santa Barbara, California, and Thompson, Connecticut, and, as a straw in the wind, the race at Chieti in an up to 750-c.c. race, thus showing the wearers of the red that even their 750s were not immune to the onslaught of the British 'tiddlers'. The total of major Cooper wins in Formula III amounted to fifty-three, including seven Hill Climb successes, and once again Ken Wharton had won the Hill Climb Championship in the bigger class. Against this, Kieft had recorded twenty-four wins, including one hundred-mile race and two Hill Climbs, Staride had come up with a rush with six wins, Leston had won five times with his Leston Special; constructed by Ray Martin, the Martin-Norton had four solid wins to its credit, the Smith-Norton had brought off a surprise by winning a hundred mile race at Silverstone, and with one win each by Paul Emery's Emeryson and Clark's C.B.P., '500' racing had become more open than at any time since its inception, for in addition to the above marques, there were other makes competing in Formula III racing, such as Arnott, Creamer, Hill-J.A.P., Leprechaun, Revis, and Walker-J.A.P.

1954 AND ALL THAT

WITH the possibility of greater competition in Formula III, the Coopers decided to rehash completely their little '500', and in January 1954, they presented the new Mark VIII, which was sleek and handsome and, in many people's eyes, the finest '500' ever built by the Surbiton firm. The chief changes from the Mark VII were the substitution of the old side fuel tanks for a scuttle mounted seven-gallon tank, the use of $1\frac{1}{2}'' \times 18$ gauge steel tubing in a new tubular structure of triangulated design, and the lowering of the body height and width, from height 2' $11\frac{1}{2}''$ and width 2' $4\frac{1}{2}''$ to 2' 8'' and 2' respectively, and the clever use of three parts only in the body, the nose, the tail and bonnet, and the undershield. Other changes were gearbox mountings: dural plates at top and steel plates on chassis. Fuel system: A.C. pump worked by cam on centre driving shaft at rear fed fuel from tank to small gravity tank behind headrest. Although no claims were made on the grounds of weight saving, the new car weighed some twenty pounds less than the Mark VII. With the official works team nominated as Les Leston and Stuart Lewis-Evans and with Moss driving one of their products whenever he could, Cooper's could look forward to the coming season with some confidence.

However, the future was not nearly so rosy in the larger class, for with the announcement that Formula I, with permitted limits of 2,500-c.c. unblown or 750-c.c. blown, would take the place of Formula II (up to 2-litres unblown), they had nothing to offer, and even worse, nothing in sight as a possible power unit excepting the Coventry-Climax FPE twin cam, $2\frac{1}{2}$-litre V8, still very much behind schedule in positive development. With no fresh orders forthcoming for the Cooper-Bristol, the firm had no alternative but to suspend production and forego their grande epreuve aspirations until such time as a very much more potent British power unit came on the scene, a sad end to a fine chassis, and a particularly bitter blow to Charles Cooper who had set his heart on winning a G.P. for Britain.

Although they had not yet come into contact in competition proper, John Cooper was well aware of the initial success of the Lotus Engineering Kit, an idea developed by young Colin Chapman of selling a sports car in sections to the enthusiast so that he could make it up himself. That from this modest beginning Colin would eventually emerge as his strongest challenger, John could not, of course, foresee.

With nothing bigger than the '500' on the stocks, the Cooper Car Company was pleased to receive an order from Peter Whitehead for a streamlined sports/racing car based on the sensational Jaguar C engine. This car, when finished, obtained many successes including first place in the Wakefield Trophy.

With the Cooper-Bristol holding its own at home, the most the marque could hope for abroad was to give the Continental cars a run for their money in the lesser races. They did, in fact, bring off a surprise win at Zandvoort, Holland, where Alan Brown won the Dutch G.P. for sports cars with Bob Chase's Cooper-Bristol.

The first big win for Surbiton was the British Empire Trophy early in April. The race was run in three heats, the first seven finishers in each case going forward to the final. Heat I was won by Peter Gammon (Lotus-M.G.) from John Coombs (Connaught) and Stirling Moss (Leonard-M.G.); heat II gave victory to Roy Salvadori (Maserati) from Tony Crook (Cooper-Bristol) and Alan Brown (Cooper-Bristol); heat III went to Duncan Hamilton (Jaguar) with Ninian Sanderson (Jaguar) second and Tony Rolt (Jaguar) third.

The Handicap was worked out on the basis of the times in the heats of the first three cars. This meant that the $1\frac{1}{2}$-litre cars were given two credit laps less 35 seconds; the $1\frac{1}{2}$- to 3-litre cars one credit lap less 20 seconds and the bigger stuff started from scratch. Gammon (Lotus-M.G.) led the field a merry dance and after five laps was leading on handicap by three seconds from Moss (Leonard-M.G.) with Coombs a close third. Following behind were Ruddock (Lester-M.G.) fourth, Threlfell (Turner) fifth, and Gallagher (Gordini) sixth. None of the bigger cars was on the leader board at this stage, but with their far greater speeds it was only a matter of time. The first to get up was Brown (Cooper-Bristol) who passed Gallagher on lap ten to take sixth place on handicap; Moss retired with clutch trouble on lap twelve, leaving Coombs in second place. At fifteen laps, Gammon was still first, Coombs second. Brown had moved up to third, Ruddock fourth, Davis (Tojeiro) fifth, and Threlfell sixth. But now the handicap began to sort itself out. At twenty laps Salvadori (Maserati) had moved up to fourth, and the inexorable Brown had overtaken Coombs and was closing up on the gallant Gammon. Salvadori had a great chance to pass Brown but made a mistake at Druids and went off course, losing some time, but the indomitable Roy still pressed the inexorable Alan who could now see the gallant Peter in his sights. The crowd had taken the last named to its bosom and cheered each time he came round. The question on everyone's lips was, could Gammon bring home the bacon. On lap twenty-two, Salvadori set up a new lap record. On lap twenty-five Brown had passed Gammon, who was being hounded by the 'Maser', the heavier car getting by on lap twenty-eight, but too late to catch the speedy Brown. Gammon gained some consolation with a Class win. With Coopers and Lotus figuring in the first three, this race was the forerunner of the duel which these two friendly rivals have fought out since and which is still not decided. The British Empire Trophy result was Brown (Cooper-Bristol), Salvadori (Maserati) and Gammon (Lotus-M.G.).

A month later, Coopers had another big car success, this time at Helsinki, where Nuckey (Cooper-Bristol) won the Formula Libre race from strong opposition including Laurent (Ferrari). It is only fair to say that Laurent was penalized one minute for jumping the start and was placed third behind Carlsson (Ford Special).

The large Coopers had to wait another three months for further successes, but this was somewhat compensated for by their winning three big races in quick succession, the Snetterton Unlimited Sports Car race on 14th August, the Dutch G.P. on 15th August, and the Wakefield Trophy on 28th August.

The Snetterton race was rather unexciting, as Whitehead (Cooper-Jaguar) took the lead on the first lap and ran away with the race. Head (Jaguar C) and Berry (Jaguar C) tried their best to make a race of it, but Whitehead nearly lapped them both.

Nuckey did very well at the same meeting in the forty-lap Formula Libre race, finishing second to Collins (4·5 'Thin-Wall' Ferrari) and beating Flockhart (B.R.M.) in the process.

On 15th August, the entry for the Dutch G.P. was divided into two heats, up to 1,500-c.c. and 1,500–2,000-c.c., run concurrently in heat I and up to 3-litres and unlimited in heat II. In the first heat, Brown (Cooper-Bristol) led all the way to gain a comfortable victory from Musy (Maserati) and Rogers (Cooper-Bristol), whilst the second heat was a Jaguar benefit with Laurent (120C Jaguar) winning from Sanderson (120C Jaguar), and Levegh's Talbot third. In the final, Brown won the up to 2 litres class from Musy with Barendregt (Veritas) third and Sanderson won the over 2-litres Class from Scott Douglas (120C Jaguar), with Laurent third. Due to a rather complicated calculation of heat and final times, the Cooper-Bristol of Brown was adjudged the overall winner of the G.P. from Sanderson (120C Jaguar) and Laurent (120C Jaguar).

With the thirty-lap Wakefield Trophy (Scratch) being a combined race with the O'Boyle Trophy (Handicap), some very varied machinery turned out, including Powys-Lybbe's wonderful, but very ancient 2·9-litre Monoposto Alfa, twice winner of the Irish race. Competing against this monster were such cars as the XK120 coupé, several M.G.s, a Porsche, a Cooper '500', a handful of Jaguar 'Cs', a Gordini, Cooper-Bristol, and Connaught, a brace of Fords, besides Whitehead's Cooper-Jaguar and quite a few other well-known makes.

On race day, McKenzie (M.G.) had the smallest handicap whilst Hamilton, Titterington, and Whitehead were on scratch. At five laps, McKenzie (M.G.) was leading on handicap followed by three other M.G.s. This order remained unchanged at ten laps, with Earl (Vanguard Special) in fifth place which he held for three more laps and then retired. Whitehead (Cooper-Jaguar) was by now leading all the 'Cs' although well behind on handicap. Gallagher (Gordini) was gaining on his handicap. At this stage, the race was marred by a tragic accident in which local driver Joe Quinn's S.A.M. Special crashed into the crowd, killing Quinn, a marshal, and a spectator. By lap fifteen, McKenzie led from Manthorpe (M.G.) and Lacy (M.G.) with Lord (M.G.) fourth, Coleman (Austin-Healey) fifth, and Gallagher sixth. At twenty laps, Lord had retired, Gallagher had passed Coleman and was now fourth to McKenzie, Lacy, and Manthorpe, but now the bigger cars were moving up the handicap with Whitehead setting the pace by clocking 147 m.p.h. on the timed quarter-mile of lap twenty. At twenty-five laps, Gallagher's fleet little Gordini was making mincemeat of the TD's and TC's and was second, and the 'Jags' of Kelly, Hamilton, and Whitehead were like cats chasing the M.G. pigeons. One lap later the cats were amongst the pigeons, and Gallagher was leading the field on handicap with Whitehead leading for the Wakefield Trophy. Only Berry (XK 120) had a chance of catching the Gordini, and on lap twenty-eight he was 22 seconds behind Gallagher, which was cut down to 12 seconds on the penultimate lap, but the latter scampered over the last lap as though all the bats of hell were after him and managed to gain the O'Boyle Trophy by a mere 3 seconds. Whitehead emerged victorious with the Wakefield Trophy, beating Hamilton (Jaguar C) and Kelly (Jaguar C), and the incredible Powys-Lybbe Alfa was fourth.

To cap a season of limited success for Cooper Formula II cars, Gerard (Cooper-Bristol) carried off the Madgwick Cup and was fourth in the Goodwood Trophy at the International September Meeting at Goodwood on 25th September.

From the fall of the flag, Gerard (Cooper-Bristol) took the lead, pressed by Keen (Cooper-Alta) but very soon Keen overdid things at Woodcote, letting Beauman (Connaught) through into second place. Riseley-Prichard (Connaught) and Gould (Cooper-Bristol) had a grand dice to see who could breathe down Keen's neck. Meanwhile a cool and collected Gerard was finding the use of 700–16 tyres on his back end a very steadying influence on the car, and it was soon obvious that he had the measure of the opposition, which allowed him to ease off a little before the end. The position behind changed not at all, with Beauman second, Keen third and Riseley-Prichard getting the better of Gould.

In the Goodwood Trophy, of twenty-one laps, Cooper's had a difficult task, but Gerard more than held his own in practice, being third fastest in a field of twenty-one.

Parnell (Ferrari) and Moss (Maserati) got away together, chased by Gerard (Cooper-Bristol), Salvadori (Maserati) and Collins (Vanwall). The Vanwall did not look too steady as the full power came in, but Collins held it well. Keen easily led the second group. As the cars came round the first time Moss had taken the lead with Collins close behind, Parnell third, Gerard fourth, and Salvadori fifth. Parnell began to drop back with piston maladies whereupon Salvadori took Gerard and made tracks for the wildly weaving rear of the Vanwall. On lap three Parnell retired and Moss began to draw away from Collins. At five laps Moss was leading Collins by about six seconds with Salvadori third, Gerard fourth, Beauman fifth, Keen sixth. At ten laps there was more daylight between the leading 'Maser' and the Vanwall, the position behind being the same. At fifteen laps Beauman had passed Gerard and barring accidents, Moss looked as though he had the race in his pocket. At twenty laps Moss was 18 seconds in front of Collins and both cars had practically lapped the field. Salvadori was third, followed by Gerard who had again passed Beauman; Keen was sixth, a lap behind the leader and in this order they finished.

In Formula III events, the Cooper Mark VIII had had a most successful season, winning every International race at home and abroad except two, plus the majority of the lesser races. The superiority of the new design with its cleverly constructed tubular chassis, allied to the inspired driving of Leston, Lewis-Evans and Moss, had become so marked as the season wore on that only Bicknell (Revis) and Parker (Kieft), were able to make a race of it, although the Staride still showed promise and did, in fact, win an International race at Oulton Park. Also Martin Headland had a victory in a Silverstone '100' with his Martin Special. Cooper '500' wins abroad included Helsinki, Eifelrennen, Hedemora (Sweden), Orléans, Bressuire, and Agen, Porrentruy (Switzerland), and Skarpnack (Sweden), and also 750-c.c. races at Chieti, Senigallia and di Terano. They won International races at home at Silverstone twice, Goodwood once, Aintree twice, Brands Hatch once, Oulton Park once, Snetterton and Crystal Palace once each.

By far the most important occurrence of the year as far as 500-c.c. cars were concerned was the emergence of the 750-c.c. race in Italy. With the complete lack of a small car to compete with the British '500', the Italians could now make a respectable race of it with their '750s', thus ensuring full spectator interest in these events.

One of the most outstanding personalities to spring into prominence in half-litre racing was undoubtedly Jim Russell of Downham Market, a thirty-four-year-old garage proprietor who, on the strength of the season's showing, was snapped up by John Cooper for the 1955 works team.

Just when all the boys were putting their cars away for the winter, the B.R. & S.C.C. (late Half-Litre Club) hit on the bright idea of staging a '500' Championship Meeting at Brands Hatch on Boxing Day and to many people's surprise, it was a colossal success. Before the meeting, Don Parker had a half-point lead over Les Leston for the big pot, so rightly or wrongly he had to prove his claim to the Championship once again at the extra meeting.

With some really wonderful racing preceding, the crowd was on its toes for the twenty-lap Christmas Trophy race, the last of the day. Leston was the hot favourite as he was the only driver with the Cooper Mark IX, an advance delivery of the 1955 model (a facsimile of the Mark VIII with disc brakes on the back and improved suspension). Ranged against him was a badly shaken Parker (Kieft) who had crashed in practice, Bueb (Cooper), S. Lewis-Evans (Cooper), Tyrrell (Cooper), Bicknell (Revis), to mention the most important challengers. To add to the interest, Father (Stirling Moss) Christmas was official starter and with his Union Jack tucked under his red coated arm 'Santa' staggered on to the rostrum, down went the flag and the field was off, except for young Lewis-Evans who stalled on the line and had to wait patiently for a shove, as all eyes were focused on the corpulent character gaily tripping off the starter's box. Meanwhile, Leston (Cooper) had not wasted his time and was leading the field coming round after the first lap. Close behind heading the pack was Bueb with Bicknell, Tyrrell, Cowley (Cooper), and Parker following. Going into Druids, Bueb put in his challenge and passed Leston. Cowley, driving really well, succeeded in passing Tyrrell and the irrepressible Bicknell closed up on Leston, and the latter had to fight hard to keep second spot. With all these dog-fights going on, nobody had noticed that Lewis-Evans had made up a lot of ground, until some of the brighter lads began to put their watches on him, only to find that he was lapping faster than the flying Bueb.

With the pace quickening all the time and with nary a soul watching his revs, something had to go, and on the fifth lap, Cowley and Bicknell began to drop back with sick engines. Bueb, driving magnificently, was actually leaving Leston behind, Mark IX and all—Parker was now well in the picture and closing up on Leston on every lap. By lap eight, Parker had taken Leston and Lewis-Evans, going like a shot from a gun, had passed Tyrrell and was in fourth place—a fine effort after giving the field half a lap start. Leston was determined to catch Parker, for the Championship was at stake, and lap after lap they were locked in the very 'daddy' of a dog-fight with no holds barred. There were thrills a-plenty and even more to come when Lewis-Evans got even closer to the *Autosport* Trophyites. The majestic Bueb had by now drawn clear away from everyone and looked a certain winner, but forty thousand pairs of eyes were riveted on the dog-fights behind.

Then Fate took a hand, for the strain of fighting off the Leston challenge proved too much for Parker, who lost his concentration for a fraction of a second and spun, letting Les through, and to make matters worse for the little man, Lewis-Evans also passed him before he could get going again.

Although he had lost much valuable time, Parker was still in the hunt and chased round as before. Now Leston was faced with another challenge, this time from the dauntless Lewis-Evans and try as he might could not shake him off, so much so that Lewis-Evans passed the Mark IX driver on the outside going round Paddock Bend, a move that left the crowd gasping. Prior to this young Stuart had put up a new lap record of 61 seconds. With no chance of catching Bueb and with his chief opponent some distance behind, Leston slowed a little, content to keep his third place. Lewis-Evans carried on as fast as ever and finally finished a brilliant second to Bueb, with Leston third and Parker fourth. By gaining an extra point, Les Leston just pipped the unfortunate Parker for the *Autosport* Championship, and with Coopers filling the first three places the race proved another triumph for invincible Surbiton.

LADY GODIVA COMES TO TOWN

HAVING been proved successfully at Brands at Christmas, the 1955 Mark IX Cooper '500' was put into series production and the basic changes from the Mark VIII were written up in the January issue of *Motor Racing* with emphasis on the new disc brake as follows: 'The hydraulically operated brake is an adaptation of the Palmer aircraft brake and is manufactured for the Cooper Car Company by the H.R.G. Engineering Co. Ltd. who made the original adaptation. Production Mark IXs will be fitted with either cast iron or malleable steel discs. There is one banana-shaped friction pad mounted to apply pressure on each side of the disc. Although the brake was fitted primarily to reduce unsprung weight to the minimum it has turned out to be powerful and smooth in operation.' Other modifications to the car included flattening the front and rear transverse leaf springs, which allowed the frame to be lowered by one and a half inches, tilting the Norton engine towards the rear at an angle of fifteen degrees, which lowered the power unit by two and a half inches, and modifying the centre mountings on the front and back springs to provide more roll resistance at the front. (This latter was conspicuously successful.) A reduction in weight by the careful machining of the front wheels allied to the much lighter disc brake and slightly shorter frame tubes meant a substantial weight reduction over the 1954 Mark VIII, with better handling qualities. This was indeed the complete lethal weapon for Formula III.

Allied to the Mark IX, the Cooper Car Company also offered the Cooper-Jaguar Mark II with D-type engine and gearbox, but their chief hopes for sports car racing were pinned on the new 1,100-c.c. Coventry-Climax engine which was due for delivery early in 1955. With Formula III safely in the bag, John Cooper was more than keen to have a go at the Lotus of Colin Chapman which had established overwhelming superiority during 1954 in the smaller sports car classes. With Jim Russell already signed, John Cooper took quick steps to get Ivor Bueb's pen to paper, and with these two worthies in the works team, the astute John was well set for the 1955 season.

THE RACING COOPERS

Cyril Kieft stepped in first with a 1,100-c.c. Coventry-Climax engined sports car which was officially announced in the 14th January issue of *Autosport* by John Bolster. Meanwhile, both Cooper and Lotus were working along the same lines, and very shortly afterwards Surbiton had their first Cooper-Climax sports car ready for testing. The most sensational departure from standard was undoubtedly the 'Manx Tail' in the use of which Coopers had followed the theory of Doctor Kamm, the German scientist, who held that the sawn off back sets up eddies which give stability equal to tail fins and, further-more, that it is a more efficient shape than the fully stream-lined back. (There is a story going the rounds which may contain a grain of truth, i.e. that as John Cooper could not get a fully streamlined car into the works truck, he decided to solve the problem by sawing off the back!) Apart from this departure, the clever chassis was basically 'Cooper', engine at rear, standard Cooper wheels, centre seating, multi-tubular space frame, I.F.S., and I.R.S., etc. The spare wheel, battery, radiator, and fuel tank were in front and the car was designed to carry forty-five per cent of the total weight of 800 lbs. on the front wheels, with over 75 b.h.p. John Cooper had tried many gearboxes without success until he finally settled on the standard Citroën gearbox with four special ERSA gears which did the trick admirably. The Coventry-Climax overhead camshaft four-cylinder 72·4 by 66·6 mm. 1,097-c.c. engine was mounted behind the driver's seat and was aligned with the Citroën bell housing by means of an adaptor plate also carrying the starter motor, the body was all-enveloping and owed a great deal to its parents, the previous Cooper record-breaking cars. Overall length—10' 10", width—4' 9", wheel-base—7' 5", and with driver aboard, plus full tank, the weight distribution was 45/55.

With the classic British Empire Trophy race designed as the first public outing, Surbiton did their utmost to get the new car ready, but unfortunately, due to various technical hitches, it was not to be. However, nine days later, the car was on the line for the Easter Monday International Race Meeting at Goodwood.

The sports car race, for cars up to $1\frac{1}{2}$ litres, was notable for a stimulating battle between the two $1\frac{1}{2}$-litre Connaughts of Leston and McAlpine and the new 1,100-c.c. Cooper-Climax driven by Bueb. From the start the two Connaughts shot into the lead with Leston and McAlpine duelling for dear life.

LADY GODIVA COMES TO TOWN

Behind these two, Moss (Beart-Rodgers-Climax) and Bueb did their level best to give 400 c.c.s to the Connaughts, but after two laps, the Beart-Rodgers had had enough and blew its top. Coombs (Lotus-Connaught) kept on the Manx-tail of the Cooper, but was unable to pass, and Brandon (Halseylec-Climax) drove very well, but could not quite get on terms with Coombs or Bueb. Chapman (Lotus) did not show to advantage at all and retired on lap two. Leston and McAlpine remained glued together for every one of the five laps with Leston leading his fellow Connaught driver over the line by a bare 1·4 seconds with Bueb third and first in the 1,100 Class, and, incidentally, well ahead of several 1½-litre cars, a gratifying start for the prototype Cooper.

The Cooper Car Company soon had its second works car for Jim Russell finished and in addition, it delivered the first privately owned car to Tommy Sopwith, who took to it like a duck to water. Meanwhile the stage was set for the International Meeting at Silverstone on 7th May and Ivor Bueb was entered to drive the works Cooper-Climax in the big sports car race.

In practice Bueb had done a 1 minute 59 seconds, which put the 1,100-c.c. Cooper well ahead of all the 1,100-c.c. and 1,500-c.c. cars. In the race, although Leston (Connaught 1½-litre) led the up to 1,500-c.c. Class for a while, it was not very long before Bueb (Cooper-Climax 1,100-c.c.) had replaced him. With Connaught, Lotus, Beart-Rodgers-Climax, and Lester-M.G. all competing for the honours in the up to 1,500-c.c. Class, the Cooper had to be very good indeed to bring home the 'lovely olly' and the Surbiton *equipe* was out in force to cheer its new driver on. Ivor responded to such good purpose that he equalled Scott-Brown's fastest lap (90·84 m.p.h.) in the 2-litre Lister. The pace became too hot for many cars and retirements included Chapman (Lotus-M.G.), broken crankshaft, Brown (H.W.M.), valve spring, Sears (Lister), accident, Scott-Brown (Lister), blown gasket, and Moss (Beart-Rodgers), ignition trouble. Bueb drove on undisturbed and led the 2-litre class to boot. It was to prove Ivor's day in the remarkable little Cooper, and even the lion-hearted Leston could not hold him, although it is only fair to mention that the Connaught driver had a sticking throttle for part of the time. The race ran out in this manner with Parnell (Aston-Martin) winning overall from Salvadori in a similar car, Bueb winning the up to 1,500-c.c. Class from the

Connaughts of Leston and McAlpine, and being placed ninth overall and ahead of all cars up to 2-litres.

The racing fraternity was quick to see the possibilities of the sports Cooper which provided a car priced at £1,350 which could more than hold sports cars at double that figure and orders began to roll in, making the little Surbiton factory very busy indeed. Not being one to sit back, John Cooper had already put the Cooper-Climax through tests with two hundred weight of ballast in the rear, and satisfied himself that the car could take a bigger engine should one be forthcoming.

Towards the end of May the 'Manx-tail' was on parade again at the International Meeting at Crystal Palace and interest was at a high pitch to see who would be the victor in the 1,500-c.c. Class of the Anerley Trophy race. Between the two leading protagonists, Leston in the 1½-litre Connaught and Bueb in the 1,100-c.c. Cooper, the honours had been even in two of the smaller meetings, Leston winning from Bueb at Ibsley and Bueb turning the tables at Brands (the last named duel being reckoned by one and all to have been the most exciting tussle seen for many a long day). At Whitsun Brands, Leston had won the Fawksham Trophy Race (sports cars up to 1,500-c.c.) and Bueb had won the Whitsun Trophy Race (sports cars up to 1,200-c.c.), but they had not met in either race.

The Anerley Trophy race was run in perfect weather, and was another complete triumph for Bueb. Leston (Connaught got away first, but Bueb (Cooper-Climax) beat him into Ramp and held an oh, so small lead coming round for the first time. Nurse (Lotus) and Hayles (Lotus) both pressed their cars as hard as they would go, but could not keep up with the two leaders. On laps two, three, and four Bueb kept his meagre lead, but Les whipped up an extra horse on lap five, and coming down Park Curve he was the proud possessor of a one-yard lead. On laps six and seven, Bueb left his braking just a fraction late in his efforts to take Leston going into Ramp, but the Connaught driver fought him off each time. On lap eight, Bueb did not leave his braking a fraction late—to the startled onlookers it seemed as though he was doing without these so-called necessities, for he charged into Ramp at an impossible speed, almost scraping the Bridge, and not one person in that vast crowd will ever believe that the age of miracles is past, for exactly one minute later there was the little Cooper shooting down past the starting line with a new unlimited sports car lap record of 72 m.p.h. in the bag. After that, even Les had to give him best, and Bueb ran out winner of the race by 3 seconds. Whew! For the record, Nurse was third.

On the previous Saturday, Jim Russell had taken the other works Cooper-Climax up to Snetterton. Here he was joined by Tommy Sopwith driving the Equipe Endeavour Cooper-Climax. Russell had not quite got the hang of the car and shunted it into a bank going through the Esses, luckily without damage to the driver. Sopwith, on the other hand, drove beautifully and well deserved the two seconds he gained in events 2 and 3. In each case, he was giving away at least 400-c.c.s, making this young driver's performance all the more meritorious. At this stage of the game it was clear that Colin Chapman, by pinning his faith on the $1\frac{1}{2}$-litre M.G. power-plant in preference to the 1,100-c.c. Climax, had made a big mistake, witness the solid record of success already achieved by the Cooper-Climax, in most cases against the best $1\frac{1}{2}$-litre cars.

With Le Mans only a few days away, the Cooper Car Company was sweating on the top line to get a car ready for Wadsworth and Brown, two amateur drivers, who, with praiseworthy spirit, had decided to have a go in the 1,100-c.c. Class. True to form the car was shipped over just in time for scrutinizing, and although technically a private entry, John Cooper very sportingly put all the facilities of the works at the disposal of Wadsworth and Brown, and in addition, secured the services of one of the greatest improvisers in the trade as Manager of the pit, to wit, John Cooper. Harry Munday, designer of the 1,100-c.c. engine was also there. In the 1,100-c.c. Class, the Cooper was opposed by Kieft, Panhard, Osca, Lotus-Climax (Colin Chapman having decided to use the Coventry engine in preference to Abington), the inevitable Porsche, and a brace of Panhards.

The Cooper marque was also represented in the larger class by the brothers Whitehead in their Cooper-Jaguar. One place where John Cooper was welcomed with open arms was the Jaguar pit, where our old chum Ivor Bueb, on the strength of John's recommendation to Mr. Lyons, had been signed on to co-pilot with Mike Hawthorn in the Jaguar team.

The Le Mans Twenty-four Hour race took place on 11th–12th June. In practice in their Class, the Cooper and Lotus showed up best; the Kieft-Turner was far slower than its sister cars with Climax engines. John Cooper took the Cooper-Climax round for several laps and found everything to his liking. For sheer speed only the Panhard looked a danger to Lotus and Cooper, but so much depended on reliability. At four o'clock in the afternoon; accompanied by all the pomp and circumstance of Le Mans, the field made its first rush under the Dunlop Bridge. At four minutes past four a flash of red denoted the passing of the dashing Castellotti (works Ferrari), hounded by the Hawthorn–Bueb Jaguar and the rest of the bigger stuff. About a minute later, the first of the 1,100-c.c. Class came shooting past—it was the Lotus of Chapman–Flockhart. Seven seconds behind the little Cooper was being chased by the Panhard of Cotton–Beaulieu, and the Kieft. The two 1,100-c.c. Porsches and the other Panhard were already some distance back. The class position did not change very much for the first few laps, and by lap four the Mercedes, Ferraris, Jaguars, and Aston Martins had already begun to lap the Class II and G cars. Notwithstanding the maelstrom all around it, the Cooper was being driven very fast and very safely, but the far more experienced team of Chapman and Flockhart kept the Lotus in front. After two hours' racing, John Cooper was well pleased with the W. and B. performance.

Then, as is well known, at six twenty-five came the horrible accident that changed a gay race into a fearful inferno and caused terrific strain on the already tense drivers. The almost untried team of Wadsworth and Brown came through the grim test with flying colours, as, in fact, did Bueb when called upon to take over the leading Jaguar from Hawthorn having been a witness of the terrible crash only seconds before. As darkness fell, the Lotus was leading the 1,100-c.c. Class by one lap from the Olivier–Jeser Porsche, with the Cooper three laps behind the Porsche, but in its turn, leading the Duntov–Veuillet Porsche and the two Panhards; the Rippon–Merrick Kieft had retired on lap forty-eight with no oil. During the hours of darkness the class position changed greatly. The Cooper suffered a fractured hose-pipe and under the regulations was not allowed to pull into the pit for repairs. Consequently W. and B. carried on and hoped for the best. They were faced with the almost impossible task of doing eight laps without water in the radiator before getting a refill, and the sturdy little Climax engine did just that, and on being allowed to slake its thirst at last, it carried on as sweetly as before.

Chapman in the Lotus had the misfortune to slide off at one fifty-five a.m. and, was disqualified for reversing back onto the course without waiting for a marshal's permission. The Chancel brothers' Panhard retired at two twenty-one with fuel feed failure, and the Cotton–Beaulieu Panhard retired one and a half hours later with gearbox failure. This left the brace of Porsches comfortably ahead with only the Cooper to make up the class. Having lost nearly two and a half hours during the night through water starvation, the Cooper had no chance of catching the two Porsches, and settled down to finish, which it managed to do, but only just, as the last three laps were touch and go with the engine by now very much the worse for wear. However, at four o'clock, twenty-four hours after the start, the Cooper finished its first long distance race and joined the select band of twenty-one finishers out of fifty-eight starters, besides being third in the 1,100-c.c. Class. With the sight of Bueb and co-pilot Hawthorn driving past the long line of cheering pits in the winning Jaguar still fresh in his mind, John Cooper was heard to remark to no one in particular: 'Can I pick 'em or can I pick 'em?'

Results	750–1,100 c.c. class	Distance	Speed
1st	Duntov–Veuillet (Porsche)	3,303·570 kms.	85·45 m.p.h.
2nd	Olivier–Jeser (Porsche)	3,155·310 kms.	81·52 m.p.h.
3rd	Wadsworth–Brown	2,789·610 kms.	72·05 m.p.h.

Having proved that the new sports car was not only fast but also reliable, John Cooper, Bill Knight, and the author began planning an all-out attack on World and International Records (Class 'G') to take place in October, and a new car was laid down for this purpose to incorporate everything learned at Le Mans.

On 18th June, at Goodwood, Tommy Sopwith had a red letter day. Driving the Equipe Endeavour Cooper-Climax he beat a strong field in Event 1 up to 1,250-c.c. and also Event 3 up to 1,500-c.c. In both races the rest of the field must have thought that they were chasing a shadow for what they saw of Tommy once he left the gate. The result of the 1,250-c.c. race was first, T. Sopwith (Cooper-Climax); second, R. Mackenzie Low (Elva); third, W. Liddell (Buckler); and of the 1,500-c.c. race first, T. Sopwith (Cooper-Climax); second, W. Liddell (Buckler); third, P. Riley (Lotus).

A week later Jim Russell gained his first success with the works Cooper-Climax taking the up to 1,500-c.c. Class on his own ground at Snetterton, where he won from Naylor (Lotus-Connaught 1,488-c.c.) and Digby (Lotus-Consul 1,498 c.c.).

An exceedingly welcome visitor to the Cooper works was Jack Brabham, the well-known Australian driver and mechanic, who, having been fascinated by Ivor Bueb's performance at Silverstone with the Cooper-Climax, suggested to John Cooper that if he could build him a similar car round the 2-litre Bristol power-plant, it would prove a worthy contender for Formula I honours. John was in complete agreement and it was decided there and then that Jack Brabham should give a hand in the assembly of the car and when it was completed, he should drive for the works.

Besides the record car and the Brabham Special, orders were received for eleven more Cooper-Climax '1,100s', a sizeable order for the small Surbiton concern.

The Brands Hatch Meeting was held on 10th July. In the event for sports cars up to 1,200-c.c., Russell, Bueb, and Gammon were all driving Cooper-Climaxes, the opposition being led by Chapman, Hayles, and Page on Lotus, and Brandon with his Halseylec. The Coopers and Lotus got away in a bunch but Russell (Cooper) soon put some daylight between himself and the field. Chapman (Lotus), Bueb (Cooper) and Gammon (Cooper) provided the excitement behind the leader and no quarter was asked or given. Russell definitely had the edge on the others and increased his lead on every lap. Whilst doing this, he put up a new class record of 63·6 seconds (70·19 m.p.h.) Chapman managed to draw ahead of Bueb and Brandon managed to pass Gammon for fourth spot. As Russell took the flag Chapman came charging down the straight with Bueb doing his best to make it a Cooper 1-2 victory. He did make up the required inches and the official result was a dead-heat for second place.

In the race for sports cars up to 1,500-c.c. Bueb (Cooper) got a flyer and was sternly chased by Jopp (Lotus), Gammon (Cooper) and Russell (Cooper). After four laps Bueb still led, but Russell had passed Gammon and Jopp and was holding second place. On lap six the two Cooper works drivers were disputing the lead which eventually fell to Russell. From then on Russell drew away from Bueb. Hayles (Lotus), Stacey (Lotus), Jopp (Lotus) and Gammon (Cooper) diced for the minor position and not until the last lap was this place occupied for good and all by Gammon, making Coopers 1-2-3.

On to the British Grand Prix at Aintree, where the main Cooper interest lay in the sports car race, the works 1,100-c.c. Cooper-Climax being driven by Ivor Bueb.

Run on General Classification, the Cooper could not hope to win outright from such opposition as the works Jaguars and Aston Martins, and even to lift the 1,500-c.c. Class it had to beat the Lotus team led by Colin Chapman in his 1,500-c.c. Lotus-M.G. and works Connaught led by Ken McAlpine, besides Les Leston driving the Peter Bell Connaught. From the start, the big cars got well in front with Astons seeming to have the legs of the Jags. By lap three Salvadori (Aston) and Collins (Aston) were 1-2, Hawthorn, Berry, and Sanderson third, fourth, and fifth in their Jags, but going very well in eighth position was the leader in the 1,500-c.c. Class, Colin Chapman. Bueb's Cooper, the smallest car in the race, was back-marker, but pluckily having a dice with Leston (Connaught), McAlpine (Connaught), and any spare 2-litre cars that might be trying to get away from the lowly '1,100'. By lap ten, having no doubt breathed fire and brimstone on his 'Loti', Chapman led both the 2-litre and 1,500-c.c. Classes. McAlpine had pushed his Connaught well past all but one of the 2-litre Class and Bueb had managed to take Leston and proudly passed Davis (Lotus-Bristol). By lap fifteen the race was led by the four Astons of Salvadori, Collins, Parnell, and Walker, with Hawthorn fifth, Chapman ninth, McAlpine eleventh, and Bueb thirteenth. With no major changes on the last two laps, the race finished in this fashion: up to 1,500-c.c. Class; first, C. Chapman (Lotus-M.G.); second, K. McAlpine (Connaught); third, I. Bueb (Cooper-Climax).

Jack Brabham entered his new 2·2-litre Cooper-Bristol in the British Grand Prix Race and hoped to put up a fair show. It was completely untried and proved the slowest car in practice. In the race it developed severe clutch slip, and although Jack did his best to keep going, after thirty laps he retired with a bent valve.

Over the August holidays there were the usual two South of England meetings, Crystal Palace International on the Saturday, and Brands Hatch International on Bank Holiday Monday. The Cooper works team was entered in both events, whereas Lotus works was entered at Crystal Palace only, although six privately owned Lotus were down to run at Brands.

There was a strong entry at Crystal Palace on 30th July in the sports car race up to 2 litres, made up of Bueb, Russell, and Sopwith (Cooper-Climax 1,100-c.c.), Page, Jopp, Coombs, and Young (Lotus-Climax 1,100-c.c.), Chapman (Lotus-M.G. 1,500-c.c.), Brandon (Halseylec), Crook (Cooper-Bristol), Anthony (Lotus-Bristol), Salvadori (Cooper-Maserati), and Rolls (Tojeiro).

Chapman took an early lead, and with Sopwith and Bueb fighting desperately for second place, the race settled down to the question of who would occupy the minor positions. As Chapman's aerodynamic Lotus-M.G. had drawn well away from the bunch, Sopwith was really driving on peak form, which caused Bueb to pull out all the stops in his efforts to edge in front. He did this on lap four, but on lap six Sopwith just would not have it and passed Bueb on the inside going into Ramp Corner, a startling manœuvre. Bueb did a Fangio-Moss up to lap nine, then rang the changes, also on the inside into Ramp Corner. This was a shaker and how the crowd loved it! However, Chapman had the race well in hand and, barring accidents, he looked a comfortable winner, so interest centred on the Bueb-Sopwith battle. Behind the two Manx cats, Anthony's Cooper-Bristol was holding off Russell's Cooper-Climax, with Salvadori (Cooper-Maserati) in sixth place. In his hurry to beat Sopwith to the chequered flag, Bueb turned in a record lap of 1 minute 8 seconds, but even then, he just could not leave Sopwith who followed him over the line with about four feet clearance.

Air Kruise Trophy, up to 1,500 c.c.

Having had a most successful Saturday, Colin Chapman turned up after all at Brands Hatch, on 1st August, with his Lotus-M.G. to give battle once again to the Cooper combination. The Air Kruise Trophy, up to 1,500-c.c., was run in two heats and a final, heat I being convincingly won by Chapman with Russell (Cooper-Climax) second and Leston (Beart-Rodgers) third. Heat II was all Bueb (Cooper-Climax) with Gammon (Cooper-Climax) second and Coombs (Lotus-Connaught) third.

In the final Gammon's Cooper, having shed its surplus fat in the Gammon manner (no pun intended), had the edge from the gate and took the lead from Bueb's similar car, with Chapman

(Lotus) third, and Leston (Beart-Rodgers) fourth. Bueb passed Gammon to lead coming round Clearways with Chapman hard on Gammon's heels. On lap two, Chapman had replaced Gammon and was closing the gap on Bueb. Another lap and Chapman had used those extra 400 c.c.s to advantage and led from Bueb and Gammon. Russell began to move up with the third Cooper and passed Gammon and Leston was really mobile in the Beart-Rodgers and was holding fifth place. Chapman had to drive on the limit to hold off the Cooper works drivers who were worrying him like a couple of terriers. Suddenly the edge went off the Lotus power unit and away went both Bueb and Russell. Chapman kept trying and held on to Russell for a lap or two, but could not overtake. Coombs (Lotus) came charging past Gammon and Leston to hold fourth place, leaving Gammon and Leston dicing it out for fifth spot. From lap twelve to the end, Bueb held off his team-mate and won by 1·6 seconds, with Chapman only a fraction behind Russell over the line. Chapman gained some consolation by putting up the fastest lap.

In Northern Ireland, at Craigantlet, the little Cooper-Climax had its baptism of Hill Climbing and performed admirably, gaining two class awards in the hands of Christopher Lindsay. This was the Wadsworth–Brown Le Mans car with plenty of racing miles to its name.

Although most of the racing stables were preparing for the important Goodwood Nine Hour Race on 20th August, the International Snetterton Meeting, run several days earlier, attracted quite a good entry.

At this Meeting, on 13th August, the events for sports cars up to 1,300-c.c. and from 1,300–1,500-c.c., were run concurrently. The redoubtable Roy Salvadori was down to drive the Equipe Endeavour 1,100-c.c. Cooper which he did to such good advantage that he not only walked away with the 1,300-c.c. Class, but was ahead of John Coombs who won the larger class with a Lotus-Connaught. The race was run in heavy rain and the slippery surface caused cars to revolve in all directions, offenders being Russell (Cooper), Smith (Lotus), Steed (Lotus) and Gammon (Cooper). Not so Salvadori, who was absolutely untouchable and came home nearly a lap in front of second man Stacey (Lotus-Climax). Retirements included Chapman (Lotus-M.G.), broken drive shaft, and Bueb (Cooper), transmission trouble. Roy's fantastic drive in the wet was not lost on John Cooper, who marked him down as

No. 1 on the approach list for Cooper, 1956. The result of the up to 1,300-c.c. Class was first, R. Salvadori (Cooper-Climax), second, A. Stacey (Lotus-Climax), third, H. P. Deschamps (Lotus-Climax).

In the 1,300-c.c.–1,500-c.c. Class, first, J. Coombs (Lotus-Connaught), second, J. C. Stocks (Tojeiro), third, B. W. Seaman (Tojeiro-M.G.).

Jack Brabham in the new Cooper-Bristol turned out for the twenty-five lap Formula I race, and showed fine G.P. form, fighting it out with great man S. M. himself who had to drive the Maserati using all his skill to get past Jack on the twenty-second lap to take third place behind the Vanwalls of Schell and Wharton.

And so on to the high spot of the British Season, 'the Nine Hours' at Goodwood, a truly International race with works entries from Ferrari, Porsche, Aston Martin, Cooper, and Lotus, besides cars from Connaught, Ecurie-Ecosse, Lister, Tojeiro, Frazer-Nash, and Singer, thirty-five in all.

The Cooper interest lay, as usual, in the up to 1,500-c.c. Class comprising twelve cars: Moss and von Hanstein (Porsche), Seidel and Steed (Porsche), McAlpine and Thompson (Connaught), Leston and Scott-Brown (Connaught), Sopwith and Blond (Cooper-Climax), Bueb and Russell (Cooper-Climax), Watling-Greenwood and Barthel (Cooper-Climax), Chapman and Jopp (Lotus-M.G.), Flockhart and Allison (Lotus-Climax), Coombs and Young (Lotus-Connaught), Page and Emery (Lotus-Derby), and Calvert and Green (H.R.G.).

The field got away to a fine start at exactly three p.m. with the sole exception of Moss (Porsche) who stalled on the line. Going into St. Mary's, Gaze (Aston D.B.3S) spun and shunted Flockhart (Lotus), completely wrecking the latter's front end, but the Aston, after a quick look-see was able to carry on. Leston (Connaught) was going great guns and led the up to 1,500-c.c. Class from Chapman (Lotus) with Moss (Porsche) cutting great chunks off the field in his efforts to get to the front after his bad start. After one hour, a grand battle was going on in this Class. McAlpine (Connaught), Leston, Moss, Bueb and Chapman had all covered thirty-three laps with Leston leading from Chapman and Moss. At the two hour mark, Moss had taken the lead and was a lap in front of the Leston–Scott-Brown Connaught and the Bueb–Russell Cooper with the Chapman–Jopp Lotus in second place half-way between Moss and the Leston–Bueb duet. At six

Charles Cooper and partner in some motor-cycle acrobatics
John Cooper, aged nine, with the first Cooper Special. Kay Don's
sister is helping

The first and second Coopers ever made

'Pa' Cooper shows John round Silverstone, 1949

The Spanish hardwear

Brandon leading John Cooper, with Parker's rear end just vanishing, 1950

Genoa, past and present: Moss, Nuvolari, John Cooper, Wharton, Charles Cooper, George Paige (was Cooper garage boy, now stock-car driver)

Cut and thrust by Brandon and Moss at Goodwood, 1951

A very determined Jim Russell

George Wicken at Silverstone, cornering *à la* Wicken

Mike Hawthorn with his father, Leslie Hawthorn, and John standing behind the victorious Cooper-Bristol, 1952

Crystal Palace: Leston (29) leads Brown (26) with Moss (27) behind, 1953

Avus, just after the prang

Moss and the Cooper-Alta, 1953

A stark study: Cooper-Bristol Mark II

Cooper works team: Leston and Lewis-Evans with John and the Mark VIII Cooper

Whoa there, Hector!
Chapman spins in front of Gammon at Castle Combe

Wadsworth and Brown at Le Mans, 1955

Salvadori leads the cars into the first bend at Monaco, 1958

Rouen: Brabham (Cooper) about to pass Schell (Maserati) with
Menditeguy (Maserati) behind

The last surviving 'round the houses' race

Avus, 1953: John and Stream-liner on the banking

Jack
Brabham
(Cooper)
and
Trintignant
(Ferrari)
in some real
cut-and-
thrust
dicing

The epic Salvadori *versus* Lewis-Evans duel in the British Grand Prix, 1958

MacLaren in action during the German Grand Prix, 1958

A fine study of Trintignant

Calmness at Casablanca
Brabham (50) and Behra (14)

Monza, 1957: Ron Searles high on the banking

The fibreglass 250-c.c. Streamliner

o'clock the lead in the smaller class had changed again, the Leston–Scott-Brown car, with the latter driving, having taken the lead from von Hanstein, who had taken over from Moss and was lapping exactly ten seconds slower on each lap. The Chapman–Jopp car was third, and the Bueb–Russell car was fourth. At seven o'clock the order had changed again, the Connaught of Leston and Scott-Brown led the class, but the Moss–von Hanstein Porsche had slipped back to fourth, second Chapman and Jopp, third the McAlpine–Thompson Connaught, and fifth the Bueb–Russell Cooper. An hour later, the order was first Chapman and Jopp, second McAlpine and Thompson, third Moss and von Hanstein, fourth Bueb and Russell, and fifth Leston and Scott-Brown. The last-named had lost nearly ten minutes in the pits changing a rocker arm. With Moss once again at the wheel of the Porsche, it moved perceptibly nearer each lap to the flying Chapman and McAlpine.

As darkness fell, things began to happen in the '1,500' Class. The Chapman–Jopp Lotus retired with a broken flywheel, then shortly afterwards, the McAlpine–Thompson car pulled into the pits with a broken rear brake pipeline and the long stop for repairs dropped them well back in the field. With two hours to go, Moss had gained a lead of five laps over his nearest challenger, the Leston–Scott-Brown Connaught, with the Bueb–Russell Cooper leading the rest of the field. Then, just when it looked odds-on on Moss walking away with the 1,500-c.c. Class, Tony Crook spun his Cooper-Bristol right in front of Stirling who failed to negotiate this unexpected hazard and collided with the Cooper, putting both cars out of the race. This left Leston in the lead with the steady little 1,100 Cooper-Climax of Bueb and Russell in second spot well in front of the Seidel–Steed Porsche. Try as it may, the Surbiton Cooper could make little impression on the well-driven Connaught, which ran out an easy winner, with Bueb and Russell second and Seidel and Steed third. The speed of these smaller capacity cars can be gauged by the results sheets which showed that the first three cars in the up to 1,500-c.c. Class were all quicker than the winner of the 1,500–2,000-c.c. Class. Actually the Leston and Scott-Brown combination was sixth overall and Bueb and Russell seventh overall in general classification; food for thought.

Exactly a week later, forty thousand people turned up to see the fun at Oulton Park. The main event was the International

Trophy race, which had attracted a first-rate entry. Coopers had the works team of Bueb and Russell entered in the 1,100-c.c. Class, and opposition consisted of Brandon (Halseylec-Climax), Allison (Lotus-Climax), and private entry Gammon (Cooper-Climax). The course seemed to suit Jim Russell who drove a steady and consistent race, well content to let Bueb make the running until half way, when the Bueb Cooper pulled in to the pits with clutch slip, which from then on was quite incurable and dropped Ivor well back to the rear of the field. Once Russell took over, he outdrove Brandon (Halseylec) and finished a lap in front, with Gammon (Cooper-Climax) third. Allison crashed badly at Old Hall Corner, completely writing off the car, but miraculously emerging from the wreck quite unhurt.

On 3rd September, the Cooper works team split up, Ivor Bueb going to Skarpnack, Sweden, and Jim Russell going to Aintree for the International. Both drivers did extremely well, Bueb winning the 2-litre Class in Sweden and Russell gaining second place behind Salvadori in a similar 1,100-c.c. Cooper-Climax, with third place going to Lewis (Lotus-Climax).

At Skarpnack, Ivor Bueb gave the 1,500-c.c. Porsche Spyders 400-c.c.s and a sound beating, winning by three seconds from Nathan (Porsche-Spyder) with Lautenschlager (Porsche-Spyder) third.

The following day, Cooper sports cars had another victory at Brands. In the 1,200-c.c. race, Peter Gammon (Cooper) drove a brilliant race to hold off Jim Russell (Cooper) and R. McKenzie-Low (Elva). Peter all but repeated this performance in the 1,500-c.c. race, only giving best to Peter Jopp's Lotus-M.G. on the last of the twelve laps, McKenzie-Low (Elva) being third again.

The most important fixture still left on the 1955 sports calendar was the Tourist Trophy Race which counted in the World Sports Car Championship. With Mercedes-Benz going all out to claim it as their own, and the works teams of Maserati Ferrari, Aston-Martin, and Jaguar (one car only) out to stop them, if humanly possible, this was destined to be the greatest and perhaps the most tragic T.T. ever. Against the background of the aforementioned greats, the smaller classes were to be just as bitterly fought, works entries being received from Cooper-Lotus, Elva, Kieft, and M.G. from home, and Porsche, Osca, D.B., Panhard, and Stanguellini from the Continent. On the tricky Dundrod circuit the under 2-litre cars were favoured to carry off the important Index of Performance. Russell and Taylor and Bueb and McDowell were the two Cooper works' combinations and in addition, there was a privately entered Cooper-Climax in the hands of Mayers and Brabham. The 1,100-c.c. Class was made up of Chapman and Allison (Lotus), Steed and Scott Russell (Lotus), Rippon and Lord Louth (Kieft), McKenzie-Low and Mainwaring (Elva), and Vard and Rudd (D.K.W.).

The race had been on for barely eight minutes when the shocking multiple pile-up at Cochranstown put the Cooper-Climaxes of Russell and Taylor and Mayers and Brabham out of the running, leaving six cars in the 1,100 Class. After six laps Chapman, going flat out, headed all cars up to 2-litres, a superb performance. The Bueb–McDowell Cooper was being motored along very steadily, but did not seem to have the urge generated by the Chapman–Allison Lotus. Still, the race was young and Bueb could well afford to play tortoise and hare. On lap twenty-four, Chapman got round in 5 minutes, ·07 second (86·96 m.p.h.), a time only equalled by the 2-litre works Maserati of Bellucci out of all the cars up to 2-litres, this with an 1,100-c.c. Climax engine.

During a burst of heavy rain, a further disaster depleted the 1,100-c.c. Class, when poor Mainwaring, on his thirty-fifth lap, crashed in the Elva and received fatal injuries. As the Rippon–Louth Kieft crashed at Leathemstown shortly afterwards, luckily no injury this time, only four cars were still running in Class 'G'. With half the race over the Chapman–Allison car led its class and also the Index; second in the Class was the Bueb–McDowell combination and third the Lotus of Steed and Scott Russell. Allison and McDowell had both relieved their fellow drivers but the pace had not slackened, in fact, if anything, McDowell began lapping faster than Bueb, a fine performance. At fifty laps it was *status quo*, with the Chapman–Allison wagon still leading the Index by a substantial margin. Five laps later, Lady Luck stepped in and the Lotus pulled into its pit with a broken oil pipe. The repair took 17 minutes 41 seconds, and put the car well behind the surviving Cooper, but still in front of the Steed–Scott Russell Lotus. Although the hare (Lotus) tried to get on terms with the tortoise (Cooper), Messrs. Bueb and McDowell thought otherwise and held off the challenge and actually gained 5 seconds on the last three laps to take the class prize by exactly that margin, with Steed and Scott Russell third.

THE RACING COOPERS

Index of Performance Cup

1st	Armagnac/Laureau (D.B.)	·99283
2nd	Moss/Fitch (Mercedes-Benz)	·98374
3rd	Cornet/Storez (D.B.)	·98356
4th	Bueb/McDowell (Cooper)	·97565
5th	Chapman/Allison (Lotus)	·97539

In the General Classification, Bueb and McDowell were tenth and Chapman and Allison eleventh. The race was won by Moss and Fitch.

There were forty-nine . starters, of whom twenty-seven finished.

Goodwood, on 24th September, and Snetterton, on 25th September, distributed honours fairly evenly between Lotus and Cooper, leaving a final encounter at the International Castle Combe Meeting.

At Castle Combe, on 1st October, the Cooper and Lotus sports cars were vitally interested in the 2-litre Trophy and the Invitation races.

With Leston (Connaught 1½-litre), Bueb (Cooper-Climax 1,100-c.c.), Chapman (Lotus-Climax 1,100-c.c.), heading the list in the 2-litre Trophy, the pace promised to be hot, so hot indeed, that André Loens (2-litre Maserati) and Salvadori (Lister-Bristol) had to fight for *fourth* position behind Leston, Chapman, and Bueb. In all, ten Lotuses, including seven aerodynamics, were being taken on by Bueb's Cooper—'taken on' being the right phrase, for the Surbiton driver kept hard on the heels of Leston's leading Connaught and headed Chapman after a hard fight, until after fifteen laps, the Connaught responded not to the treatment meeted out by its jockey, and cried enough, or nearly so, for its harsh cries echoed from the rear end of the field. Bueb, seeing a beautifully clear track in front, kept it that way and pulled off a ten to one shot by a shade over eight seconds, leaving some rather red faces among the Lotus boys. After him came A. C. B. Chapman (Lotus-Climax), second, and R. F. Salvadori (Lister-Bristol), third.

In the Invitation Race, up to 2,000-c.c., with the mixture as before, Chapman (Lotus) took the lead, followed by Bueb (Cooper), and Leston (Connaught). After one lap Bueb displaced him, and whilst attempting to regain the lead, Colin spun and dropped back to eighth position. Leston battled vainly with Bueb, but once again the Connaught cut up rough, leaving Jopp (Lotus-M.G.) in second place. Leston's Connaught regained its tune, Les got Chapman in his sights and the two began to work their way through the field. On the penultimate lap, Chapman edged past his team-mate, Jopp, and took up second station, the rather weary Connaught could not, however, follow him past and had to be content with fourth place. Loens had one or two spectacular moments before retiring the 'Maser' with a locking brake.

To keep the records straight, Colin Chapman and Ivor Bueb met once again in a ten-lap race a week later at Brands Hatch, with honours this time going to Colin, who set up a new sports car record of 72·47 m.p.h., doing the lap in 61·6 seconds.

All the activity in the sports car field had somewhat overshadowed Formula III racing where the Cooper marque continued to maintain its strangle-hold, once again making a clean sweep of all the important races at home and abroad including three major Italian 750-c.c. races at Castello di Terano, Caldaie, and Cozenza. Although Ivor Bueb and Jim Russell had both driven for the works, their own private duel throughout the season had been fought with tigerish ferocity and each meeting between the two had been a heart stopper. As the season had progressed and Russell and Bueb raced neck and neck for the National 500-c.c. Championship, the rivalry between the two reached new heights in savage cut and thrust, so much so that even the most seasoned spectators breathed a sigh of relief when their races finished. But no one could have been more relieved than John Cooper when the season wound up with Jim and Ivor each in one piece! John was convinced that had they gone on much longer something terrible must surely have happened. Russell won the Championship with thirty-one points against Bueb's twenty-nine points, third and a long way behind was S. Lewis-Evans with twelve points. Just when John Cooper had made up his mind to tell Messrs. Jim and Ivor that the old ticker would not stand the strain of another year's racing with the two incorrigibles, Ivor forestalled him by deciding to concentrate on the larger stuff during 1956. John gave him the 'here's your hat, what's your hurry?' routine.

1955 had been an outstanding year for British drivers, with Moss second to Fangio for the Championship of the World, Tony Brooks' surprise victory in the Syracuse G.P. with the Connaught, Jaguar wins at Sebring and Le Mans, Moss winning the Mille Miglia and the Targa Florio with Peter Collins, the last two honours falling to an Englishman for the first time ever. And most important of all many bright new stars were appearing after cutting their first teeth, so to speak, at English Club meetings. This healthy state of affairs could be directly traced back to the solid background of Formula III racing, and this nursery had already produced such stars as Bueb, Collins, Hall, Lewis-Evans, Allison, Moss, Russell, Wharton, and Leston, to mention but a few.

The British Hill Climb Championship had resulted in a dead heat between Tony Marsh and Ken Wharton, both Cooper-mounted; the R.A.C. eventually awarded the Championship to Marsh.

WHO WANTS A GOLD CUP?

FOR the 1956 season Coopers fielded their well-tried sports car, but with some significant improvements. A high-lift camshaft had been designed by Coventry-Climax which had proved very successful during the World Record attempt at Montlhéry in October 1955, the increase in power being in the region of 9 b.h.p. Consequently this was now fitted as standard; larger, more powerful brakes were also fitted, 10" against 8". The cockpit had been slightly enlarged to give the driver more comfort, and in the light of the experiences at Montlhéry, heavier 'shockers' were now fitted on the rear end, cutting out the tendency of the back of the 1955 model to wander. The Formula III car, now Mark X, remained the same, it being thought that this singularly successful vehicle could easily stand another season. The line up of pilots for 1956 was settled as Roy Salvadori, No. 1, with McDowell and Jack Brabham, when available, on sports cars, and Jim Russell on '500s'. The inclusion of Roy in the team was a sound choice, as John Cooper hoped that sometime during the year Coventry-Climax would deliver the long awaited 'double knocker' $1\frac{1}{2}$-litre engine which, with the new chassis design on the drawing board, would provide Salvadori with something approaching a Grand Prix car, to compete in the new Formula II (up to 1,500-c.c. unsupercharged) class announced by the F.I.A.

In February, Colin Chapman brought out his new brain-child, the Lotus Mark XI. With a dry weight of about seven and three quarters hundredweight, this beautifully proportioned little car made even the 1955 Mark X look old fashioned. Chapman, aided and abetted by the clever Costin boys, was determined to wrest the blue riband for sports cars, be it from Cooper, Porsche, Osca, or for that matter Vanwall, should they be inclined to produce sports cars of 1·1-litre capacity.

During the winter months many sports car adherents hover between Hornsey and Surbiton making up their minds, or perhaps having their minds made up for them on either a Cooper or a Lotus. To the casual observer it is often very amusing to see the rather cool reception a known Lotus exponent gets on his arrival at Surbiton or vice versa, but surprisingly enough, before the bod is much older, he is shown the absolutely latest gen with the cheerful threat of 'now take that back to . . . and let him put that in his pipe and smoke it', for Colin and John are firm friends, at least as firm as two people can be who stay awake many a night scheming how to outdo each other.

One welcome item of news filtered through from the Continent to the effect that the Ecurie Flandre, led by the popular Anglicized Frenchman André Loens was building a new Formula III Norton-engined car to be known as the 'Loweno'.

Jack Brabham had taken his Cooper-Bristol to New Zealand for the G.P. on 7th January, but a cracked gearbox housing put him out of the race, won easily by Stirling Moss in his Maserati from the Ferraris of F. O. Gaze and P. N. Whitehead. Three weeks later Brabham did much better with a sound second place to Reg Hunt's Maserati in the hundred-mile South Pacific Championship in New South Wales. Kevin Neal also got his more orthodox Cooper-Bristol into the money with a fine third place in this event. Brabham also added the Australian G.P. to his off-season's bag.

Back in England, the season started in earnest at Goodwood on 17th March. Keith Greene, piloting a brand new Cooper-Climax '1,100', drove very convincingly to take pride of place in the Novices five-lap Handicap. However the Loti made mincemeat of the opposition in both the five-lap Scratch Race up to 1,250-c.c. and the similar race up to 1,500-c.c., taking all four places in each case, it being only fair to point out that there were no Cooper-Climaxes in either race.

The first test of strength between Lotus and Cooper was due to take place at the end of the month at Sebring, Florida, and although Lotus had already been seen in the United States, Cooper sports cars were making their debut. The entry list showed one 1,500-c.c., and two 1,100-c.c. Lotus and two 1,100-c.c. Coopers. The practice period eliminated the 1,500-c.c. Lotus-Climax when Len Bastrup, co-driver with Colin Chapman pranged it, fortunately without injury. It was now a straight fight between the two 1,100-c.c. Lotus, driven by Sheppard and Smith and Mr. & Mrs. Wyllie respectively and the two works Cooper entries driven by Cracraft and Byron and Hugus and Bentley, all eight drivers being American. At the last minute, another Lotus was accepted, this being a privately entered car driven by Attaway and Parkinson, so the scales were tilted slightly in favour of Lotus.

A late change of drivers put the experienced Colin Chapman

in with Joe Sheppard, and at ten a.m. the race started. At twenty laps, Class 'G' (three Lotus, two Coopers, one Osca) was being led by the Chapman–Sheppard Lotus, with the Attaway–Parkinson Lotus second and Cracraft and Byron third, the Osca of Lucera and Marcotulli having retired on the eleventh lap. On lap forty-nine, Attaway and Parkinson's Lotus retired with a broken oil lead, which left the Chapman–Sheppard Lotus in the class lead with the Wyllie–Wyllie Lotus in second place, having overtaken the Cracraft–Byron Cooper. The position changed again shortly after the third hour when the Chapman–Sheppard car was disqualified when its mechanics spun the rear wheels to start it after the starter motor had burned out. With the two Coopers still going very steadily only the Wyllie family now stood in the way of a class win. At this stage the 750-c.c. D.B. driven by Le Mans experts Armagnac and Mercador was easily leading the Index of Performance and also the 1,100-c.c. Class as well. At seven hours, Wyllie Incorporated still led the class from Hugus and Bentley, but shortly after, a cloud of smoke denoted that Madame Wyllie was the not so proud possessor of a large hole in the crankcase of the Lotus, a malady that even Doc Wyllie could not cure. It now looked fairly certain that Coopers were going to do the old 1-2 in the class as both engines were running in the true Climax manner. However, in twelve hours many things can happen, and after a hundred and seventeen laps, the Hugus–Bentley Cooper retired with a flat battery. This left only one car still competing in the class so wily Wyllie got his well ventilated Lotus ready to try and complete the last lap and qualify for second place in the class. The wonderful little D.B. was still leading the Index, but due to bad pit organization it ran out of fuel during the tenth hour, letting the Porsche of Herrmann and von Trips take over the lead, onto which it held until the end. The Cracraft–Byron Cooper ran on undisturbed to triumph for the Surbiton firm, and Doc Wyllie staggered round for a final lap to take second spot, but definitely the honours rested with Coopers. In the General Classification, the Cooper finished twenty-first, the Lotus twenty-fourth and last finisher, and the fleet little D.B. sixteenth and ahead of the complete M.G. works team.

With Sebring out of the way, Colin Chapman returned home post haste to do battle with John Cooper who had in the meantime equipped his works team with bored out 1,100-c.c. Climax engines, now rated as 1,460-c.c., of which Coventry-Climax were making twelve only to tide over until the 'double knocker' was ready.

April 2nd, and the 1956 season really began to kick with meetings at Brands Hatch and Goodwood and the racing contingents were out in strength. During the winter the main sports car drivers had settled on their individual choices and the 1,460-c.c. engined Coopers were driven by Cooper, Salvadori, Russell, Leston, Bueb, Moss, and Dennis Taylor. The Lotus drivers were Chapman, Bicknell, Allison, and Hawthorn. Also over the winter, working from the other end, Peter Gammon had severely modified his 1,100-c.c. Cooper-Climax and with a 'hang the expense' attitude, succeeded in knocking off nearly 110 pounds in weight against the standard, with results shown later in this chapter.

At Goodwood, on Easter Monday, the Lavant Cup, up to 2-Litres, took place. Here Salvadori (Cooper-Climax 1,460-c.c.) had to compete with full 2-litre stuff in the shape of Gerard (Cooper-Bristol), Coombs (Lotus-Connaught), Young (Connaught), Davis (Lotus-Bristol), Somervail (Cooper-Bristol), Rodgers (Sun Pat Special), and Tyrrell (Cooper-Bristol). However, Leston was backing him up with the Willment Shop Cooper-Climax 1½-litre. From the start, Salvadori took the lead, hounded by Gerard with Young third and Leston fourth. Tragically, Bert Rodgers was killed on this lap when the Sun Pat Special crashed at Lavant. Salvadori held on to his lead with Gerard trying his level best to get on terms, but without success. Leston soon withdrew when one of his S.U.s worked loose, leaving Salvadori on his own to fight off the Connaughts and Bristols. Les had no cause to worry, for Roy forged ahead and ran out a clear winner from Gerard and Young. In the paddock, Bob Gerard was seen giving the Cooper-Climax engine a quizzical look, as well he might.

In the Sports Cars race, up to 1,500-c.c., again Salvadori (Cooper) was outstanding. Ably backed up by Russell in the other works Cooper, he easily claimed the first prize and Leston (Cooper) having taken third position, it was a 1–2–3 victory for Coopers.

Coopers were having a heyday at Brands as well, every race being won by the marque. About Peter Gammons' Cooper mods the less said the better. None of the other competitors could get near enough to see, for Peter skated home in both the sports car races. One kind scribe remarked afterwards that Peter had found a few more horses since the previous season—

the horses were the same, but they had a lighter load to carry, an object lesson for even the mighty Cooper Company. The result of the race for Sports Cars up to 1,200-c.c. was first, P. D. Gammon (Cooper-Climax); second, T. Barnard (Lotus-Climax); and third W. S. Frost (Lotus-Climax). In the Sports Cars up to 1,500-c.c. race, first, P. D. Gammon (Cooper-Climax); second, T. Barnard (Lotus-Climax); and third, D. J. Hayles (Lotus-Climax).

On the day's showing at both circuits, it certainly looked as though the balance of power remained firmly in Cooper's grasp, and the Hornsey firm could not have gone home feeling at all happy.

But worse was to come. The Lotus versus Cooper battle was due to be continued at the classic British Empire Trophy Race at Oulton Park on 14th April, so Colin Chapman led his team on to the field determined to stop all this Cooper nonsense once and for all.

The race was being run on Handicap with three sixteen-lap heats and a twenty-five-lap final, the heats being divided as Heat I—up to 1,500-c.c., Heat II—1,500-c.c.–2,700-c.c., and Heat III—2,700-c.c. plus.

In the starting grid were twenty-two cars, eight Lotus, ten Coopers, two Maseratis, one Connaught, one Halseylec. Out of these, there were ten 1,460-c.c. Climax-engined cars, four Lotus driven by Chapman, Allison, Bicknell, and Hawthorn, and six Coopers driven by Moss, Salvadori, Bueb, Russell, D. Taylor, and Leston. Bueb made a fine start in the heat and led the pack by several yards—right round Old Hall Corner, down into Cascades he fought them off. Moss had darted through the second row stalls, so to speak, and was mixing it with Chapman, just behind Bueb's 'Manxtail'. Also well in the hunt were Leston and Russell. After the long dash to Knicker Brook and then under the bridge at Clay Hill, the position remained unchanged, but in his desperate attempt to keep ahead of the demoniac mob at his heels, Bueb overdid Druids and crashed, the car landing upside down, but Bueb escaped, luckily without serious injury. Chapman then took the lead from Moss with Leston, Russell and Salvadori following in that order. Moss seemed to be having trouble steering his car and did not look too happy. On lap two, Chapman had settled down to lead by about three seconds from Moss. On lap three Russell took third place from Leston, whose car seemed to be losing its edge. Lap four saw Salvadori begin to move up, as did Hawthorn. On lap five Leston had slipped well back and the order was Chapman, Moss, Salvadori, and Hawthorn. Moss continued to have trouble with the handling of his car, and on lap seven Salvadori passed him. Chapman drove impeccably and held a lead over Salvadori of about four seconds, winning at an average speed of 83 m.p.h. On lap fourteen Hawthorn passed Moss and the heat ran out in that fashion.

The glum faces of the drivers of the larger cars after this race had to be seen to be believed, but the officials brightened them up a little by altering the handicap for the final so that cars over 2,700-c.c. started from scratch, those from 1,500-c.c.– 2,700-c.c. were given twenty-five seconds start and those up to 1,500-c.c. were given forty seconds start.

With a forty second start, the smaller cars made hay whilst the sun shone in the twenty-five-lap final, and by the time the large cars started they were almost up to Knicker Brook, which, in any language, is a long way ahead. (In the light of subsequent happenings, it is anybody's guess whether a scratch race would have changed things at all). Moss had shot in front from the off, hounded by Salvadori, Taylor, and Chapman, with Hawthorn fifth. After four laps the larger cars had not made the slightest impression on the $1\frac{1}{2}$-litres, and most were actually losing ground. The position up front was still Moss leading, but now he was being pressed by Chapman, then Salvadori, Hawthorn, Leston, and Russell. The order remained the same at ten laps. Musy (Maserati), winner of the unlimited heat, tried all he knew to make up some leeway on the Climaxes, but even a fast lap in 1 minute 57 seconds was parried by a similar effort from both Moss and Chapman, so he stayed as he was. Flockhart (Jaguar) was also trying hard, but could only just manage to keep Taylor's Cooper in his sights, Dennis being seventh overall. On lap sixteen, by dint of limit driving, Chapman passed Moss to lead for the first time, but Moss pressed him relentlessly and two laps later, Colin made the mistake that cost him the race, he shot into the tricky Druids Corner much too fast, braked too hard and spun, letting Moss through to take the lead once again.

The pace of the two leaders can be assessed by the fact that although Chapman lost about eleven seconds during his spin, he still retained his second place in front of Salvadori. With Moss now firmly in the lead, the race became something of a procession with Moss, Chapman, Salvadori, Hawthorn, Leston, and Russell in that order; only Flockhart's Jaguar, closing up very slowly on Russell's Cooper, seemed to have any chance of getting on the marker board, but in fact Russell held him off fairly easily and crossed the line seven seconds to the good. Reporting on the race, *Auto Course* noted that the first six places in the final were taken by single overhead camshaft 1½-litre Coventry-Climax-powered cars. And they remarked that, 'When the new twin overhead camshaft 1½-litre engine appears some time next year, it looks as if the big cars may well prefer to stay at home on twisting circuits'.

A week later, at Aintree, Colin got some of his own back on the Surbiton boys, for Lotus registered wins in both classes of the smaller sports car race. In the 1,001-c.c. Class, Chapman beat off the challenge of Peter Gammon, promising Tony Marsh and M. G. McDowell, all on Coopers, but not before Gammon had led him a rare old chase, a fine effort from private entry Gammon against the full works entry of Chapman. In the 1·1–2-litre Class, Hawthorn (Lotus-Climax) showed his best form, which meant that there would be no chance for any other driver to come in first, for did not somebody say that on form, one Michael Hawthorn is most definitely the world's No. 1, not excluding Juan Fangio, and this was just such a day. The two classes finished thus: up to 1,000-c.c.: first, C. Chapman (Lotus-Climax); second, P. Gammon (Cooper-Climax); third, M. G. McDowell (Cooper-Climax). Up to 2,000-c.c.: first, M. Hawthorn (Lotus-Climax); second, R. Salvadori (Cooper-Climax); third, R. G. Bicknell (Lotus-Climax).

Yet soon afterwards the tables were turned again, this time at Silverstone on 5th May, and in no uncertain manner. The Cooper works team consisted of Salvadori and Brabham, the latter replacing Russell officially as Cooper's second string. The 1,100-c.c. and 1,500-c.c. Classes were run concurrently.

Salvadori drove a fantastic race in the Cooper works '1,500'. He completely outdrove Chapman (himself no slouch). Colin, desperately trying to catch up, spun after several laps, letting Brabham with the other works Cooper through into second place, and although the Lotus driver pulled the last ounce out of his car and repassed Brabham, he was quite unable to do anything about Salvadori's lead, which increased on every lap. Brabham had very bad luck after a first-class drive, when on lap eighteen his gearbox packed up. Leston (Cooper-Climax) then took over third place, and, just to rub it in, Salvadori put in a lap at 96.67 m.p.h. and was an easy winner of the 1,500-c.c. Class by 30 seconds from Chapman.

In the Class 'G' part of the race Allison, in the works Lotus, had led the field for several laps with the main trouble coming from Gammon (Cooper), MacDowell (Cooper), and Marsh (Cooper), none of whom looked like catching him. On lap nineteen, after Brabham's retirement with gearbox maladies, Allison was seventh overall and well in front of such potent machinery as Brooks' Lotus-Connaught and Bonnier and Naylor in 1½-litre Maseratis. Gammon had made up a lot of ground after being left at the post at the start, but his chances of overhauling Allison seemed rather remote. However, on the twenty-second lap, Allison retired with a broken suspension, leaving Gammon comfortably in charge of the 1·1 Class for the next three laps—hard luck on Allison, but that's racing. The result of the 1,100-c.c. Class was: first, P. Gammon (Cooper-Climax); second, M. MacDowell (Cooper-Climax); third, A. E. Marsh (Cooper-Climax). In the 1,500-c.c. Class: first, R. Salvadori (Cooper-Climax); second, C. Chapman (Lotus-Climax); and third, L. Leston (Cooper-Climax).

On 30th April at the Brands Hatch Meeting, a new star appeared from out of nowhere, one Graham Hill, a twenty-seven-year-old mechanic of the Lotus Engineering équipe, who, having borrowed a works car for the day, proceeded to make meat balls out of the habitual Brands mob, won the 1,100-c.c. sports car race, came second in the 1,500-c.c. sports car race, broke the 1,500-c.c. sports car record, and then went home, no doubt to continue work on the Hornsey cars. 'Many a flower is born to blush unseen' etc. On 10th May, the author took the 1955 Cooper-Climax 1,100-c.c. record car up to Djurgards-loppet, Finland, and registered a modest second place in the up to 2-litre sports car race, behind Eric Brandon in the new Halseylec-Climax, with André Loens (Maserati) third. This popular Finnish race, run in a park full of about ninety-eight thousand people proved to have a funny side. The race was run over twenty-five laps, and from the start Nellemann (Cooper-Climax) took the lead, closely followed by Brandon (Halseylec) and Loens (2-litre Maserati). After one lap on this narrow circuit, Brandon feinted to the left and Nellemann, looking in his rear mirror pulled slightly over whereupon Brandon darted over and passed him. Smart work. After eight laps, Loens literally forced the heavy 'Maser' past Nellemann's

Cooper; soon after, the latter retired with lack of oil pressure.

This left me in third place. It seemed that at this stage my Cooper had the legs of the 'Maser', and I was soon on André's tail, but to get past was another matter. The steering of the Italian car seemed very shaky and André was fighting it all the way. I tried to pass him continually for about five laps, but found it impossible, and having nearly run off the track a couple of times, I decided that discretion was the better part of valour and took up station in third spot. After a few laps like this, the car was running so sweetly, I decided so try and catch André again (he was by now about 500–600 yards ahead), so I pressed on steadily lap by lap. I made up ground chiefly on braking, as both cars seemed to have the same amount of speed up the straight. Coming down the hill towards the corner leading to the finishing line, I was very surprised to see the 'Maser' motoring quite sedately well into the left hand side of the road, so here was a chance to have one more attempt to pass. I figuratively closed my eyes and put my clog down and was past; the look of amazement on André's face was something I will never forget, and lo and behold! I was round the corner and the chequered flag was waved. A second later, the blue Maserati came thundering by, almost deafening me. André was really mad. It appeared that after he had managed to fight me off in the earlier stages of the race, he had looked in his side-mirror and seen that I had gradually begun to trail farther and farther back, so he had wiped me off. Having been given the signal that he was on the last lap he had relaxed a little and not bothered to see what was going on behind until it was too late. I don't believe that he ever did forgive me for that little affair.

The race meetings were coming up one after the other in great profusion, sometimes two or three in a day, so on Whit Monday, the Lotus–Cooper contingents were split up between Crystal Palace and Goodwood. On Whit Sunday a well supported Brands Meeting saw victory in the 1,200-c.c. Class for sports cars go to Cliff Allison's works Lotus-Climax, second place to Stacey (Lotus-Climax), and third to Hill (Cooper-Climax). Gammon was blackflagged when well up among the leaders, as his Cooper looked dangerous after going off course. Chapman won the 1,500-c.c. Class for sports cars fairly easily from Brabham (works Cooper-Climax) with Leston (Cooper-Climax) third. A welcome newcomer to Lotus–Cooper racing,

Archie Scott-Brown (Lotus-Climax) was fourth. Leston obtained a Cooper sports car win in the twelve-lap Handicap race, beating the Scott-Brown Lister-Maserati and Shale's Austin-Healey.

Crystal Palace Meeting

Moss (Cooper-Climax) was a hot favourite in the Anerley Trophy Race, up to 1,500-c.c., at the Crystal Palace meeting. His main opponents were Leston (Cooper-Climax), Hill (Lotus-Climax), Gammon (Cooper-Climax 1·1), Moore (Cooper-Climax 1·1), and Hall (Lotus-Climax 1·1). Leston and Moss got away together, and Moss edged in front going into Ramp, but Les overtook him before they got to South Tower Corner. Moss did not like this at all and put up a dazzling performance in his efforts to take Leston. The latter would persist in staying in front, a clear case of dazzle-dazzle or something, but Leston did us proud, he beat the great Moss over the line by one-fifth of a second. Although the other cars were dicing wildly, they were completely overshadowed by Mr. M. and Mr. L. up front. Hill took third place.

In the Norbury Trophy Race, up to 1,500-c.c., the big question, could Leston put it across Moss again, was very soon solved by the Master himself. The answer—no! Moss screamed into the corner first with Leston at his heels, obviously not caring about his poor little Climax engine and using valve bounce not the rev counter as a guide. He flew round the course at such a fantastic speed that the sports car record was broken once again, this time at 77·22 m.p.h. Although Leston tried his level best to hold 'The Champ', Moss pinned him back and took the flag 1·2 seconds ahead. Hill again took third place.

Over at Goodwood, the excitement was also intense, the main interest centring on the twenty-six-lap race for sports cars up to 1,500-c.c. The duel this time was fought out with no quarter given or taken by Hawthorn (Lotus 1·5) and 'The Boss' himself, (Lotus 1·5). Hawthorn took the lead on lap one with Allison (Lotus 1·1) determined to make a race of it. Shortly afterwards, Bicknell (Lotus 1·5) gave way to Chapman (Lotus 1·5) who occupied third place for half a lap and then passed Allison into second place. At this point, Chapman passed Hawthorn, then Hawthorn passed Chapman, then Chapman passed Hawthorn (shall we dance?). This went on and on and on and the drivers were enjoying it, the crowd was enjoying it, the only one who was not enjoying it was Jack Brabham (Cooper 1·5) lying fourth, who considered he should be lying first, but his Cooper thought otherwise. The two leaders raced neck and neck, and lap after lap the lead changed until at last Hawthorn's car was magnetized by Colin's and for a brief second they stuck together going round Madgwick. Hawthorn demagnetized his car hurriedly and Chapman shot off again, but his partner had to pull into the pits for a front wing to be hammered out. Hawthorn started again, but now had to be content with second place. Brabham, still unhappy, finished third.

These results meant that honours were even on the day between Surbiton and Hornsey.

Behind the scenes at Cambridge (Lister), Hornsey, and Surbiton, the race was on to see who could design the best Formula II car capable of taking the Climax 'double knocker' which was nearly ready. At Coventry the brake had shown 140 b.h.p. at 7,000 revs and more to come, so it looked as if at long last a British made engine was about to arrive with sufficient power to take on the Continental engines in Formula II with a fair chance of success. Peculiarly enough, Charles Cooper was not enthusiastic about this new engine. His view was that it would be no better than the single overhead camshaft engine. On the other hand, John Cooper felt just the reverse; he could not wait to get his first prototype engine for testing (Climax had promised one each to Cooper and Chapman), his view being that the extra thirty-five to forty per cent power could be used usefully throughout the range. Charles insisted that nothing in the new design made him think that the engine would have a better or smoother power curve than that of the single knocker 1,500-c.c. engine.

There was also a decision to make as to whether to use the single 1,500-c.c. engine or wait for the 'double knocker' for the new Cooper due to be made to attack World Records in Class 'E' early in October, the idea being to bore the engine out to just over 1,500-c.c. to enable it to qualify for Class 'E' (over 1½- and under 2-litres). After a lengthy discussion, John, Charles, Bill Knight, and I finally agreed to ask Coventry-Climax to try and cast a 'meatier' block from the 1,460-c.c. single o.h.c. engine and bore this out to about 1,510-c.c. This was a bit chancy as the 1,460-c.c. engine was already bored out almost to its maximum. However, Mr. Windsor Smith of Climax said he would try. There had already been a certain amount of talk amongst race organizers about putting on some good Formula II races with substantial prize money, so John and Charles thought that if they could adapt their Formula III design to take the larger Climax engine they would have a head start on the other marques and would without doubt, clean up in the Formula II races which they hoped would be arranged for later in the season. The order went into the factory to stop all work on sports cars and concentrate on the new Formula II and by using the single o.h.c. engine, the new Cooper would be ready to race in weeks instead of months. By stopping all development on sports cars, Coopers were virtually handing the blue riband for sports cars over to Lotus on a plate, but as it turned out, the gamble on Formula II paid off big dividends.

Notwithstanding all the urgent development going on in the factory, Coopers were heavily committed to Esso to compete in many other sports car races, one of which was the City Cup for sports cars up to 1,500-c.c. run on the Bõavista road circuit in Portugal on 16th June.

In its 15th June issue, *Autosport* announced the arrival of the brand new Formula II Cooper-Climax with a two page spread, although artist Theo Page had to scratch around the Cooper works to get all the pieces in one place for the illustration. The new car had a single o.h.c. Climax engine fitted, but with slight modification, could easily take the twin o.h.c. when it arrived. It was a fine compromise between the Formula III Cooper and the Sports Racing Cooper, including the best points of each. The engine was in the rear, driving through the Citröen/Ersa four-speed gearbox. *Autosport* described the car thus: 'Broadly, the new Cooper follows closely the very successful sports-racing machine, and retains the well tried Cooper system of independent suspension by means of transverse leaf springs and wishbone. The rigid frame is made up of welded steel tubes, the side members forming a curve towards tapering points front and rear, with additional strengthening in the shape of transverse tubes, and a hoop-shaped structure behind the driver.' They went on to say: 'Accessibility of all components has been carefully studied. The front portion of the body shell pivots forward like that of the "500". The radiator assembly is carried far forward in the nose, and also pivots with the shell. A vee-shaped duct conducts warm air from the radiator and out of the body between the front wheels. The water header tank is located just behind the driver's head, and is bolted on to lugs attaching to the "hoop". The wheels are cast separately from the brake drums and are of the now familiar turbo-spoked pattern. The periphery of each drum is finned laterally, and cold air is deflected to the brake-shoes via the wheel spokes and holes drilled in the drums. No back-plates are used at the rear. There are three fuel tanks; one fitted forward of the facia panel and smaller tanks on either side. The offside fuel tank is recessed and permits space for the driver's foot. Twin S.U. petrol pumps are located under the driver's seat to feed the two S.U. carburettors. It is possible that double-choke Webers may be tried. The rear part of the body shell is hinged to move backwards, leaving the engine and auxiliaries well-exposed for working on. Two twin-branch exhaust manifolds terminate in a single large diameter pipe. A clever gearbox selector is used, by means of which neutral can be found separately *via* an arrangement of cambs.' Which just about summed up the whole thing.

The specification of the model was given in *The Autocar*, 13th July 1956, as follows:

Engine

Make	Coventry-Climax FWB
Position	Rear in unit with transmission.
No. of cyls.	4—in line.
Bore and stroke	76·2 m.m. × 80 m.m. (3″ × 3·15″).
Displacement	1,460 c.c. (89·2 cu. in.).
Valve position	O.H.C. in-line valves.
Compression ratio	8·6 to 1.
Max B.H.P.	100 at 6,000 r.p.m.
Max B.M.E.P.	168 lb./sq. in. at 4,250 r.p.m.
Tank capacity	12 Imp. galls.
Battery	Motor-cycle type 6-volt.

Transmission

Gearbox	Citröen special close ratios
Overall ratios	Top 3·63, 3rd 4·64, 2nd 6·58, 1st 9·82 (with 3·10 final drive ratio). Other final drive ratios available 3·44 or 3·87.

Chassis

Brakes	Lockheed hydraulic; 2-L.S.F. and R.
Suspension	Independent, transverse leaf springs and tubular steel lower wishbones F. & R.
Steering	Rack and pinion.
Tyre size	450"—15" F. 525"—15" R.

Dimensions

Wheelbase	7' 5".
Track	F. 3' 9½"; R. 3' 11".
Overall length	11' 1".
Height to headrest	2' 10½".
Ground clearance	4⅜".
Dry weight	694 lb. (6¼ cwt).

For the race in Portugal, the works team of Brabham and Salvadori with Cooper-Climax '1,500s' was faced by works Lotus Allison and Bicknell (driving Lotus-Climax '1,500s') plus the inevitable 1½-litre Porsches and Maseratis. The course suited Salvadori down to the ground and after having clocked fastest time in practice, he put on a terrific show in the race to lead from start to finish. Although Roy won by a little over a minute, it was certainly not a walkover, for the Portuguese drivers (mostly amateur) shook the British 'pros' rigid and Bicknell (Lotus), Brabham (Cooper) and Allison (Lotus) had to drive on the limit in their efforts to hold Messrs. Nogueira and Simoẽs with their brace of Porsche Spyders. Both Brabham (gearbox trouble) and Allison (engine caught fire) had to retire, and Nogueira managed an easy second, over one and a half minutes in front of third man Bicknell.

On June 23rd at Aintree, the Lotus and Cooper works teams met briefly in the 10 lap sports car race. Chapman purloined the 1,500 c.c. prize and MacDowell the 1,100-cc. one, so honours were even.

Then came the important 12-Hour Sports Car Race at Rheims for cars up to 1,500-c.c.

As Charles Cooper was not over-keen to have John flitting off with the works team so soon after returning from Portugal and also as the first prototype Formula II Race was due very shortly, neither of the factory cars appeared at Rheims. This was very largely offset by Stirling Moss being there with his Cooper-Climax with Phil Hill as co-driver. Colin Chapman was there with a works car driven by Ivor Bueb and Mackay Fraser, the up and coming 'coffee' man from Brazil. Also entered were two 150S Maseratis driven by Michel–Berger and Bourillot–Perroud, one Osca driven by Chiron–Maglioli, five Porsche Spyders driven by Mesdames Bousquet–Pondi, Frankenberg–Storez, Goethals–Goethals, Buff–Seidel and Harris–Hacquin. Other entries included a Cooper-Climax entered by the British Army and driven by Power–Hiam, the well known D.B. of Laureau–Armagnac and Blanche–Pons (Ferry-Renault), the last two being 750-c.c., and a works Gordini driven by Madame Thirion–Loyer. As it turned out, the race was a complete triumph for the Porsches with three finishers out of five starters placed first, second and fourth.

At 10 a.m. the race started. Moss (Cooper), easily fastest in practice, remained true to form and was first away from the Le Mans start. Mac Fraser got away last, the low back axle ratio hindering him. Stirling came round the first time seven seconds in the lead and going like a 'sputnik', but due to last minute preparation, the car was in no fit state to last 12 hours and after leading the rest of the field by the 'length of a street' for 30 wonderful minutes (even Alf Francis began to look hopeful), it drew into the pits with a faulty carburettor setting and from then onwards, it was consistently in trouble, finally retiring with overheating caused by weak mixture.

When Moss pulled in, the Chiron–Maglioli Osca took the lead, Maglioli keeping his foot well down, built up a sizeable lead over second man the Frankenberg–Storez Porsche, which was now being chased by Fraser in the Lotus, going faster and faster as he got to know the car (he had never even sat in a Lotus before). Also going extremely well was the fleet little Gordini, driven by Loyer at this time, and now lying third. Mackay Fraser kept closing the gap and on lap 17, he was on Loyer's tail; on the next lap he passed and went haring after von Frankenberg's Porsche. With only an eighth of the race completed, gloom was thrown over the the crowd when the news came through that Anne Bousquet had failed to negotiate the left hand bend behind the pits; her Porsche had overturned with fatal results. Although Moss (Cooper) had been calling into his pit with monotonous regularity, he was still putting in some wonderful lap times, one of which was 2 min. 45·5 secs., or 112·16 m.p.h. At noon Hill took over the Cooper which was getting very rough and after a few fits and starts, he retired.

Mackay Fraser had by now passed von Frankenberg (Porsche) and was second to Maglioli's Osca and gaining fast. Just after noon, Mac brought the Lotus into the lead and now had come through the field from last place to first, a superb performance. Chiron (Osca) took over from Maglioli in second place; third and fourth respectively were the Porsches of von Frankenberg and Seidel. The Army Cooper had withdrawn with a blown gasket, so the Cooper race was already run. British prestige now rested on Mac's Lotus which at 1·0 p.m. drew into the pit to hand over to Bueb to well earned applause. After a refuel and change of front tyres, the car got away in second place. Trouble then struck both leading cars; first the Lotus stripped a gear and the von Frankenberg–Storez Porsche passed it and then Chiron's Osca retired with a damaged rear bearing. A rather one-sided battle now took place between the 3-speed Lotus and the leading Porsche with the Seidel–Buff Porsche steadily circulating in third place just in front of Madame Thirion's Gordini which she was driving beautifully. In fifth place was the Bourillot–Perroud Maserati. Unhappily, at 4.5 p.m. the Thirion–Loyer Gordini went out with magneto trouble.

As the race progressed, the Lotus gradually lost its Austin A30 gears until only top gear remained, but still it pressed on. At 5 p.m. Bueb handed over to Mac who was determined to finish. The leading Porsche was proving very heavy on tyres which tended to slow it a little, whilst Mac kept plodding on still only a lap behind the von Frankenberg–Storez Porsche. Then a new challenge came from the Bourillot–Perroud Maserati which passed Mac and lay second until close on the tenth hour, when it disappeared with transmission trouble. An hour before the race finished the oil pump on the Lotus seized, so Mac did not get a place after all. However, the race did his prestige some good and his boss must have been pleased with him so that was something. After this the von Frankenberg–Storez Porsche cantered home, followed by the Goethals–Goethals Porsche, and third place was taken by a 'baby', the 750-c.c. Ferry–Renault, driven by Blanche–Pons.

Although this race proved once again that the Loti and Coopers had the necessary speed, it did not prove that they had the reliability to go with it and until this latter useful quality could be obtained, the slower Porsche would remain a very considerable thorn in the side of the smaller British sports cars in these long races.

At home, the Surbiton works were rushing to complete the new Formula II car for the Silverstone meeting on 14th July. Roy Salvadori was entered to drive it in the first race to be held under the Formula. As the great day drew near, there were persistent teething troubles, not the least of which were roadholding problems, eventually solved by fitting '500' springs.

Formula II Race.

Salvadori was in charge of the only genuine Formula II car in the race. Chapman, back from a very successful foray at Rouen, entered his '1,500' sports car stripped of its unnecessary fitments, and tried to kid himself that he didn't care, but there it was in black and white, one gleaming Cooper, so Charles and John had scooped the pool and Colin had been left behind. The question still to be answered was 'would it work?'. Salvadori supplied part of the answer by putting up the fastest lap in practice—1 min. 49 secs. or 96·67 m.p.h.

21 cars entered the race, 20 sports cars in various stages of undress, and Salvadori's. Brabham drove the works sports Cooper, Bueb, Marsh, Parnell, Leston, McMillan, Summers and Taylor their own private Coopers, Chapman, Allison and Bicknell drove works Lotus, Hill, Frost, Hall, Somervail, drove private Lotus, Pilette (Gordini), Naylor (Lotus-Maserati) Russell (Lotus-Connaught), Richards (H.A.R.) and Burgess (Osca) made up the field.

Everybody imagined that Salvadori would lead from the gate, but Chapman thought that even if he did not have a Formula II car, he would beat it and give it the 'horse laugh'. So he shot off the line like one possessed and got a sizeable lead almost before Roy had got moving. Coming round the first time, it was Chapman (Lotus), Bicknell (Lotus), Bueb (Cooper) and Salvadori (Cooper Formula II). Some of the knowledge-able folk began to shake their heads sadly (but then knowledge-able folk always do). On lap five Salvadori was lying second, having passed Bueb and Bicknell having retired (those who know began to nod their heads slightly). Chapman, in a desperate effort to hold off the inevitable, pulled out all the stops and did a lap in 97·93 m.p.h., but on the tenth lap, Roy was past (those checked caps began to nod vigorously). From then onwards, Salvadori built up a bigger and bigger lead, crossing the line 30·6 seconds in front of Chapman; Bueb's Cooper beat Allison's Lotus for third place. As Salvadori crossed the finishing line, little knots of knowledgeable folk were busy with the 'I told you so' routine. Charles and John Cooper were extremely elated with their new 'infant'.

The time was fast approaching for the Le Mans classic and as was the case in 1955, the Cooper Car Company had again handed over their entry to private owners, this time to the two Americans, Ed Hugus and John Bentley. Chapman was taking the race much more seriously and had three works cars entered, one 1,500-c.c. and two 1,100-c.c.

24-Hour Sports Car Race, Le Mans, July 28th/29th.

Once again, John Cooper was assisting in the pits, but even with his tremendous drive behind them, Hugus and Bentley could hardly be said to have much chance of success in this race, more particularly as this was the first time either had driven in Europe. But self-appointed pit manager, John Cooper had given instructions out of the corner of his mouth and between puffs on an empty pipe, namely 'to have a go', to which the Americans replied in their slow, lazy drawl, 'What revs do you want down the straight, John?' All of which would have been completely misunderstood by 'Papa' Cooper had he been there, for Charles calls a spade a spade, as Alf Francis, amongst others, knows to his cost. But to get down to business, entered in the 1,100-c.c. class were five cars, Allison–Hall (Lotus), Bicknell–Jopp (Lotus), Dumazer–Campion (V.P.), 'Py'–Dommée (R.B.) and Hugus–Bentley (Cooper)—a rather slim class out of a total entry of 49 cars. The race was run in the most appalling weather and 13 cars retired due to accidents. The Allison–Hall Lotus hit the biggest dog in France on the Mulsanne straight and Allison, who was driving, had a very lucky escape. One car was disqualified and twenty cars retired with mechanical troubles. This left a mere fourteen finishers, and surely these could not include our American friends, or perhaps they were fourteenth. But oh dear no, there it was for all to behold, Hugus and Bentley (Cooper-Climax 1,098-c.c.), eighth overall, and second in the class to the Bicknell–Jopp Lotus. Surely after this performance, if his American cousins had said to John, 'We were getting 8,200 down the Mulsanne, John,' he would have just grinned and replied, 'You've sure spluttered a bibfull babe.' The results of Class 'G', 750–1,100-c.c., were: first, R. Bicknell and P. Jopp (Lotus)—253 laps, fourth, Index of Performance; second, E. Hugus and J. Bentley (Cooper)—252 laps, fifth, Index of Performance; and third, H. Dumazer and A. Campion (V.P.)—210 laps.

August Bank Holiday week-end was a very busy one for the Cooper works team. They were due to race the sports cars at the Nurburgring, Germany, on the Sunday and then fly back for Salvadori to compete in the Formula II Race at Brands Hatch on August Bank Holiday Monday.

The Nurburg Sports Car Race was really a case of bearding the lion in its den, but the 1½-litre Coopers were going so fast these days that John Cooper was eager to try his luck against the works Porsche in a shorter dice. In this race, five Porsches started, together with four East German Streamlined A.W.E.s. Moss drove a Maserati 1½-litre, as did Behra; Pillete (Gordini), Perdisa (Maserati), Miss Haskell (Maserati), Brandli (Sauter), Hicks (Lotus) and Piper (Lotus) completed the field. Salvadori (Cooper) was quite at home on this most difficult of all circuits, but Brabham (Cooper) wisely felt his way round slowly but surely, having realized that a first timer could come unstuck very quickly.

In the race, Salvadori got away first and led for a short time, only to be passed by von Trips (Porsche), but before the Porsche driver had completed one lap, he burst his engine. Herrmann (Porsche) and Barth (A.W.E.) had passed Salvadori who now lay third. On lap two, Moss also passed Salvadori. Brabham was in ninth spot, steady, but taking no risks. On lap four, Barth retired with engine trouble, leaving Herrman in first position, Moss second, and Salvadori third. Herrmann settled down comfortably in the lead, but Salvadori and Moss were having one hell of a dice. Although both cars were not running on peak form, Moss's being undergeared and Salvadori's having rear shock-absorber trouble causing the car to hop about, neither factors stopped these two from fighting it out and during the ten minutes odd of each lap, each got ahead of the other at different times. Finally, Moss set up a new lap record of 10 minutes 13·3 seconds, which did increase the gap over Roy by about ten seconds. Herrmann's Porsche beat the Maserati by under three seconds in the end after leading by 18 seconds at one time. Brabham brought his Cooper home safely in seventh place.

At Brands Hatch on 6th August, storm and tempest made the meeting more like a Water Carnival. The important race was the Television Trophy for 1,500-c.c. sports cars, but Coopers were much more interested in the Formula II race.

THE RACING COOPERS

The Television Trophy Race was run in two fifteen-lap heats and a twenty-lap final, and all the local lads were engaged in this one, plus Mike Hawthorn (Lotus 1,290-c.c.), a new boy at Brands, who had gladly accepted a Lotus drive when the stick-in-the-muds in Germany had refused his entry at Nurburg. Heat 1 was won as it should be by Hawthorn with the smaller Lotus, mainly on superb cornering on a nasty, muddy, wet track. Heat 2 was taken by Ivor Bueb (Cooper-Climax) after Colin Chapman (Lotus-Climax) had spun off, and Roy Salvadori had spun into a flag marshal's post. Salvadori appeared shaken after the accident, but did not realize that he had broken some ribs in the encounter (or at least ignored the pain) and carried on, anxious to have a go in the Formula II race. In the final, Bicknell (Lotus-Climax) obtained a well deserved success after Taylor (Cooper-Climax) had led for eight laps, Brabham (Cooper-Climax) for two and Bicknell himself for the remaining ten laps. The result of the final was: first, R. Bicknell (Lotus-Climax), second, J. Brabham (Cooper-Climax), third, D. Taylor (Cooper-Climax).

In the Formula II ($1\frac{1}{2}$-litre unsupercharged) event, once again the Salvadori Cooper was the only real Formula II car in the race, and although rather a slow starter it carved its way through the field of sports cars until on lap five it took the lead and from then on it was no race. Roy finishing well ahead of Bicknell and Taylor. A feature of the Formula II races had been the large number of retirements of sports cars trying to keep up with the new Cooper, no doubt due to over-revving. The engine mortality was much greater than usual. (Although Salvadori won this race, he was in great pain and after doggedly competing in the first leg of the Formula Libre race with the Formula II car, he had to be taken to hospital.) Jack Brabham drove the single seater in the second leg of the Formula Libre race and finished third.

Now that the Formula II car had been thoroughly tried, and not found wanting, the Coopers were prepared to accept orders for them. They had already got a second works car well under way and orders were received from R. R. C. Walker for a car for Tony Brooks to pilot and from Ken Wharton.

A week's respite and then the Lotus-Cooper duel was resumed at Oulton Park in the *Sporting Life* Trophy Race.

Rain, rain, rain; only Noah and the Ark were missing on this occasion. The B.R.S.C.C. seriously thought of scrubbing the meeting, but compromised by shortening the main races. The *Sporting Life* Trophy was cut to ten laps. The big boys were out in force: Moss (Cooper-Climax), Hawthorn (Lotus-Climax), Salvadori (Cooper-Climax), Brabham (Cooper-Climax), Allison (Lotus-Climax), Hall (Lotus-Climax), Bicknell (Lotus-Climax), Bueb (Cooper-Climax) and Gammon (Cooper-Climax), being among those present. The race started in a cloud of spray with Moss shooting into the lead, hounded by Hawthorn, with Salvadori, Hall, and Allison in a close bunch, just behind the two leaders. To the drivers it must have seemed like driving through a river during a deluge, and things could not have been more difficult, but both Moss and Hawthorn were prepared to dice, come what may, and coming round for the first time, these two were almost side by side. Salvadori, always a tough nut to crack (this was only two weeks after his accident) waded through the morass in his efforts to catch the two leaders who kept disappearing under the odd ton of *aqua*. After a time, Roy discovered Mike's Lotus and got past only to be retaken by the lion-hearted Hawthorn in double-quick time. Going up the hill towards Knicker Brook, as they chased through the fastest part of the track, Mike got into serious trouble right on the corner, his car skidded, caught on a wheel and somersaulted right in the path of Roy's Cooper. It was, as Roy told me later, the most terrifying moment of his life. By a miracle Roy ducked slightly as the Lotus came flying over him and this undoubtedly saved his life because it actually dented his helmet. The unfortunate Mike was thrown out and landed many feet away, escaping with slight injuries. Two accidents in two weeks was too much even for Roy, who retired from the race. Moss, left to his own devices drove on steadily to victory whilst behind him two waterlogged Lotus 1,100-c.c.s, with Hall and Allison squelching in pools of water, finished second and third.

For the Goodwood Meeting, on 8th September, out came the Salvadori single-seater Cooper, entered this time in both the Woodcote Cup and the Sussex Trophy. As a bit of advance publicity, Roy made fastest lap of all the classes when he averaged a practice tour at 89·23 m.p.h., or 96·80 seconds.

The Formula II Cooper was again slow off the line in the Woodcote Cup (2-litre racing and sports cars), but once it got weaving, Chapman (Lotus-Sports) and the gang were just not in the race. Roy won, easing up. Several paid up members sought the minor role which eventually went to Chapman with

Leston (Cooper-Sports) just pushing Bicknell (Lotus-Sports) out of the money.

In the Sussex Trophy (1,500-c.c. racing and sports cars), again, Roy gained an easy victory over Chapman and Leston, an eyebrow or two being raised when it was announced that the Cooper had lapped in 1 minute 35·4 seconds—90·57 m.p.h.

Salvadori's personal record with the Formula II car at this stage was four races, four wins. But the real test had yet to come, for the *Daily Herald* Gold Cup and a cool thousand pounds were waiting for the winner of the Formula II race to be held at Oulton Park on 22nd September. Before this important event, Coopers had an engagement to fulfil at Avus, Germany.

On 16th September the Berlin G.P. for sports cars up to 1,500-c.c. took place. As at Nurburg, Coopers were faced with works Porsches and A.W.E.s. In practice both Brabham and Salvadori did well, Salvadori's Cooper making second fastest time with Barth's A.W.E. making No. 1 grid. Avus suited the streamlined Cooper very well and Roy in particular went to bed the night before the race well pleased with himself. But an unkind twist of fortune changed things completely on race day. In practice the Cooper team had been using their own fuel, brought over in the transporter, on which the engines ran perfectly. Having run out of it, they were forced to use the local stuff which played havoc with their carburettor settings, with consequent loss of power.

The race was notable for one of the most spectacular crashes ever seen on any track when von Frankenberg in the new experimental works Porsche went right over the top of the banking, the car falling about eighty feet to the ground and bursting into flames. Von Frankenberg was thrown out into a tree as the car toppled and although he smashed through the tree onto the ground, it broke his fall and the German escaped with his life, a million to one chance. At the time of the crash, he had been leading the field, followed by von Trips (Porsche), Salvadori (Cooper), Herrmann (Porsche) and Brabham (Cooper). At this point, von Trips took over and was never headed. The two Coopers were running very unevenly and peak power was necessary to hold off the strong opposition. Half way through the race Salvadori had to give best to Herrmann, Rosenhammer (A.W.E.) and Thiel (A.W.E.). Brabham drove well under the circumstances and when his team-mate ran out of fuel on the penultimate lap, took over his fifth place, which he held to the end, Roy finishing sixth.

WHO WANTS A GOLD CUP?

Home again, cursing but intact, Salvadori and Brabham picked up their Formula II cars from Surbiton and hopped up to Oulton for the Gold Cup race. Roy had not made room on his sideboard for the enormous Trophy, for to quote his own words: 'I didn't fancy my chances.' Readers of the book *Alf Francis—Racing Mechanic* will note that on page 314, Alf insinuates that the Coopers deliberately held up delivery of the Rob Walker Formula II engine to prevent him from 'modding' it, as he puts it. Also he says that John and Charles secretly increased the compression ratio of the two works cars, giving them 6 or 7 b.h.p. more than the standard engine. At the same time, he says he spent two weeks at the Surbiton works helping with the assembly of the Pippbrook Garage Cooper, and that in any case, Tony Brooks would have won the race if it had not been for Alf's own clottishness in fixing four brand new tyres on the car instead of running on part worn ones. In the cold light of day, all this does not make sense, firstly if Coopers had wanted to put one across Rob Walker, they would hardly have allowed Alf Francis to have the run of the works whilst he helped with the assembly of the car, particularly as anyone who has ever been in contact with the Cooper works knows that no Cooper secrets are safe from Ernie, the foreman, Doug, 'Whiskers', or Ron or any of the boys. Someone, repeat, someone, would most certainly have told Alf Francis if John and Charles were thinking of modifying the standard engine. Secondly if, as Alf says, Tony Brooks would have won the big race in any case with half worn tyres, is it his considered opinion that Tony could have given Roy Salvadori a beating even though he was giving away 6 or 7 b.h.p., or about five per cent total power? Tony may be good, but he is certainly not that good. It sounds like sour grapes to me.

The eagerly awaited Lister Formula II car did not turn up for the Gold Cup race, as the small Cambridge concern had run into adhesion troubles with the back end of its promising little car, Chapman's prototype single seater Lotus was not ready, so it was left to Coopers to wave the flag of Formula II *vrai*. Brooks in the Rob Walker Cooper, put up the fastest practice time in 1 minute 55·2 seconds (86·28 m.p.h.), followed by Salvadori, 1 minute 55·6 seconds, and Brabham, 1 minute 56·8 seconds; thus the front row of the grid was controlled by three Cooper Formula II cars. The next fastest time was clocked by Chapman in 1 minute 57·2 seconds, and this just beat Wharton's time in the fourth Formula II Cooper, so Colin had the satisfaction that in practice at least, his sports car had 'the legs' of one of the new invincible Coopers.

The Race: Salvadori proved the fastest 'trapper' tearing into Old Hall Corner several yards in front of the snarling pack, comprising second position Brooks, third Brabham, fourth Wharton, fifth and sixth positions being fought out by Chapman (Lotus-Sports) and Flockhart (Lotus-Sports). Going round Esso Bend and accelerating up to Knicker Brook, the leading Cooper was perceptibly gaining on its fellows and by the time Lodge Corner had been navigated, Roy's Cooper had a lead of over eighty yards and was gaining fast. At this rate, he had already earned twenty-five pounds of the thousand-pound prize. Going round the second time, the order had not changed, but Chapman's Lotus was right on Wharton's tail. On lap three, the former took the latter, but was still well behind the three single seater Coopers. On each succeeding lap, Salvadori increased his lead over Brooks and Brabham, and after ten laps led by 11 seconds (two hundred and fifty pounds sterling in the bag?). Brabham, surely the most improved driver of 1956, had managed to pass Brooks and Flockhart had stepped in front of Wharton in place number five. On lap eleven, Bicknell (Lotus-Sports) braked too late at Cascades; the brake locked and the unfortunate Reg went sliding backwards straight into Upper Lake, with an almighty splash. An undamaged Bicknell soon emerged to wander dejectedly back to the pits.

At the five-hundred-pound mark of this thousand-pound race, Salvadori led by 14 seconds from Brabham and Brooks with Flockhart fourth, in place of Chapman. (Mac) Fraser (Lotus-Sports) driving with a blown gasket, was being slowly roasted by the flames, and, true to form, was humming 'Baby, it's cold outside' as he went round. Of the rest, Leston (Cooper-Sports 1,500) duelled mightily with Cliff Allison (Lotus-Sports 1,100) for seventh place. On lap twenty-four Brabham had foul luck, the lead to the electric fuel pump coming away from its moorings, the sorting out of which cost Jack nearly four minutes and virtually put him out of the race. Chapman was also in trouble having used up all his 'anchors'. Salvadori continued his devastating drive and was now lost to view of second man Brooks who led third man Flockhart by over a minute. At the seven hundred and fifty-pound mark, the position was unchanged, and as he motored 'sedately' up to Knicker Brook on the closing laps, Roy did not perceive

Anthony coming down from Cascades, so our hero decided to spare the horses a little and finally coasted into victory, plus a thousand pounds, plus one large goblet, 27 seconds in front of challenger Brooks, with Flockhart a very cheerful third. With only one fuel tank aboard, the Cooper had used up nearly all its Esso, and one lesson learned from this race was that more fuel tanks would be required for 1957.

The third Shell G.P. for sports cars was due to be run on 23rd–24th September at Imola, Italy, but due to lack of entries, it had been postponed to the 29th–30th, and the help of the R.A.C. had been sought to bolster the list. The net result was Lotus works entry—Colin Chapman, Cliff Allison, and Mackay Fraser, and Cooper works entry—Jack Brabham and Roy Salvadori, and private entry Alan Mackay with a 1,100-c.c. Cooper Sports. (The last named gentlemen is well remembered by the author as the vendor in the sad case of the Austin Transporter of doubtful heritage, sold to him for a hundred and forty pounds on the recommendation of a third party who shall be nameless, as really first class and 'going like a bomb'; it certainly went like a bomb, but in addition, it made a noise like a bomb; the last offer received for this noble chariot was 'you give me a fiver and I'll take it away.') But to get back to the story, such was the enthusiasm of Mackay for punishment that he was prepared to borrow Mike Anthony's transporter and drive night and day down to Imola (roughly in the centre of Italy) for the princely sum of eighty pounds starting money, plus, of course, the glory of the chase! He actually left the Cooper Car Company's works at eleven o'clock at night, he had to drive to the coast, cross the Channel, and then drive flat out without sleep to Imola to be in time for practice. Having successfully negotiated this hurdle, Alan Mackay had to retire after only five laps of the race owing to lack of oil pressure. Of such an indomitable breed are racing drivers made!

The Imola G.P. sports cars up to 1,500 c.c., although an International race, it was not supported by Ferrari or Maserati; this left Castellotti, the leading Italian driver, free to drive a works Osca in addition to Musso and Cabianca. From France came works Gordinis headed by da Silva Ramos, Leston drove the Willment Speed Shop Cooper '1,500', Bonnier (Maserati), Naylor (Lotus-Maserati) and the Cooper and Lotus works teams completing the issue. From the start of the race, it was quite clear that it was touch and go between Osca, Lotus, and Cooper. Allison (Lotus), always a go-getter, soon took the lead from Castellotti (Osca), followed by Salvadori (Cooper), Brabham (Cooper), Musso (Osca) and Cabianca (Osca). Allison managed to hold off Castellotti for eight laps at which point the Italian just edged in front by mere inches. The two leaders were many seconds ahead of the two Surbiton drivers, who in their turn, had already mastered the Oscas of Cabianca and Musso. On lap twelve, Allison spun off course and crashed, without damage to himself, leaving Castellotti easily in the lead. Salvadori, now second, began to make up ground and cut a second or two off the arrears each lap. Brabham closely followed his team-mate in third position. Chapman's Lotus had shed all gears except top so he was no longer a menace. On lap thirty. Salvadori ran into trouble and retired with distributor drive failure.

This left only Brabham as the meat in the Osca sandwich, the position being first Castellotti, second Brabham, third Musso, fourth Cabianca, fifth Mackay Fraser, the last named being too far behind to present a real challenge. Brabham, very much on his mettle, began to carve large slices off the Castellotti lead, necessitating the 'hurry' sign from the Italian's pits. Not wishing to disappoint his lads, Castellotti put in a new lap record at 89·98 m.p.h. (some going on this circuit!), but even this did not shake off the Australian, who was driving a masterly race. Although he was clearly closing on Castellotti on each lap, Jack had left his effort too late and the race ran out with the Osca driver heading the Cooper over the line by 39 seconds, with Musso 35 seconds further back, third. The general opinion amongst the British contingent present at the meeting was that Jack Brabham was fast approaching No. 1 rank in world driver class.

The last big race of the season was the Rome G.P., which John Cooper coupled with the record attempts to be made at Monza Autodrome. As Jack Brabham was unable to take his place in the Cooper works team, it was decided that should the Record car still be in one piece after the attempts, a spare standard 1,100-c.c. Climax engine would be fitted and I would take Brabham's place in the works team for the Castelfusano race.

On 15th October we were successful in breaking seven World Records in Class 'E' and on the following day, we added one more record to the bag from Class 'G', all of which are dealt with in detail in the chapter 'The Record Breaking Coopers'. As the car was still in one piece, the 1,100-c.c. engine was put in and the transporter was despatched to

WHO WANTS A GOLD CUP?

Rome. Roy Salvadori, Bill Knight, John Cooper, and I followed in a Lancia Aprilla that I had hired in Milan. I drove for about seventy miles, and then John got fed up with my snail-like pace and took over until we reached Rome. About the journey in between, little can be said except that when we started my little Aprilla was a dainty little chick with well shod tootsies, but when we landed in Ostia she was an old battered fowl, scarcely worth boiling. My admiration for Denis Jenkinson, and Lou Klemantaski has decreased, as *they* have not driven with John Cooper over the Mille Miglia course, although the fact that Roy would persist in putting his foot on John's accelerator foot every time he attempted to slow down might have made me a shade uneasy. I remember vaguely whilst getting up off the floor for the hundredth time and climbing back onto the seat, that I noticed a strong smell of burning which later turned out to be the most complete blow-out of a back tyre I have ever seen; the outside tread and outer rubber had just come away from the inner and outer walls. Mind you, we were only doing seventy m.p.h. at the time of the puncture, so no real harm was done. On thinking back I will always be grateful to the hire car firm for only charging me twenty pounds for repairs to the Aprilla. It must have been nearing Christmas.

Although there were six separate races in the Prix de Rome, on 20th–21st October, each of one hour's duration, the British cars were only interested in two, the up to 750 c.c. racing, and the sports cars up to 1,100-c.c. and 1,100–1,500-c.c. run concurrently. The winner of the G.P. was to be the car putting up the fastest time in any one of the six races.

We were all very keen to see how Colin Davis, driving the Ray Petty Cooper-Norton 600-c.c., would fare against the 750-c.c. Stanguellinis and Giaurs in the up to 750-c.c. racing event. As it turned out, we need not have worried, the great 'Sammy' would have been proud to see young Colin run the opposition into the ground to win by over five m.p.h. from second man Pirocchi (Stanguellini) with Branca (Moretti) third.

The strong line up in the 1,500-c.c. Class of the sports car race up to 1,100-c.c. and 1,100–1,500-c.c. comprised Musso, Cabianca, and Castellotti (Oscas), Bonnier, Boffa, and Garavaglia (Maseratis), Salvadori and Leston (Coopers), Flockhart and Allison (Lotus), Naylor (Lotus-Maserati) and Consolazio (Ermini). In the 1,100-c.c. Class, the line-up was Fraser and Piper (Lotus), Owen and Jackson (Coopers), ranged against nine Oscas led by Rossi and Bernabei and five Stanguellinis led by Peduzzi. Fastest practice times were: 1,500-c.c. Class, Salvadori—2 minutes 21 seconds, and 1,100-c.c. Class, Fraser —2 minutes 31 seconds. These times so discouraged Jean Behra that he withdrew from the 1½-litre Class and drove only in the 2-litre Class. After practice in the Cooper camp we were feeling jubilant, as Roy's time was only a shade slower than the fastest 2-litre cars, and he reckoned that he still had quite a bit in hand. Back at our hotel that night, Roy talked us all into believing that he could win the G.P., there being no doubt that the four-mile Castelfusano circuit suited the light and fast Coopers and Lotus cars very well. It was also, surprisingly enough, a top gear circuit all the way round.

In the sports car race, Salvadori, Castellotti, Musso, and Naylor were on the front row of the grid, two green cars and two red ones, all 1,500-c.c., and on the second row were Leston, Flockhart, Mackay Fraser (Lotus 1,100-c.c.), Cabianca; most of the other 1,100-c.c. cars were behind, together with Allison, who had put up a slow time in practice. From the fifth row, where I was situated, I saw Salvadori make a wonderful start, and when I lost sight of him he was well ahead of Castellotti and Musso. Going round on the first circuit, it was rather like travelling to Brighton on a Sunday afternoon, most of the Oscas and Stanguellinis seemed to be crawling along; without overdoing things in any way I must have passed about ten cars on the first lap.

My own personal job was to try and keep within striking distance of Mackay Fraser and Piper, the two leaders in my class, but I am afraid that I lost sight of them very quickly and did not see them again until the race was over. On the second lap, Salvadori had toured in 2 minutes 20·6 seconds, and was building up a lead. As we came round for the third lap, I was shocked to see Roy's Cooper parked at the right-hand side of the track and out of the race. As we settled down, I was having a private dice with Rossi's Osca, which I could beat for accelera-tion up the long straight, and I managed to get in front of him after about six laps. The sun was shining very strongly right into the drivers' eyes as they came up the straight past the pits, and I for one could not see my pit signals at all, so I had no idea what position I was in.

As the race wore on, parked cars began to appear at odd parts of the circuit. I saw Allison's Lotus, then Flockhart's, and a few laps later, Leston's Cooper on the far side of the circuit. At this rate, I thought I might even get up with the leaders. I was still managing to hold off Rossi's Osca and I had passed Bernabei's early on, so at this stage I was reasonably happy. I was soon shaken up. I was using the Dunlop tyres specially prepared for the records at Monza and these had been milled so that the treads were ground slightly to a point in the middle of the tread and a slight over-correction going round the rather sharp right-hand corner after the long straight caused the car to go off balance. Luckily, having had the same experience at Monza the previous week, I managed to get the car back under control, being as delicate as I could with the steering wheel; having frightened myself to death I slowed a little and very soon Rossi passed me.

From then onwards I chased him, but without success, in fact he seemed to be getting more speed out of the Osca, and left me behind going along the uphill straight. I kept a weather eye out for Mac or Piper in case they had dropped out of the race, but no luck, and shortly before the end Musso's Osca passed me in a hurry, and about three laps before the finish Naylor bagged a corner with his Lotus just as I was about to claim it. I chased Brian for the remaining laps and followed him to the chequered flag and to the pits to the accompaniment of much handclapping from above the pits. As I had experienced this sort of thing before, I was quite blasé. I had enough sense to know that it was not for me (it was recognition for Naylor's fine drive into second place in the 1,500-c.c. class) and that was that. On enquiry I found that Roy, Cliff, and Ron had retired with the same malady, namely stripped fibre timing wheels. Obviously something would have to be done in this direction for 1957. Although the race must have been a great disappointment to both John and Roy, they shrugged it all off with nary a word, two grand sportsmen. Jean Behra (2,000-c.c. Maserati) won the G.P. on General Classification. The result in the sports cars up to 1,100-c.c. was first, M. Fraser (Lotus); second, D. Piper (Lotus); third, G. Rossi (Osca); and fourth, A. Owen (Cooper). In the race for sports cars up to 1,500-c.c., first, L. Musso (Osca); second, B. Naylor (Lotus-Maserati); third, G. Cabianca (Osca); and fourth, J. Bonnier (Maserati).

A pleasing result at Brands on 14th October had been Tony Brooks' victory in the Formula II race, and Jack Brabham's new record for the class in 59·40 seconds was not to be sneered at.

Both Coopers and Lotus had had a wonderful year, but the shrewd move of the former in turning over to Formula II cars so quickly had swung the pendulum in their favour. For the orders for the new Cooper were coming in fast, and in all ten were received, which meant that when Chapman got his new car going, he would have a very lean order book. (It may seem strange that ten orders can make such a difference, but in this type of racing, once people like Wharton, Leston, Brooks, Marsh, Wicken, Whitehouse, Brown, Beart, Naylor and West-cott have purchased a car, there are not many drivers prepared to buy at around £2,200 to make another car a paying pro-position). In sports car racing the Cooper '1,500' had more than held it own with Lotus but in the 1,100 c.c. class it was slipping back rapidly, only Peter Gammon's ultra light car being able to take on the Lotus XIs with any great success. As the season wore on, Coopers were prepared to gamble this pawn to gain a rook in the shape of Formula II cars and forsook sports cars entirely for 1957, only making them for very special orders.

Going over the season's racing, the Cooper '500' had once again carried all before it at home winning thirty important races, with Moor's Wasp gaining the sole victory for the other marques. Abroad, the Loweno, driven and constructed by André Loens, had put up a fine show finishing only a neck behind Kuhnke's Cooper in a great race at Narbonne, and being placed second on two occasions at Roskilde Ring, Denmark. It had also led the race for many laps at Djurgard-sloppet, only to break down with victory in sight, but apart from these isolated instances, it had been Cooper all the way. Colin Davis had won the big race at Castelfusano with the Petty-Cooper 600-c.c. and Tony Marsh had again won the British Hill Climb Championship with his Cooper. Formula II racing had been like Formula III, all Cooper, for they had won every race including the valuable Gold Cup. By using the Formula III car as a prototype for the larger Formula II car, they were able to steal a comfortable march over the opposition, whereas Lotus and Lister had to start completely from scratch.

For winter relaxation, Jack Brabham took the works 1,500-c.c. sports car 'down under' for an extensive season of racing, the results coming through with rather monotonous regularity all through the winter, that Jack had knocked them for six again.

SUEZ, DARK CLOUDS, AND THEN A SILVER LINING

WITH interest in '500s' flagging, Coopers did not bother to alter the Mark X, now Mark XI. Several 'mods' were carried out on the Formula II car ready for 1957: first and foremost, the chassis was lengthened two inches to take the new 'double knocker', and the nose was lowered two inches. The sides of the body were widened in order to take three larger fuel tanks and the widening continued right back past the cockpit giving more shape to the back part of the body. Coopers also did away with the hole in the tail, and widened out the cockpit by about two inches. Having done this, John Cooper set the lines burning to Coventry for them there 'double knockers'.

Then Nasser played his nasty little hand. As Suez, petrol rationing, and attendant troubles are still fresh in our minds, there is no point in dwelling on these unfortunate incidents, but at the time things looked very black. Brands Hatch and Mallory Park Meetings were both cancelled because of the petrol restrictions, and the fuel and oil companies were not willing to make any arrangements with drivers or firms for bonuses, so motor racing as such came to a dead halt. At Coventry-Climax, there was at this time an order on hand for forty twin-overhead camshaft engines, forty thousand pounds worth of engines at selling price, and the firm was very, very worried because if the order went through, as planned, for delivery early in the year and we were not 'de-Nasserized' by that time, it would suffer heavy loss. For several weeks all the news was bad and Charles Cooper could almost see himself retiring to Box Hill of necessity and not by choice. The biggest headache for Charles and John was how to keep their skilled labour force employed and there was much scratching of heads by all and sundry on this thorny problem.

During one of John's brainstorms he had designed a three-wheeler and had gone so far as to get the frame made up (this was for us to attack three-wheeler records). When the wheels were fitted to the contraption and some kind person sat in it, the thing had tilted, so John had turned 'Charlie' as the saying goes, and hung the frame up in the roof of the works 'for future development'. During the crisis, the three-wheeler was brought

153

down and John and Co. converted it into a four-wheeler and this passed some of the time away very pleasantly.

It was left to the late Ron Searles, Cooper's Factory Manager, Chief Mechanic, Designer, Errand Runner and Head Cook and Bottle Washer, to come up with the idea that saved the day: The Cooper Racing Driver School. This started with two modest advertisements in *Autosport* and *Sporting Life* and became an immediate success, in fact to this day, the waiting list of would-be drivers is as long as when the scheme began.

At the beginning of January, Cooper's received their first twin-camshaft Climax engine which was immediately put into the Formula II chassis and taken down to Goodwood for testing by Roy Salvadori and John Cooper. (Climax had by now decided to carry on with the order for the 'double knocker' engines, so providing there were no cancellations, the Cooper Car Company had to deliver nine cars within the next few months.) The tests proved rather disturbing, the twin o.h.c. unit did not deliver anything like its real power under 5,000 revs, with a maximum of 7,500 revs. Also the carburation was wrong and it took several weeks before the trouble was cured. It seemed almost as though Charles Cooper had been right from the beginning and that the single cam motor was more useful. However, as time passed, most of the teething troubles were ironed out and the twin o.h.c. proved its worth, not before giving its patrons a *big* shock when Tony Brooks, driving the Alf Francis-tuned single cam Cooper, beat up the works twin o.h.c. Coopers of Salvadori and Brabham at Goodwood.

The new engine is now known as the F.P.F. It is a four-cylinder unit, bore 81·2 m.m., stroke 71·1 m.m.; capacity 1,460-c.c. developing 141 b.h.p. at 7,000 r.p.m. on 100% octane fuel; compression ratio 10 : 1, maximum torque 108·5 lb. ft. at 6,500 r.p.m. Maximum b.m.e.p. 181·5 lb./sq. in. at 6,500 r.p.m., weight 255 pounds.

The 1957 season started off with the very sad news coming through from New Zealand that the popular Ken Wharton had lost his life in the race for the New Zealand G.P. Ken's wonderful run of five R.A.C. Hill Climb Championships in succession, each time with his little Cooper, will always be remembered with admiration by all who knew him.

Cooper works drivers for 1957 were Roy Salvadori and Jack Brabham. There was a very big snag over Salvadori as, in addition to driving for Coopers, he had also contracted to drive for Aston Martin, whose works team manager was now Reg

Parnell, and, of all things, the B.R.M. The latter was a very surprising decision as Roy had told me many times that he had absolutely no confidence in the B.R.M., and with its past record, I can't say that I blamed him. Nevertheless, Roy is a professional racing driver and I suppose the May-Berthon set-up offered him attractive terms. However, this meant that Aston's and B.R.M. had first claim on Roy's services, so it looked like trouble for Cooper's every time they clashed with Astons. Owing to their commitments with Reg Tanner and Esso, Cooper's had to build a works sports car with 'double knocker' engine in addition to their two Formula II cars. So, with three cars and one full-time and one part-time driver, they were not very well placed.

Once the Ministry of Power allocated petrol for a limited number of U.K. race meetings, things in general began to settle down and Cooper's could plan the season's programme. Several more orders for Formula II cars came in and in every case, the car was wanted urgently, so, as usual, from being a lot of layabouts, as Reg Tanner might describe them, the whole Cooper organization turned from calm to panic. Jack Brabham, on his way back from Australia with the same size in hats, broke his journey to drive the R. R. Walker–Alf Francis single o.h.c. Cooper-Climax in the Syracuse G.P. in Sicily on 7th April.

Brabham (Cooper Formula II), was aided in the race by Wicken (Cooper Formula II) and Whitehouse (Cooper Formula II). As all three were 'single knockers' they had set themselves a hard task in taking on the Formula I might of Maserati, Ferrari, Vanwall, and Connaught. However, two out of three of the Coopers finished, Brabham in sixth place and Wicken in seventh, so they were far from disgraced. Moss, in the Vanwall, did everything but win the race for Britain, but was baulked by fuel injection trouble which took him back from the lead into sixth place. Breaking the lap record regularly with cool indifference, Stirling fought back to finish in third place. With four British drivers and one Australian in the first seven, how the international racing scene had changed!—the result being: first, P. Collins (Ferrari); second, L. Musso (Ferrari); third, S. Moss (Vanwall); fourth, P. Taruffi (Maserati); fifth, I. Bueb (Connaught); sixth, J. Brabham (Cooper Formula II).

The day before, in England, the B.R.D.C. had run the British Empire Trophy race at Oulton Park, and there was the gleaming new Cooper sports car, complete with the latest

F.P.F. engine, a potential winner of the race, and nobody to drive it. Reg Parnell had firmly put his foot down, Salvadori would *not* be allowed to drive for Coopers in the B.E.T. The race was not going to be a handicap this year, but three separate class races with the fastest outright time winning the Trophy, and Reg wanted the B.E.T. for a wonderful start to his new Aston-Martin appointment and was not taking any chances by letting Roy drive the fleet little Cooper. That two lads from another tiny firm in Cambridge should thwart Reg's ambition must be considered only poetic justice.

Owing to the petrol restrictions, the B.R.D.C. had some misgivings about this meeting—they wondered whether people would be able to get to the course. However, in their usual fair manner, they arranged that all entries should get ten pounds starting money, but should the attendance be over a certain amount, this would be doubled or trebled. This also applied to the prize money—minimum first, a hundred pounds; second, fifty; third, twenty-five; to be doubled or trebled *pro rata* with the attendance. The B.R.D.C. need not have worried as the crowd was the biggest ever at Oulton and twelve thousand cars turned up, so we all received thirty pounds. After practice it was obvious that the winner of the race would come from either Class 1,200-c.c. to 2,000-c.c. or over 2,000-c.c. The first race for cars up to 1,200-c.c. was a Lotus benefit with six Lotus out in front dicing all the way, the eventual winner being Graham Hill, with Dickson second and Ashdown third.

The second race, for cars from 1,200-c.c. to 2,000-c.c., was also Lotus dominated with four Lotus entries out of nine starters, the rest being three Listers, one A.C., and one Cooper (mine). The race developed into a 'needle' match between Flockhart (Lotus) and Chapman (Lotus), with Naylor's Lotus bringing up the rear. On the first lap, I had the misfortune to switch off the ignition in my rather small cockpit by catching the key whilst turning the wheel sharply. It took me a few seconds to find out what was wrong (moral—always check to see that your hand cannot switch off the ignition key, and if there is any danger of doing so, file down the head of the key). At the head of the queue Chapman briefly took the lead, only to lose it a few laps later when he spun going into Cascades. From then onwards Flockhart took charge, and although Chapman passed Naylor who had got in front when the former had spun, he could not make up any time on Flockhart. Moore (Lister-Maserati) lost 1 minute 16 seconds at the pits through a fuel leak, but rejoined the field as Naylor's Lotus came past and pressed the former so much that Naylor spun off leaving the steady Frost (Lotus) to take third place, to Flockhart, first, and Chapman, second.

In race No. 3, over 2,000-c.c., Scott-Brown really put it across the Astons and private Jaguars. After a bad start he finished the first lap 2 seconds in front of Salvadori's works Aston with Cunningham-Reid on the other works Aston, third. It says much for Salvadori's driving that although he was going at one hell of a lick, it looked as though it was an easy drive, but with only fifteen and a half hundredweight to tow and a neat 3½-litre Jag. under the bonnet, the Lister-Jaguar was uncatchable. The race became a procession, but with a big query, could the untried Brian Lister creation last out? This it did to win the race, plus the Trophy, plus three hundred pounds prize money, plus great smiles from J. Eason Gibson and George Eyston, and hearty congratulations from Aston Martin drivers Salvadori and Cunningham-Reid, who were second and third respectively. What wonderful encouragement for great-hearted Brian Lister after all the disappointments, and could one think of a better example of David and Goliath than Scott-Brown versus works Astons? There was one certainty, it was not a Cooper day, with Lotus taking the first six places in Race No. 1 and the first three places in Race No. 2. The highest we came was seventh in the 1,100-c.c. and fifth in the 1,200–2,000-c.c. We missed Brabham and Salvadori that day.

On 23rd March at Sebring, Colin Chapman and Joe Sheppard had won the 1,100-c.c. Class with an American couple T. Hallock and M. Goldman second in a Cooper; Colin had also managed third place in the Index of Performance. John Cooper and I had been hoping that Coventry-Climax would have been able to deliver the new 750-c.c. engine in time for this race—they had promised one each to Coopers and Lotus —as if they had, Bill Knight and I would have taken one of the Cooper Car Company's entries in the race and gone for the Index of Performance. As the engine did not arrive, regretfully, we had to cancel this plan. We still hoped that the engine would come later in the spring, so that we could use it for record attempts, but although Colin Chapman received his and won the Index of Performance at Le Mans with it, the Cooper 750-c.c. block was lost somewhere between the Climax factory and that of a sub-contractor, so there remains only one in existence and Chapman has that little item, for which I personally would give my eye teeth.

From Northern Ireland came the news that Jim Meikle had converted a Cooper '500' into the Meikle Jet Car, and what is more, it worked!

Keen interest had been aroused by the Goodwood meeting, on 22nd April, because both Cooper and Lotus were entered with Formula II cars with twin o.h.c. Coventry-Climax engines for the first time, and the organizers had allowed them to compete in the Glover Trophy against the 'heavy' stuff like Vanwall, Maserati and B.R.M. Despite petrol rationing, fifty-five thousand people attended and witnessed some fine racing. In practice, Tony Brooks, driving the Rob Walker Formula II Cooper 'single knocker', put up fastest time of the Formula II cars.

With Salvadori on the B.R.M. and Brooks on the Vanwall, Brabham was the sole defender for Coopers in the Formula I Glover Trophy Race. Moss (Vanwall) got in front from the flag, followed by Brooks (Vanwall), Flockhart (B.R.M.) and Lewis-Evans in the strange looking new Connaught. Salvadori (B.R.M.) was out of the race on the first lap when he spun off course with a locking brake. The leaders soon came round— first Moss, second Brooks, third Flockhart, fourth Lewis-Evans, fifth Fairman (Connaught), and then, very close together, Brabham (Cooper) and Russell looking rather strange and very stern in a Maserati. Moss tried to leave Brooks lap by lap, but our dentist friend was not having it, and a few yards was the best that Moss could do. Then Brooks stopped with a broken throttle linkage, leaving Lewis-Evans to take up the chase as Flockhart had slipped back with a badly spinning B.R.M. Moss stayed well in front of the field until he succumbed to the same trouble as Brooks, leaving the Lewis-Evans Connaught 'Dart' in the lead followed by team-mate Fairman and the still struggling Flockhart B.R.M. Then some way back came Brabham's Cooper being chased by the stern Russell. Brooks started again and put up the fastest lap in 1 minute 29·6 seconds (96·43 m.p.h.), but he was by now too far behind to alter the issue. So the race ended with Lewis-Evans walking home a good 20 seconds in front of Fairman and Flockhart fighting the B.R.M. into third place, Brabham fourth and Russell fifth.

In the Lavant Cup, Formula II race, with Salvadori and Brabham together and both on Cooper twin o.h.c. Formula II cars, at last John Cooper had his full works team. Allison drove the sole Lotus Formula II car and Brooks had command of Alf Francis's favourite car, the Cooper with the single-cam engine, which, as mentioned previously, made a shocking mess of its twin-cam brothers and won fairly easily from Brabham and Flockhart, after Salvadori and Allison had both retired shortly after the start. The low down power certainly paid off in this case, as Alf Francis had forecast.

With the constant need for more and more engine power always before him, and also Charles Cooper's oft-repeated wish for an engine to take on the Formula I cars in his mind, John Cooper put the position squarely before Wally Hassan at Climax; could he bore out the new 1,460-c.c. engine to 2-litres or over? The answer was 'Yes', if a special crankshaft with new liners and pistons was manufactured, the cubic capacity could be increased to 1,960-c.c. and later 2·2 litres. That staunch supporter of British racing cars, Rob Walker, then came upon the scene and agreed to bear the cost of the new modified engine which was ordered with the Monaco G.P. in view.

In the Monaco G.P. on 19th May, the sixteen starters were Fangio, Menditeguy, Schell, Gregory, Gould, and Scarlatti in Maseratis, Collins, Hawthorn, Trintignant, and von Trips in Ferraris, Moss and Brooks in Vanwalls, Flockhart in B.R.M., Lewis-Evans and Bueb in Connaughts, and Brabham in a Cooper. Against opposition of this calibre, the Rob Walker Cooper équipe could not hope to win, and after practice Charles and John would have settled gladly for a place in the first ten.

The Race: At two fifty p.m. down went the flag and away went sixteen cars in a blur of red and green, contrasting strangely against the white pavements and the blue sea and sky. With two hundred and four miles to cover the cars had to get round each tricky corner a hundred and five times, and one small error of judgement on the narrow road could cause a multiple pile-up, witness 1936, 1950, and 1952. After all the noise as the cars shot into Gasometer Corner, a hush fell on the massed crowds round the start, including Their Royal Highnesses Prince Rainier and Princess Grace, who occupied the Royal Box directly over the Cooper pit. Then the snarl, once, twice, thrice, and still more as the field chased round Ste. Devote corner, and quiet again for what seemed an eternity, then a false alarm, all heads turned to see who was coming through in the lead. Was it green or red, Fangio or Moss, or perhaps Collins or Hawthorn?

This unique type of 'round the houses race' can best be compared to a bull-fight. You have the colour, excitement, spectacle, thrills, peerless skill, and the biggest draw of all, the duel with death, and the crowd can smell blood and perhaps unconsciously with a car race, they are looking for someone to crash, just as much as they are hoping that the bull will out-manœuvre its tormentors and topple the hated picador, or catch the gallant matador off his guard just when he kneels and bows, to the plaudits of the crowd. These primitive feelings must go back a long way, but, civilized or not, we cannot resist the drama of it all.

And then the roar and almost before we realized it, four or five cars shot by and it was Moss leading from Collins and Fangio, being tailed by Hawthorn and Brooks. There was just time to wonder how five cars could get round in such close formation when the next batch went by, then one by one the slower cars passed, already some distance behind after one lap. The hush, then the snarl and then roaring through Tir aux Pigeons Tunnel—Moss came tearing along pursued by Collins and Fangio, with Schell now very much in the picture, fourth, shadowed by Brooks, Menditeguy, and Hawthorn. Fangio did not appear to be in a hurry for a change, and was content to let Moss and Collins make the running. Whether it was intuition or plain common sense, only Fangio could say, but on the third lap it paid big dividends when Moss, the leading Vanwall driver, made a mistake (an easy thing to do with those red devils on his heels). He came up to the chicane too fast, braked too hard, the brake locked and the Vanwall smashed into the safety barriers. Collins, too close to get out of trouble, was hit by one of the long wooden poles displaced by Moss and as poor Peter swerved desperately to the left, he caught the flying pole straight into his front wheel and radiator. Fangio, just that fraction behind, squeezed through the narrow gap and was away. Hawthorn, not so fortunate, collected the remaining flying débris, hit Brooks' car lightly, threw a wheel and finally mounted the nearside bonnet of Collins' Ferrari (which Peter had left in a hurry). Mike missed a ducking in the harbour by mere inches and what could have been a nasty accident left the three British boys with nothing worse than a few bruises.

Whilst everyone was excitedly discussing the news, around came Fangio with Brooks holding him, so Tony's car had come to no great harm. Brabham, lying fifteenth on lap three, was now tenth, a meteoric climb in one lap. Fangio opened up a gap of 5 seconds on Brooks, who was quite happy to leave it that way. Then there was a twenty-second pause for von Trips' Ferrari followed by Menditeguy and Schell in the brace of Maseratis, and some distance back a regular patron of the arts, Horace Gould led the third pack. On lap eight Brabham picked up another place and was ninth. He was settling down very well, and from now on steadily lapped in 1 minute 50 seconds, getting down on lap twenty-one to 1 minute 47·7 seconds, which compared very favourably with both Fangio and Brooks. People were now beginning to take notice of the little Cooper. By this time it was in fifth place; in front were Fangio, Brooks, von Trips, and Schell in that order. Two laps later Schell retired with broken suspension links, after hitting the kerb at Ste. Devote, and J.B. was now fourth and 63 seconds behind Fangio. As a point of interest, Jack lost four and a half seconds per lap to Fangio for the first eight laps, but from lap eight to lap twenty-four he reduced this to 1·7 seconds per lap, and on lap twenty-one his time was only one tenth of a second outside the World Champion's. This car was certainly shaking the populace, but Coopers would have to start thinking soon, for Jack had to come in to refuel. Meanwhile he was certainly 'having a go'.

The race was following a set pattern out front. Fangio had the situation well in hand, and any time he felt like it put in a lap in 1 minute 45 seconds, which was a little too fast for Brooks; von Trips was a safe third, and Brabham fourth at thirty laps. At forty laps the position was the same. Bueb (Connaught) retired on lap forty-seven with a split fuel tank, leaving ten runners, but now Menditeguy was really motoring and caught and passed Brabham and von Trips to take third place. The Cooper had become everybody's favourite, and each time it came round it was loudly cheered. Menditeguy came unstuck very badly at the nasty chicane, crashed into a lamp standard; the car was a 'write-off' and poor Menditeguy received facial injuries, luckily not too serious. The order was now Fangio, Brooks, von Trips, and Brabham, and Rob Walker decided to call Brabham in on the sixty-second lap. In came the Australian, some fine pit work from Alf Francis, John Cooper, and two helpers, but the car would not start! Panic, a few swear words then a hefty push from all and sundry and Jack was away, and all this in fifty seconds—time enough for Gregory and Scarlatti to shoot by, but on lap sixty-five Scarlatti was out with no oil pressure and with Flockhart out on lap sixty with a broken camshaft drive, we had only seven cars to watch, or eight if Bueb (Connaught) could still be counted. He had re-started after a pit stop of forty-two minutes and was trying to finish.

We were all prepared to see Fangio, the Master, win, but were keeping our fingers crossed for courageous Tony Brooks, still second, and now we saw that Brabham had overtaken Gregory's Maserati and was fourth again. It had to come sooner or later, and here it was. The wags were calling 'Brab' Jack the Giant Killer, we were getting very worked up over the Brabham-Gregory duel which was keeping the race alive. Gregory nosed in front of Jack, but the fantastic little Cooper had the edge on the 'Maser' and repassed. Bueb finally called it a day, Fangio eased up a little as he was some way ahead of Brooks, and seeing the 'Boss' slackening somewhat, Tony's pit gave him the 'leaden boot' sign to which Tony reacted and lapped between 1 minute 48 seconds and 1 minute 49 seconds. It was a wonderful change to see a green car challenging for an outright win, and with 'Brab' still fourth, we did not have to hope for a miracle. Fangio lapped von Trips, the race was running its course, and just when we were resigned to the finishing order, very much more drama—on lap ninety-six von Trips had an engine seizure, causing him to spin round and hit a barrier coming towards the Casino. Von Trips was unhurt, but his race was finished, so by looking at the faces of the Cooper family, one could gather that their prodigy was third.

It was mentioned that Fangio had lost a gear, but even if he had, he was still lapping in 1 minute 49 seconds, and although Brooks had made up over three seconds on lap ninety-seven, barring accidents, he could not now catch the Maserati driver. There were only three laps more to go. Jack was driving hard to hold off Gregory, but his pit now had a worried look as it seemed that he was slowing. Yes, he was, but no, it must be all right, for next lap, he was back to 1 minute 48 seconds. What a car, this Cooper. The ninety-ninth lap, 1 minute 49·6 to Gregory's 1 minute 49·5. He was due round now for his hundredth tour . . . 1 minute 50 seconds . . . 1 minute 55 seconds . . . 2 minutes . . . Gregory had gone by . . . 2 minutes 5 seconds . . . 2 minutes 10 seconds. . . . John looked a bit sick; this was the worst part, the waiting. Lewis-Evans and Trintignant had gone by, but still no sign of Jack. A couple of minutes passed and then someone with fieldglasses spotted Jack pushing the Cooper. Whew! so Jack was safe! The figure in the distance got progressively larger as the wiry Australian pushed No. 14 down the harbour road. The minutes were passing and according to the chart, Jack could not possibly push the car to the line before Lewis-Evans made up the leeway and beat him to it. Gregory was already home in third place, then over went Lewis-Evans for fourth place. The very partisan crowd did not seem to mind when the Connaught driver took this position, but when Trintignant crossed the line in fifth place, there were a few groans. However, after eight minutes of hard pushing, Jack was home, with an official sixth place. The crowd cheered up and gave the laddie from 'down under' a wonderful reception and the next day, the international motoring press collected our Jack to its bosom in a big way, along with the little Cooper, and both were stars of the first magnitude. Brooks and Vanwall also received rave notices for being second in a Grande Epreuve after all the weary years of waiting. The result, after all that, was: first, J. M. Fangio (Maserati); second, C. A. S. Brooks (Vanwall); third, M. Gregory (Maserati); fourth, S. Lewis-Evans (Connaught); fifth, M. Trintignant (Ferrari); and sixth, J. Brabham (Cooper).

The Monaco success was a big step up the ladder for the Cooper Car Company. Until that time they had not been considered as serious Formula I contenders, but for the rest of the season, the G.P. organizers were more than keen to have them, and consequently they were invited to compete in all the big G.P.s with lovely lumps of starting lolly thrown in. The works team had never had it so good. As John Cooper put it to me recently, the Cooper Car Company lived for the rest of the season on Monaco.

About a thousand miles from Monaco, at Brands Hatch on 19th May, some of the private owners of double o.h.c. Cooper-Climaxes were out on their maiden flight. In the two Formula II races, George Wicken, Tony Marsh, and Bill Whitehouse had to take on the Francis-tuned Cooper single o.h.c. driven by Peter Gammon, which could be a very tough proposition, especially around twisty Brands. Apart from Peter, the rest of the entries were standard sports cars, which, on form, should have been well outclassed.

In the first Formula II race, Wicken (Cooper Formula II) took the lead, never to lose it throughout the ten laps, and won by nine seconds. Opposition to the Cooper single-seaters came from Ian Raby, who brought his 1,100-c.c. ex-Gammon Sports Cooper right into the middle of Whitehouse, Marsh, and Gammon, and Raby pressed on regardless, which Messrs. W., M., and G. did not like at all. Gammon (Cooper Formula II) soon retired, leaving Whitehouse and Marsh to puzzle out why they should have spent two thousand two hundred pounds on a new car, when fourteen hundred would have sufficed. Whitehouse did manage at long last to get the 'Puddle Jumper' in his rear mirror, but Marsh spent his time surveying the 'Manx Tail' of precisely the same car that he disposed of earlier in the year.

In the Second Formula II race, again Wicken made the running after Whitehouse had led for one lap and then retired with transmission trouble. Raby used his Cooper as a lawn mower and retired with a broken 'shocker', Gammon got the Francis Cooper on the move and drove very nicely to take second place, with Marsh third.

On 29th May, Connaught Engineering announced that owing to financial difficulties, they were completely withdrawing from racing. This was a very serious setback to British aspirations in Formula I, more so as after John Heath's magnificent show on the Continent Connaughts had assumed the H.W.M. mantle to such good effect—instance the Syracuse G.P. win of Tony Brooks amongst other grand successes—that the demoralizing effect of the B.R.M. débâcle had been almost wiped out. Still, life went on, and with Connaught out the Cooper 1,960-c.c. car would be able to step into the breach and give Vanwalls a hand in upholding the country's prestige.

With Le Mans in the offing, Coopers had kept their sole entry and had plans for a sports 1,100-c.c. car to be driven by Jack Brabham and Ian Raby. Lotus had already received acceptance of a 1,500-c.c. and 750-c.c. car and an 1,100-c.c. car was on the reserve list. The 750-c.c. car surprisingly had a rather difficult time gaining acceptance, and it seemed as though the French were not too anxious to have competition in Class 'H'.

Whitsun, always a full programme for motor racing, was also a busy time for the Cooper works team, with Brands on 9th June and Crystal Palace on 10th June.

With Lotus and Cooper out in full force at the Brands Hatch Meeting on Whit Sunday, with Formula II cars and sports cars, this meeting promised to be a hot one.

SUEZ, DARK CLOUDS, AND A SILVER LINING

Main interest in the sports cars of 1,100-c.c. to 2,000-c.c. was centred on Salvadori with the Cooper 'double knocker' and Chapman with the Lotus 'double knocker' sports cars. Archie Scott-Brown was determined to see them both off in the new Elva, which unfortunately did not start as an exhaust valve dropped in practice and the car could not be repaired in time.

Chapman made a magnificent start, whereas Salvadori was left at the post. You just cannot do this sort of thing and get away with it with Chapman, and although Roy worked his way through the field with great gusto, he was unable to catch Colin, and came second, with Frost (Lotus-Climax single o.h.c.) third.

In the Formula II race, Part 1, Brabham and Salvadori drove the two twin o.h.c. Coopers, and Mackay Fraser and Cliff Allison the two works twin o.h.c. Lotus. Also competing were private entries Leston and Wicken with their Cooper twin-cams, and Brooks with the Alf Francis Special Cooper.

Salvadori got away to take an early lead from Brooks, Allison and Brabham, but coming down the back straight, Brabham began picking off his opponents, and passing the grandstand on lap one, he was leading from Mackay Fraser and Allison, with Salvadori fourth. On lap two, Brooks shot off the course at Pilgrim's Rise and was out. Brabham piled on the pressure and increased his lead over the field, and Salvadori took Allison and later Mackay Fraser to take second position by the half-way mark, but Brabham won, easing up a little with Salvadori second and Mac third.

In Part 2 of the Formula II race, once again Salvadori took an early lead from Allison and Wicken, with Brabham a slow starter. Wicken retired after one lap with valve trouble and Salvadori retiring one lap later with engine trouble, so Brabham took over the lead from Allison and Fraser. This order was extremely short-lived as Allison retired on lap four, leaving Mac to uphold the Lotus tradition and win the race, if possible. This, the American was unable to do as he was shedding gears every lap, having but one on lap six. Brabham carried on undisturbed and won yet again with Fraser second and Leston third.

The aggregate winners of two races were: first, J. Brabham (Cooper Formula II); second, H. Mackay Fraser (Lotus Formula II); and third, L. Leston (Cooper Formula II).

From Brands the circus moved nearer town to Crystal Palace. With roughly the same entries in the two Formula II races as at Brands Hatch, the main interest was whether the Lotus team could improve on their Brands Hatch showing.

In the London Trophy Race, Formula II, Part 1, again Salvadori in the Cooper 'twin' got away first, leading the field round the circuit, followed by Brabham in the sister car, Fraser in the Lotus 'twin', and Wicken in his private Cooper 'twin'. Fraser soon faded out with transmission trouble, leaving Wicken in the minor position. Many people who had seen the previous day's racing at Brands expected Brabham to overtake Salvadori, but this time Roy had the bit between his teeth and led all the way to register his first Formula II victory over Jack. Wicken was third.

In Part 2, as in Part 1, the race was enlivened by a terrific duel between Salvadori and Brabham with no holds barred. With John Cooper content to let his two boys fight it out, the grim contest between works Coopers was strangely reminiscent of the dog-fights of a year or so ago between Bueb and Russell. This time, Brabham got ahead of Salvadori, with Wicken close behind. Roy pressed Jack with all his might, but unfortunately lost a gear whilst so doing, which dropped him back. Wicken picked him off, but Roy passed again, but with a draw-back in the 'cog' department, could not catch Jack, who was not lazing about as he had set up a new circuit lap record. Wicken once again passed Salvadori and held him until the end.

The Aggregate Winners of two races were: first, J. Brabham (Cooper Formula II); second, R. Salvadori (Cooper Formula II); and third, G. Wicken (Cooper Formula II).

In the sports car race, 1,100-c.c. to 2,000-c.c., Chapman had some redress as he just pipped Salvadori at the post to win the race with his Lotus 'twin'.

Back at Surbiton there was an argument, as Roy felt that he, as No. 1 driver for Coopers, should get the best prepared car (which he was sure he was not getting). Jack, for his part, said that if he worked on a car, then that was the car that he was going to drive, which made sense. It was another case of a first class driver-mechanic having the advantage over another first class driver who was not a mechanic. A compromise was reached over a beer in the pub adjoining the works to the effect that Jack and Roy would have their own cars, but that Jack would be responsible for seeing that both cars were in A.1 condition. It meant quite a lot of extra work for the Australian, but he possesses great pride in the Cooper Car Company which he feels gave him his first real chance, so to him, in all things, it's

Cooper first and last. It is pleasant to record that at this time Roy and Jack are firm friends and make a fine works team.

Six days later the Cooper works team was engaged at Montlhéry in the Prix de Paris, with MacDowell taking Salvadori's place in the team.

This race was run something on the lines of an all-in contest. Eligible were Formula II cars, sports cars and grand touring cars. Naturally, amongst this mixture, the stark little Cooper 'twins' were the best bet, however Brian Naylor had also taken the trip and his brisk Lotus-Maserati was not going to be sneezed at. Tony Marsh and Ivor Bueb were representing private ownership with their Cooper 'twins' as was Sir Gawaine Baillie with his Formula II Lotus and 'Jabby' Crombac (an expert on this track) was down to drive his sports 1,100-c.c. Lotus. Amongst other notables was Goethals (550 RS Porsche).

Without too much effort Brabham and MacDowell took their Formula II Coopers off the front row of the grid well ahead of all except Naylor's Lotus-Maserati. Brabham led, but not by much, and as they went round the road circuit, MacDowell was giving nothing away and 'Brab' was putting his foot down hard. Naylor motored behind the two leaders very swiftly. By the end of lap one the works Coopers were well out in front and gaining on everything except Naylor's Lotus. Lap two was a repeat, but on the following lap, Naylor began to move up on the leaders and the 'Maser' part of the Lotus was coming into its own. At this stage the Lotus was certainly going faster than the Coopers, but Brian soon hit trouble and had to retire just when the race was getting exciting. It was now a question of by how much Brabham could beat MacDowell, or so he thought. But any man who can lap faster at Dundrod than Ivor Bueb is certainly no push-over, and before very long instead of No. 91 leading No. 90 it was 'bicki-burki', but not for long, as the lean one took over once again and stayed ahead. At a respectable distance behind, Tony Marsh, in his first Continental race, was leading Ivor Bueb in a similar car, and fifth, in front of Goethals' Porsche, lay Baillie's Lotus. Brabham, in peak form, managed to hold off MacDowell who drove brilliantly, and Marsh did likewise with Bueb. And just to make the story complete, Baillie dashed Goethals' hopes. 'Jabby' Crombec, without the aid of 'Bolstair', won the 1,100-c.c. Class, which made everybody happy, most of all 'Jabby'. So a good time was had by all. No rain and no accidents, a triumph for Montlhéry.

Exactly one week later, almost to the hour, the great Le Mans race would be finishing, and already feverish activity was going on all over Europe. Chapman had his 750-c.c. and 1½-litre Lotus accepted, and in addition two private owners had their 1,100-c.c. Loti down to run. Against this, Coopers had but a singleton entry, the 'hack' Cooper sports 1,100-c.c., still being used for the School at Brands. It was certainly not up to the usual Cooper high standard, but the Cooper family was completely engulfed in Formula I and Formula II and was not particularly interested in Le Mans. It says a lot for the Cooper chassis and Climax motor that after doing about three hundred laps at Brands twice a week for many months, the 1,100-c.c. was driven back to Surbiton, looked over, made ready as quickly as possible, despatched to Le Mans, driven there for the full distance, sent back, driven down to Brands again on the Tuesday ready for 'hacking' and according to Ron Searles, its engine was still ticking over like a bird. Only Coopers could get away with such audacity!

Le Mans proved a complete triumph for Colin Chapman, as not only did he win the Index of Performance with the prototype 750-c.c. Lotus-Climax and take second place with the 1,100-c.c. car, but he also took first, second, and fourth in Class 'G' which made the dogged third in the class of Coopers look very lean. This was, without doubt, Chapman's greatest ever success, yet with their outstanding past record Coopers could have shared it just as easily if they had put themselves out to get another 750-c.c. motor made. It seemed a painfully high price to pay for Formula II superiority. The results were thus:

Index of Performance	1st	C. Allison and K. Hall (Lotus 744-c.c.)
	2nd	Mackay Fraser and J. Chamberlain (Lotus 1,100-c.c.)
	3rd	L. Cornet and J. Perrier (D.B. 744-c.c.)
Class 'G':	1st	Mackay Fraser and J. Chamberlain (Lotus 1,100-c.c.)
	2nd	R. Walshaw and J. Dalton (Lotus 1,100-c.c.)
	3rd	J. Brabham and I. Raby (Cooper 1,100-c.c.)
Class 'E':	1st	C. Allison and K. Hall (Lotus 744-c.c.)
	2nd	L. Cornet and J. Perrier (D.B. 744-c.c.)
	3rd	P. Chancel and P. Hemard (Panhard 744-c.c.)

The only fly in the ointment so far as Chapman was concerned was the 1½-litre Lotus with twin o.h.c. Climax engine, which went like a rocket in practice and broke the 1½-litre lap record, but just before the end of the practice period, a valve dropped, ending its racing career for the present. At about this time, Climax were having great trouble with valves dropping in their 'double knocker' engines, and this did, in fact, get so serious that they decided to suspend production until the trouble could be ironed out.

Jointly combined at Rouen a fortnight later were Rob Walker and Cooper cars. Having been invited to compete in the French G.P. they fielded between them the bored out 1,960-c.c. Cooper plus two 1½-litre Coopers, one being used as a reserve. With Salvadori driving a Vanwall, the works lads were Brabham and MacDowell.

There were 15 starters in the French G.P.: Fangio (Maserati), Behra (Maserati), and Musso (Ferrari)—front row grid, Schell (Maserati) and Collins (Ferarri)—second row, Salvadori (Vanwall), Hawthorn (Ferrari), and Trintignant (Ferrari)—third row, Menditeguy (Maserati), Lewis-Evans (Vanwall—fourth row, Flockhart (B.R.M.), Mackay Fraser (B.R.M.), and Brabham (Cooper)—fifth row, Gould (Maserati) and Mac-Dowell (Cooper)—sixth row.

Behra almost jumped the gun, and got well in front of the field led by Musso and Fangio and Mackay Fraser, who was well up in the B.R.M. The wait after the cars had been lost to view round Virage du Nouveau Monde seemed timeless but was actually under two minutes. Then Musso buzzed by, leading a pack of screaming red and green cars, comprising Behra, Fangio, Schell, and Mackay Fraser, surprisingly fast in the B.R.M. Howling along in the van of the next batch of cars were the two game little Coopers. On lap two, Fangio had a slight brush with Behra but managed to get past, and coming past the pits it was Musso, Fangio, Behra, Collins, and Schell, with Mac in sixth place with the B.R.M. On lap three, Salvadori slid coming round Virage du Paradis (not very well named!) and dropped oil on the circuit. Collins, coming up behind did everything but lose the Lancia-Ferrari, but got round, not so Flockhart who hit the oil patch fair and square, causing the B.R.M. to slide and hit a concrete post at the side of the track, the car overturning and throwing out the unfortunate Ron. Luck was with him, as he escaped with bruises and a suspected cracked pelvis bone.

On lap four Fangio took over from Musso. On the next lap Gould's Maserati had a complete rear axle seizure right in the path of Brabham's Cooper; Jack did everything possible to stop, but rammed some straw bales, putting the car out of the race. With three cars already out, was this going to be a repetition of Monaco? But the race now settled down to its set pattern, Fangio building up a bigger lead all the time over Collins, who was second, and Musso, third. MacDowell's Cooper was gradually slipping back, occupying eleventh position in front of the ailing Lancia-Ferrari of Trintignant, and on lap twenty-four the latter retired. On lap twenty-five Mackay Fraser retired after a gallant drive; he was hearing strange groans from deep down in the B.R.M. and suspected the worst. On lap twenty-six Salvadori retired with a broken valve spring, and three from twelve leaves nine, meaning that MacDowell's Cooper was ninth. But now Brabham had taken over from him and was trying very hard. The Cooper and Lewis-Evans's Vanwall were the only green cars left in the race. Lewis-Evans driving very potently held fifth place at thirty laps, behind Fangio, Musso, who had retaken Collins, and Behra.

Lap thirty-one saw the end of the Vanwall which drew into the pits and retired with overheating and seized steering. On the same lap, Menditeguy blew the Maserati engine to pieces going towards the hairpin. Brabham was now seventh, the only green car still running, and the race was not even half over. This sort of thing could not keep on happening, and from lap thirty-one until the finish, there were no more retirements, although some of the cars ran in anything but first-class condition. Behra's Maserati was by far the worst, and on its sixty-ninth lap it gave up the ghost just before the finishing line, whilst Behra, oily, filthy, and nearly suffocated by fumes from the broken exhaust, waited grimly for Fangio to finish, so that he could push the Maserati over the line for a place. Brabham's Cooper was still going well, but after losing about eighteen seconds a lap for so long, it had no chance of catching Behra to get into the money. It did finish a far from disgraced seventh, the only British finisher. Fangio drove a masterly race to win from Musso by over fifty seconds with Collins third.

Three quick engagements followed for the Cooper team, the Rheims G.P., the G.P. of Europe and the Caen G.P., all within the space of three weeks, so it was certainly 'panic stations'.

SUEZ, DARK CLOUDS, AND A SILVER LINING

In the Rheims G.P., Formula I, on 14th July, again the Cooper 1,960-c.c. was the odd man out, put in for the dollar lolly and also in the hope that most of the regular G.P. cars would fade out, there being a very faint chance that the 1·9 could hold the big boys on this extremely fast circuit.

The Race: competing were Fangio, Behra, Schell, Gregory, Gould, Bueb, Piotti, Halford, Bonnier, Godia, and Menditeguy (Maserati), Musso, Collins, Hawthorn, and Gendebien (Lancia-Ferrari), Lewis-Evans and Salvadori (Vanwall) and Brabham (Cooper).

The start was sheer pandemonium for M. Roche, one of the organizers, whilst attempting to stop some of the cars from push-starting (this being against the rules) waved his yellow flag for the offenders to desist, which all and sundry took to mean 'get going, brother', which they did. M. Roche made a split second decision and ran for his life. One second more and Behra would have nailed him, as would Lewis-Evans, who seemed to be weaving in the same direction as our portly friend. Jack Brabham was also a victim of this false start as he was waiting for John Cooper to bring up his crash hat and goggles and these were passed to him after all the other cars had gone. Lewis-Evans took the lead from Musso and Fangio, and behind them were Hawthorn and Collins, then Salvadori, Behra, Schell, and Gendebien. Coming round for the first time, the Lewis-Evans Vanwall led by about a hundred yards from Musso, with Fangio third. The green car began to pull away slightly on each lap, and with Collins already in the pits with severe engine trouble, those up front were Lewis-Evans, Musso, Hawthorn, and Fangio, the last two having a private duel which was occupying most of the spectators' interest. At ten laps the green Vanwall was 13 seconds up on its nearest challenger, Musso's Ferrari, with Hawthorn's Ferrari third and ten seconds up on Fangio's Maserati as the 'Maestro' had spun on lap nine. Last man, rather sadly, was Brabham in the Cooper.

At twenty laps, the fleet Vanwall had lost three seconds to Musso and Fangio had taken third spot from Hawthorn, who retired on lap twenty-seven with a deranged engine. But now Lewis-Evans was in trouble with oil escaping from an engine breather and this was blowing onto the driver, clouding his goggles. As the Vanwall driver slowed, Musso piled on the pressure and passed the green car on lap thirty-four. With Fangio and Behra in sister Maseratis grimly tussling for the minor position and Lewis-Evans losing ground all the time, the gaps between second, third and fourth soon decreased, and on lap forty-eight the struggling Vanwall was passed by both. Schell, with yet another Maserati, was fifth. Brabham was still motoring and had not dropped a valve, which was something at least. Just before the end, Fangio spun on some oil at Thillois and received a nasty knock from a brick wall hidden behind a straw bale, which retired car and driver. This let Lewis-Evans up into third place behind Musso and Behra and the race finished in that manner. Brabham finished in twelfth place after a tidy drive.

Practising for the Formula II race were Trintignant (Ferrari V6), Salvadori and Brabham (works Cooper Formula II cars), Lucas, Marsh, Wicken, Leston, Gibson, England, Whitehouse, and Nixon (private Cooper Formula II cars), Moore and Thackwell (Cooper Formula II single o.h.v.), Allison and Taylor (works Lotus Formula II cars), Mackay Fraser (works Lotus-Climax sports), Frost and Armstrong (Lotus-Climax sports), Goethals (Porsche $1\frac{1}{2}$-litre sports) and Simon (Osca $1\frac{1}{2}$-litre sports). Strangely enough, fastest practice time was put up by Salvadori in the reserve works Sports Cooper with double o.h.c. Climax engine. In this Roy did 2 minutes 38·7 seconds, with Brabham second fastest in 2 minutes 39·6 seconds and Wicken next with 2 minutes 40·3 seconds. The lone Ferrari could not approach any of these times and was having a hard struggle to keep up with Marsh who finished fourth fastest in practice. The two Lotus Formula II cars tried hard, but showed no real form. The long, fast straight of the Garenne-Thillois stretch suited the Cooper sports down to the ground, the streamlining offsetting its greater weight over the more open Formula II car. During the second day's practice a valve head broke off Bill Whitehouse's 'double knocker' Cooper.

With Salvadori taking over the Formula II Cooper in the race, Whitehouse saw an opportunity to get a drive after all, and cajoled John Cooper into giving him the very fast Sports Cooper to drive. Twenty cars came under starter's orders, and with twelve Coopers against one Ferrari the odds looked slightly lopsided. Not so, as once the race started, it was clear to see that the V6 Ferrari had sold everybody a pup—not only could it keep up with the fastest Cooper, but actually it had better brakes. From the drop of the flag there were only three cars in it, the two works Coopers and the Ferrari. On a circuit that could easily make a race look like a procession, these three cars burned up the course, only yards separating all three lap after lap. In all, the lead changed thirteen times, which must constitute a record. Time and time again during the course of a single lap, it would change. It was voted by experienced racegoers as almost as exciting as the famous Hawthorn–Fangio duel in 1953, which is saying something.

Naturally sympathy lay with the under-dog, the lone Ferrari, but it was not needed, for Trintignant on form is a sight for sore eyes. All the nice things being said about the Frenchman could not alter the fact that both Brabham and Salvadori were also driving the race of their young lives. On the debit side of this really great Formula II race was to be the sad loss of two of the most popular drivers who had ever raced cars, Bill Whitehouse, who crashed approaching Thillois Corner, and Mackay Fraser, whose car overturned going into the fast corner past the pits. Meanwhile, the race up front had sorted itself out into a speed versus brakes duel between the two Coopers and the Ferrari. Trintignant could brake later on the corners than both Brabham and Salvadori, but the Surbiton lads could pass on acceleration on the straights. Thus there was nothing to choose between them, although Coopers had the moral advantage with two against one.

Coming up to the half-way stage, Trintignant was a yard or so ahead, but on lap eighteen Salvadori had taken him again. Some way back, Lucas and Marsh were going at it hammer and tongs in their efforts to purloin the minor position, with Lucas obviously highly delighted with Alan Brown's Cooper. Still in the race, and the sole surviving works Lotus, was sixth-placed Mackay Fraser in the sports car, in front of Goethals' Porsche. On lap twenty-five Coopers lost their moral advantage with a vengeance when Brabham's Cooper dropped a valve after that worthy had taken the lead from Roy and Maurice and knocked up a new lap record of 2 minutes 38·2 seconds. It was now even pegging and Enzo's boys looked relieved, but not so the Cooper Car Company. Here it would seem that crossed fingers or a prayer to the mighty valve would be more to the point. Salvadori did not seem to worry at losing his team-mate and still held off Trintignant as they came round for the twenty-sixth time and lapped Mackay Fraser (Lotus), who, having been given the 'hurry up' sign from Pit Manager Colin Chapman, decided to tuck himself in behind the two leaders and get a tow. This proved so effective that the American was able to follow them through when they lapped Lucas and Marsh, bringing the Lotus up to third place. Unhappily, poor Mac misjudged his speed going into the fast corner towards Gueux on the thirtieth lap and crashed very near to where Annie Bosquet was killed the year before in the race where, so ironically, Mackay Fraser had his first drive in a Lotus and made such a wonderful impression.

With only a few more laps to cover, Salvadori was keeping down to 7,200 r.p.m. against a safe limit of 7,500 r.p.m. in his efforts to beat the valve bogey, but even with these revs he was able to race neck and neck with the Ferrari. Lucas was in third place, having disposed of the Marsh challenge and the steady Goethals was keeping his Porsche on the same lap as Lucas and Marsh. The leading duellists marched on side by side for one more lap, then as Salvadori slowed, it became quite clear that the crossed fingers and prayers were unavailing as one more valve had dropped and the Cooper challenge was no more. Roy staggered round for three more laps and then parked his car by the finishing line ready to push it over when Trintignant crossed for the last time. With Salvadori parked, Lucas and Marsh were able to move up a place and finished second and third to Trintignant's Ferrari, only a yard or so dividing them, after a magnificent race. John Cooper had no cause to worry over the showing of his cars at Rheims, for only valve trouble stopped him from getting four cars in the first five in this important race.

The superlative Vanwall victory overshadowed all else in the British G.P., Aintree, 20th July. The entry comprised Fangio, Behra, Menditeguy, Bonnier, Bueb, and Schell (Maserati), Brooks, Moss, and Lewis-Evans (Vanwall), Brabham and Salvadori (Cooper), Hawthorn, Collins, Musso and Trintignant (Ferrari), Fairman and Leston (B.R.M.) and Gerard (Cooper-Bristol).

The race was televised to millions of viewers, who saw three separate parts of it. The first showed Moss (Vanwall) leading from Behra (Maserati)—which must have raised their blood pressure—then later, Behra leading from Hawthorn (Ferrari)—black depression—and the final flash, Moss leading from Musso (Ferrari) until the end (too drunk to turn off the football match!). The race: Behra took an early lead chased by Moss and Brooks (Vanwall) with Hawthorn hard on their tails and Fangio (Maserati) left a little at the post. Going into Anchor Crossing, Behra, keeping well in, led Moss by a length, with Hawthorn almost in Moss's driving seat. Moss took Behra at

Canal Curve and came past the pits with a bare second's lead, the order behind being Brooks, Hawthorn, Collins (Ferrari), Schell (Maserati), Musso, Fangio, Menditeguy (Maserati), Leston (B.R.M.) and Lewis-Evans (Vanwall). On lap four, Hawthorn had passed Brooks and Lewis-Evans was moving up rapidly with the third Vanwall. On each lap Moss took the Vanwall round like a rocket and by lap ten was a shade over seven seconds in front of Behra's Maserati, the order behind being Hawthorn a yard behind Behra, then Collins, Musso, Brooks, Lewis-Evans and Fangio. Salvadori (Cooper) and Brabham (Cooper) were getting mobile lying twelfth and fourteenth respectively. On lap twenty-one, Moss came flying in to his pit to have a quick check. A plug lead was pushed firmly in and he was away again, but in thirty-five seconds he had dropped to seventh place, so fast was the pace. Two laps later, Moss came in again to his pit with nothing cured and a hungry look every time Brooks came round; 'come in' brought Brooks in on lap twenty-seven and Moss was in the race within 27 seconds, and on lap thirty he was seventh. Forty seconds behind him, now in ninth place, was Salvadori, with Brabham in eleventh position. Leading by 5 seconds from Hawthorn's Ferrari was Behra driving with great aplomb, followed by Collins, Lewis-Evans, Musso and Fangio.

With ambition driving him Moss began to carve huge slices off the cars in front; his was an impossible task, or so it seemed, but at forty laps, he was in fifth place and Salvadori was seventh. So both of these young men were moving up. On lap forty-nine, Fangio retired his tired Maserati with broken valve gear. On lap fifty-three Collins's Ferrari lost all its water and retired, and at sixty laps Moss was fourth and Salvadori sixth, with Brabham eighth, and both Coopers were running with no signs of valve trouble. Came the sixty-ninth lap with Dame Fortune smiling on Moss but not on the gallant Behra, for with the race in the bag barring trouble Behra did have trouble with a capital T, a disintegrated clutch putting him right out of the race. The luckless Hawthorn ran over a large piece of metal which punctured his rear tyre, putting him out of the main picture although he re-started in fourth place after a tyre change. On lap seventy Moss had taken the lead from Lewis-Evans with Musso third, Hawthorn fourth, and Salvadori fifth—three green cars in the first five, with Brabham seventh behind Trintignant's Ferrari! On lap seventy-three Lewis-Evans stopped on the circuit with a broken throttle linkage, seriously depleting the all-conquering green cars, and casting some doubt on Moss's car. Now Salvadori's trim little Cooper was fourth and still going strong, but Brabham did his seventy-fourth tour and then packed up with no clutch. Two green cars retired in two laps, what else could happen. Fortunately, nothing did to Moss who won from Musso and Hawthorn to the great delight of the vast crowd, but once again the Cooper was pipped, the gearbox casing split open and Roy had to do his now familiar pushing over the finishing line, to be beaten into fifth place by Trintignant. Still, even a fifth place against such mighty opposition was magnificent.

Having seen the entry list for the Caen G.P., on 28th July, Coopers were quietly confident. Maserati, Ferrari, and Vanwall were not competing and they were faced with works opposition from B.R.M. only, the rest of the cars being privately entered.

Behra surprised everyone by getting Mays and Berthon to supply him with the No. 1 B.R.M. and as Schell, who broke a piston on his Maserati in practice, also got a drive in B.R.M. No. 2, this certainly strengthened the B.R.M.'s hand, especially as Behra put up fastest practice time in 1 minute 21·1 seconds, against Brooks' second fastest of 1 minute 23·6 seconds in the Rob Walker 1·9 Cooper. Salvadori did 1 minute 24·5 seconds in the works Cooper, and Halford 1 minute 26·2 seconds in his well-known Maserati. Brabham was somewhat slower in the works Cooper 1,500-c.c.—1 minute 27·5 seconds. With two cars on the front grid, Coopers were smacking their lips in anticipation of their first G.P. win, only the B.R.M. standing in their way, a car well known for its unreliability.

The Race: Owing to the narrow road, the cars were lined up in pairs. With Brooks and Behra in front and Salvadori and Halford in the second row, Cooper's plan of campaign was for Brooks and Salvadori to tuck in behind Behra and without stressing their rather delicate engines too much, to wait for the big bang. Brabham in the $1\frac{1}{2}$-litre was to hold a watching brief. Came the start and everything went according to plan, except that Behra took the B.R.M. away so quickly, that Brooks and Salvadori were panting some distance behind on the very first lap, but Hawthorn had led the G.P. cars in the past, remember? Now Schell, who had never driven a B.R.M. before (which was probably an advantage) began to get the feel of the car and was tailing third man Salvadori who was driving very confidently behind Brooks. On lap three Schell took Salvadori, and

Brabham had to retire with ignition trouble—sad, but Coopers still had Brooks and Salvadori driving strictly to instructions and the race was over eighty-six laps.

On the other side of the fence, neither Behra nor Schell had any personal knowledge of the B.R.M. saga and were driving them as G.P. cars should be driven, a case of 'fools rush in where angels fear to tread.' On lap seven Schell had overtaken Brooks and now the B.R.M.s were 1–2 and giving the French crowd their money's worth, passing and re-passing one another in great style for lap after lap. As both the B.R.M.s were getting a little too far ahead, Brooks speeded up and attempted to get on terms with Schell. Meanwhile, Salvadori had taken over Brabham's watching brief and although still on the same lap as the B.R.M.s, was taking things easy. So far so good. Brooks made up some ground over the next ten laps, but the B.R.M.s were really motoring and the two local boys were having great fun. However, we had seen the B.R.M. flatter only to deceive many times before, so not to worry. The little game continued, soon to be interrupted the wrong way when Brooks drove into the pits for heavy water replenishments—this was not cricket at all! Twenty-seven laps and the two B.R.M.s were going as well as ever. The planners were getting a little hot under the collar. However, the big bang did come on the fifty-ninth lap, and Schell brought No. 2 B.R.M. in minus many essential parts to retire for good and all. Previously Brooks had packed up with a clutchless Cooper. Now what were the planners to do? Only twenty-seven more laps to go and Behra looking as though he could go on for ever.

Suddenly the penny dropped, perhaps it had been unwise to hang back and wait for those big bangs, but now it was too late as Behra was 30 seconds in front of Salvadori, which meant gaining over a second a lap, which Roy could not do, if the B.R.M. kept going. He was given the 'leaden boot' sign at last and went all out, but this time Behra and B.R.M. were irresistible and although Salvadori cut down the lead by over half a second per lap, he was too late. The B.R.M. did not blow up; it won its first Continental G.P. It gave Behra a wonderful ride and it gave the two greatest optimists in the game, Mays and Berthon a much needed boost after all those soul-destroying years out on a limb. As to Coopers, they lost their greatest chance to date due to over-confidence. Still, Salvadori's second place was not to be ignored. Steady Halford in the Maserati 250F was third.

Coopers appeared next in Germany, at Nurburgring on 4th August, with Salvadori driving the works 1½-litre and Brabham driving Rob Walker's similar car. They were backed up by private owners Marsh, Naylor, Gibson, and England, all, of course, entered in the Formula II section of the G.P.

In this part of the race Porsche had entered three works sports cars driven by Barth, de Beaufort, and Maglioli. As the 1½-litre Ferrari did not appear, the rest of the entry was all Cooper, so it was a straight fight between Porsche and Cooper. Fastest practice times were Salvadori 10 minutes ·06 seconds for Coopers, and Barth 10 minutes ·02 seconds for Porsche. The Coopers were standing up to the bumpy ride very well indeed, but Nurburgring to Porsche was like Brands to Cooper so they were tough opposition.

In the race Barth and Salvadori got well away from the other Formula II cars and duelled continuously for ten laps with both Barth and Salvadori taking turns in leading the section. However on lap ten, Salvadori retired with a fractured wishbone. As Brabham had already retired with transmission failure, it was left to the private Coopers to give the Porsches a run for their money, and Naylor stepped into the breach. He was not able to get on terms with either Barth or Maglioli, the two leaders, until the last named fell out with engine trouble, but although Naylor was putting in some beautiful laps, Barth had a very definite edge on him and would not be harried. Marsh had a great deal of trouble but kept going until the end to take fourth place behind of Beaufort's Porsche 1,500 RS. Only four cars finished the race.

The next day, having flown back from Germany, Salvadori and Brabham drove Formula II cars at the August Bank Holiday Brands Hatch Meeting.

As in so many races this season, Brabham was untouchable and won both Formula II heats, taking the Rochester Trophy and actress Rita Royce round the circuit for several laps. This outing prompted Jack to ask Rita whether she would like to co-pilot with him in a twenty-four hour race!

The final aggregate of heats 1 and 2 was: first, J. Brabham; second, G. Wicken; third, R. Moore.

And so to the next major G.P., at Pescara on 18th August.

Representing the Cooper marque were Salvadori and Brabham with the 1·9 Coopers, but having to give away over half a litre on the long straights in addition to suspension difficulties made getting into the money a very slim chance indeed. However, all this experience on G.P. circuits would stand the Cooper Car Company in good stead in 1958.

The race confirmed the results of the British G.P. and once more Moss gave the red cars a pasting, winning the G.P. for Vanwall and Britain by 14 seconds from World Champion J. M. Fangio (Maserati) and Schell (Maserati). Brabham drove his usual plucky race and finished seventh, but Salvadori went off the road and bent his rear suspension on the fourth lap. Roy was unhurt.

At Surbiton, as at Hornsey and Cambridge, it was all hands on deck in preparation for the International Silverstone Meeting on 14th September.

The main race of the day was the *Daily Express* Trophy race in which all the cars competed, Formula I and Formula II.

Brabham and Salvadori were driving the 1·9 and 1·5 Coopers respectively and Brooks had charge of the Rob Walker 1·9 Cooper. Vanwall, Maserati and Ferrari were not present, but B.R.M. fielded three cars driven by Behra, Schell, and Flockhart, and after Behra's victory at Caen, they were firm favourites in the Formula I section. In addition to the Coopers and three B.R.M.s, there were the private Maseratis of Gregory, Gould, Bonnier, Bueb, and Halford, Stuart and Gerard (Cooper-Bristols) and Rozier (Ferrari). In the Formula II section Salvadori, Marsh, Ireland, Leston, Wicken, Hill, Cunningham-Reid, Burgess, Gibson, Thackwell, Russell, and Moore were down to drive Cooper Formula II cars. Hall, D. Taylor, H. Haylor, and Allison were listed to drive Lotus Formula II, and also entered were the Lister-Climax Formula II and de Tomaso's Osca.

After practice on Thursday and Friday, Brooks in the Francis tuned Cooper 1·9 had overwhelmed with wonder the racing fraternity by returning a lap time of 1 minute 43 seconds, which equalled the course record. The Lister-Climax still had teething troubles and after using up all its oil was scratched.

In the Trophy Race final with three B.R.M.s on the front row of the grid, together with Gregory's Maserati it looked odds on that Mr. Owen's lads would bring home the bacon, as only Brabham in the 1·9 Cooper and Bonnier and Gregory in their Maseratis stood in their way. All the other Coopers and Lotus were 1,500-c.c. cars and as such could have little chance in the race overall. Still the battle for Formula II honours looked more exciting.

As it transpired the form book was correct, and once Behra

got in front he literally ran away with the race. Schell and Flockhart kept their stations behind the team leader and the only weakness in the whole set-up was Flockhart who might have been caught by both Brabham and Bonnier at different times. As it happened, Brabham retired on the twenty-third lap after having been in the pits previously with a serious oil leak and Bonnier piled on the pressure and nearly, but not quite, overtook Flockhart on the very last lap.

With the race a foregone conclusion up front, the Formula II part presented much greater interest as with Allison really motoring at last with the Formula II Lotus, Salvadori was having to pull out all the stops to hold him off. The Cooper driver had made a fine start and had worked through the field into sixth place, when, much to his surprise, he could see Allison in his mirror and try as he might, Roy just could not get that awful vision out of his mind (Roy has had enough trouble with Lotus Sports cars and now this!) The hectic chase went on and on, but on lap thirteen, Cooper No. 1 lost all his anchors which was not conducive to a dice of this kind, consequently, Allison took the lead and burnt up the track with a new Formula II record of 1 minute 46 seconds. Meanwhile cars were falling by the wayside, Brooks' s.o.h.c. Cooper, valve trouble, Ireland (Cooper) half shaft, Russell (Cooper) engine trouble, Thackwell (Cooper) oil pressure and sans brakes, Salvadori was using the gearbox to the full and it was a miracle that it did not burst. Wicken (Cooper) was gunning for Salvadori but could not quite catch the works job. Allison, travelling extremely fast, had by now built up a big lead and thought fit to ease a little with unfortunate results as in so doing, he lost his vital concentration at Becketts Corner and tore into the barricades, damaging car, but not driver. This gave Salvadori the Formula II race on a plate with an easy win over Wicken and Marsh.

With Goodwood scheduled for 28th September, Coopers returned to Surbiton with very mixed feelings. They welcomed the competition offered by the Lotus Formula II car, realizing that this would be the life blood of the Formula, but at the same time, after having things all their own way for so long at home, it was quite a shock to find that Colin Chapman had caught up so quickly. With their unbeaten home record at stake, the entire Cooper concern worked day and night to get their works cars on the line at Goodwood in absolutely first-class condition, and every part was checked and counter-checked by both John Cooper and Jack Brabham. John in particular worked himself to a frazzle, and things were not made easier for him by the fact that another prototype Cooper was expected any moment by Madame Cooper. Of course, things could have been arranged differently, but who could have foreseen that Chapman would have nearly beaten the Formula II Cooper so late in the season. At least that was John's story and he was stuck with it.

The long hours of hard slogging at Surbiton paid off handsomely in the Woodcote Cup, Formula II race, for Salvadori and Brabham had the race in their pockets from the flag and the only point to be resolved as they tore round at the head of the queue was, simply, Salvadori or Brabham? All the marques were in at the start, and Brooks had broken the lap record in practice with the Rob Walker Cooper 1·5. The Lister Formula II was not fast in practice, but made the line up. Hill and Allison drove Lotus Formula II cars at a high rate of knots, but were outclassed by John Cooper's super night-work jobs. This was the pay-off so far as Jack and Roy were concerned and their duel made this ten lapper the fastest race ever at Goodwood. Roy drove one of his finest races to lead Jack by a hairsbreadth all the way. Time and again, the latter tried to get by, but could not pull out the necessary nth. At one point the Australian nearly came unstuck—it looked dangerous, it was dangerous, but you would never get Jack or Roy to agree. Just a friendly dice would be their opinion, but to all and sundry, it was a 'bloody' battle settled by Salvadori winning by a half-second. Allison drove a steady race in the Lotus Formula II to finish third.

One week away was the Gold Cup Meeting at Oulton Park, and Salvadori had no intention of letting the little gold bauble slip from his grasp.

With a thousand pounds and the Gold Cup at stake, the Formula Two-ites were out in force. The Cooper Car Company had its biggest ever entry, four Formula IIs driven by Brabham, Salvadori, Russell, and Burgess, Rob Walker had two Formula II Coopers driven by Brooks and Cunningham-Reid, Lotus Engineering had three Formula II cars driven by Allison, Hall, and Hill, the Lister Formula II car did not turn up, there was a sports Willment driven by Stuart Lewis-Evans, Richards with the H.A.R., and all the rest were private Formula II Coopers, with Wicken, Marsh, Ireland, Leston, Nixon, Bueb, Halford, Gibson, Moore and Flockhart driving, plus Dennis

Taylor in a Lotus Formula II and Stoop with a 1,220-c.c. Cooper Formula II

Fastest times in practice were shared by Marsh and Allison in 1 minute 50·4 seconds, and this on a track about which Roy Salvadori has often said if you break two minutes, you are amazed that you have got round so fast.

The Race: Brooks had bad luck once again, for as he let in the clutch, his 'diff' went west. Brabham, on the inside, soon took the lead, followed by Hill, Marsh, Allison, and Salvadori. Brabham was finding that something extra over his rivals and was already building a lead. Nixon ran out of road, but rejoined the field. As the race settled down, Brabham remained firmly in front, but Allison and Salvadori having passed Marsh and Hill were second and third. The order following was Hill, Marsh, Burgess, Ireland, Wicken, Hall, and Russell. Allison put in a lap at 1 minute 53·6 seconds, a new official Formula II record. On lap four both Richards and Ireland retired. Brabham had increased his lead over Allison and Salvadori, with Hill coming along very swiftly and now in front of Marsh. On the next lap Hall came into the picture in fifth place having passed Marsh, Salvadori was putting on a spurt but his engine did not sound au point and Hill began closing up fast.

At this point, the Lotus driver broke Allison's few minutes' old Formula II record with a 1 minute 53·2 seconds lap. The gap was not widening between Allison and Brabham, and at ten laps the order was Brabham, Allison, Salvadori, Hill. At this stage, Russell ran out of road and retired and the leaders were now lapping the tail enders, always a dicey-do. Here Brabham got through, but Allison was baulked, losing a few yards. It was Cooper, Lotus, Cooper, Lotus, Lotus, and Salvadori was already in trouble. On lap fifteen Hill overtook Salvadori, who pulled into the pits very shortly afterwards with his engine sounding very rough. He was away again in a few seconds, but his hopes of retaining the Gold Cup were fast disappearing. Brabham was still the undisputed leader, but with Brooks and Russell out, and Salvadori in trouble, Lotus with second, third, and fourth positions were giving Coopers plenty to think about. But within the space of another four laps, both Hill and Hall were in the pits for lengthy repairs, putting them out of the running. Cunningham-Reid with the Rob Walker s.o.h.c. Cooper retired with a broken water pump and Salvadori regained his third place, with no hope of catching either Brabham or Allison unless they ran into trouble. Fourth place had been purloined by Marsh, and Burgess was putting in some good work with the fourth works Cooper.

A lot of oil had been spilt on the course and Wicken hit a bad spot, losing control, his Cooper flipping and crashing into a wall, Wicken coming off very badly with a broken leg and other injuries. In this hectic race, retirements were coming in thick and heavy—Dennis Taylor with a broken oil pipe, Halford with overheating, and Leston, after a lovely ding-dong with Burgess retired his Cooper with a broken drive shaft. At the half-way stage the order was Brabham, Allison, Salvadori, Marsh, Burgess, Flockhart. Now Brabham, going like a bomb, was rounding Old Hill Corner as Allison came round Lodge. Salvadori's Cooper sounded very 'ropey', and after a few more laps it packed up altogether, Roy having to push it in. Marsh and Burgess consequently moved up a place, one lap behind the two leaders. At forty laps Brabham still led by an increased margin from Allison, with Marsh third and Burgess fourth. Brabham did not slacken for a second, but Allison, realizing that it was hopeless, stopped thrashing his motor and prepared to take an easy second place. Burgess had no chance of catching Marsh and the race ran out in this form. Flockhart, on his maiden drive with a Cooper, drove a fine race to finish fifth.

Back at Surbiton, the works were at it again, preparing the Record car for the forthcoming Monza attempts on International Class 'G' records, (note: see chapter on records), and the 'F' car with a 1·9 Climax engine was being put through the mill in preparation for the Moroccan G.P. Salvadori was listed to drive this car and Brabham was engaged by Rob Walker to drive the Alf Francis Cooper 1·9. The arrangements had been for the Cooper équipe to use Rob Walker's transporter, cutting down the transport cost.

Five works teams were represented in the Moroccan G.P. at Casablanca, on 27th October, namely Vanwall, Ferrari, B.R.M., Cooper and Maserati, Godia (Maserati) and Lucas (Maserati) being the only private entries. 'Asian 'flu' was an additional hazard with which many of the drivers had to contend and Stirling Moss had a very bad dose and could not drive; Schell, Fangio, Hawthorn, and Collins had milder attacks which rather upset their driving. John Cooper, Jack Brabham, and Roy Salvadori were out for a holiday in the sun and hang the expense, after a hectic racing season. Quite frankly, they were not greatly interested, knowing full well that they were somewhat outclassed once again, particularly on road holding. They were out to have the final bash preparatory to getting the new modifications done to the car for 1958.

One of the chief worries in 1957 with the 1.9 had been the gearbox; the modded Citröen box had done wonders since 1955, but with the big increase in power since the d.o.h.c. era, it just could not stand up to the extra strain. John Cooper had overcome this by designing his own box in conjunction with 'Whiskers', the open necked shirt genius back at the works. Although all the jigs had been made, the complete article was not ready in time for Casablanca, hence the holiday feeling.

Both Cooper drivers took the practice period very easy, saving their real efforts for the race, but in spite of a 'cotton wool' practice period, Brabham broke the clutch on his car.

Race day arrived and the two Coopers did battle for strictly limited periods, Brabham's gearbox only lasting four laps and Salvadori's just over twelve. Having come all this way, Alf Francis had a brainstorm and slid quietly away to the Pippbrook Bus, returning very speedily with a new gearbox tucked underneath his arm which he proceeded to change for the rattle box already in Brabham's car. This job, which normally takes about two hours, was accomplished in forty minutes and a highly delighted Brabham shot back into the race, as the leaders came round for the twenty-eighth lap. Raymond Roche, the race organizer, took a very dim view of this manœuvre, viewing that what Roche could see at the pits, Roche knew about, but what went on behind the pits Roche knew nothing about and in any case, changing a gearbox in forty minutes was against Trade Union regulations. All this added up to a slanging match with Rob Walker and a black flag for Brabham. One regulation that Roche had forgotten was that a black flag, by F.I.A. ruling, requires a number on it, so none of the preoccupied drivers took the slightest notice. This made the said Roche hopping mad so he stuck the flag into the faces of all and sundry with the surprising result that one Juan Manuel Fangio came in with a most contrite look on his face, so Juan must have had something on his conscience. The World Champion was waved off again, immediately, and then the organizer got most browned off and told Rob Walker to call his man in or . . . ! so in came Brabham to the applause usually given to a conquering hero and off went Roche to the boos usually reserved for a heavily moustached villain!

For the record, Behra (Maserati) put it across his rivals but Lewis-Evans drove a wonderful race to bring his Vanwall into second place, nearly a minute ahead of Trintignant's B.R.M. With seven finishers out of fourteen starters, G.P. racing was now a fifty-fifty chance.

Jack Brabham made arrangements to take the 1·9 Cooper to New Zealand for the G.P., which from his showing on this side of the world could easily be Jack's first 1958 success. A very strong portent of things to come was the Brands Hatch Boxing Day Meeting, where Brabham's Cooper had the new five-speed John Cooper-'Whiskers' inspired gearbox. Using the 1·9 engine, Brabham broke the lap record, became the first man to lap the extended course in under fifty-nine seconds, and won the Formula Libre race by the length of a street, which concluded the Cooper programme for 1957.

COOPER'S CHALLENGE FOR WORLD CHAMPIONSHIP HONOURS

Having had some success with their Formula I cars during 1957, Coopers made up their minds to concentrate on a full season of G.P.s for 1958

During the winter, John managed to get a team of three new works cars made, comprising two Formula I cars and one Formula II car; however, the latter was sold almost immediately and replaced with a further Formula I car. Once more the works relied on Salvadori and Brabham with third string Ian Burgess currently running the Cooper Training School.

Improvements to the cars included disc brakes, coil spring shock-absorbers and double wishbones on front and back in place of the ordinary Newton shock absorbers with single wishbones; the body was two inches wider with a bucket seat which was much more comfortable, the curly-leaf spring was replaced by a $1\frac{3}{4}$-inch flat spring, and the car had a new anti-roll bar. Another important point was that Cooper's were now on Dunlop R.5s, a really superb new tyre.

The power mills in the Cooper works cars were two 1·9-litre Climax and one 2·2-litre Climax, the 2·2 giving 193 b.h.p. at 6,250 revs. and the 1·9s giving 180–181 b.h.p. at 6,500 revs.

It had hardly been 1958 a bare three weeks when news came through from the Argentine of one of the greatest upsets in G.P. racing since the German G.P. of 1935, when the great Nuvolari smashed the might of both Auto Union and Mercedes-Benz and won the race with a completely outclassed Alfa-Romeo. This time it was the Italians' turn to suffer, with both Ferrari and Maserati having to lower their flags to a little green Cooper driven by an equally great driver, one Stirling Moss. As news came through about the same time that Jack Brabham had also won the New Zealand G.P. with a Cooper-Climax, the double stroke of good fortune left even the unshakeable Cooper family slightly dazed.

The Argentine G.P. was held on 19th January, 1958. Owing to the rather tardy notification of the type of fuel the race was to be run on, both Vanwall and B.R.M. were unable to get their cars ready in time, but Ferrari and Maserati fielded their strongest teams, led by Hawthorn and Fangio respectively.

With Vanwall out, canny Rob Walker seized his opportunity and managed to persuade Moss to drive his Alf Francis modified Cooper-Climax 1·9 Formula I car.

The complete entry list for the event was: Ferrari—Hawthorn, Musso, and Collins; Maserati—Fangio, Behra, Schell, Menditeguy, Godia, and Gould; Cooper—Moss.

Came race day, and at four-thirty p.m. sharp away went the field with Fangio, Behra, and Hawthorn bunched in front. Collins only got as far as the first straight when a half-shaft snapped, retiring poor Peter from the race. With one lap behind him, Behra led from Hawthorn, Fangio and Moss. Already it was noticeable that Moss could conduct the light little Cooper into the corners a good deal farther before braking than his heavier rivals. On lap four, Hawthorn had obtained a thin lead over Fangio and Behra, and Musso had edged in front of Moss who was having trouble with a gear sticking in second. By by-passing this notch, Stirling began to pile on the pressure and took Musso and tailed Behra, who was now third behind Hawthorn and Fangio.

Soon afterwards, Fangio led the pack, and Hawthorn's Ferrari seemed to be losing some of its punch; Menditeguy spun and this dropped him back alongside Gould, whose somewhat slow progress rather displeased the crowd. But now Moss was really in the picture, and by lap twenty he was past Behra and Hawthorn and nosing fast towards Fangio, who strove desperately to hold him off. When Moss did a lap in 1 minute 42·9 seconds Fangio replied with one in 1 minute 42·8 seconds. With Moss hammering away, Fangio went faster and faster, finally getting down to 1 minute 41·8 seconds, an absolute lap record. This was a shade too fast for Moss, but it was also a shade too fast for Fangio's tyres, which were showing signs of wear. Nevertheless, the Master pressed on to the very nth degree hoping to build up a sufficient lead for a change of tyres, but Moss would have none of this, and when on the thirty-fifth lap Fangio dashed into his pit, the Cooper driver hustled past in no time at all. With Fangio away after a forty-second pit stop in fourth place, the effect of the shock began to wear off and the crowd realized that the Cooper had a distinct chance of an out-and-out victory.

At the half-way stage, Moss still led by a substantial margin and both Behra and Musso were having tyre troubles; Moss kept going and at fifty laps was 27 seconds ahead of his nearest challenger, Musso, who had passed Behra. Hawthorn now came back onto the leader board, his Ferrari having suddenly regained its urge, and very soon he had passed Fangio, whose Maserati was overheating. Now both Musso and Hawthorn had the bit between their teeth and chased the impudent little Cooper very hard indeed. Moss was master of the situation, however, and at sixty laps, was 35 seconds ahead of second man Musso. A hasty confab in the Rob Walker pit and out went the sign for Stirling to slow and if his lucky stars were in the right place, he would be able to run through the race without a tyre change.

The situation now became very tense: twenty laps to go and a lead of 35 seconds. Now the Ferrari boys were tearing chunks off those precious seconds every lap. This was Moss at his finest; with an iron will, he forced himself to go slower and slower, yet seeing each time he came past his pit how his lead was shrinking. With ten laps to go, 28 seconds separated Moss from Musso, with Hawthorn barely five seconds behind his team-mate. Now the canvas was beginning to show through on one of the Cooper's tyres. Stirling slowed still more and Musso was gaining at the rate of three seconds a lap; still Stirling did not lose his head, and nursed his failing tyres on and on. Meanwhile, Hawthorn slightly shunted Menditeguy's spinning Maserati, which lost him a second or two; Fangio retained a steady fourth place but could not challenge for absolute honours. Five laps to go and only 15 seconds stood between Musso and his goal! Still Moss cruised round. The pattern stayed the same. Four laps to go, the lead stood at 12 seconds; three laps . . . two laps . . . only 6 seconds. . . . One lap, and only yards separated the red from the green! Surely after all this Stirling was not going to be caught, but what a jockey Moss would have made, for with the most perfect timing imaginable he waited until Musso was right on his tail and then pressed round the last lap and into the finishing straight just that tiny bit faster than the Ferrari driver, to win by 2·7 seconds, with Hawthorn nine seconds behind his partner. A brilliant driver, backed up by a wonderful car and team of mechanics and pit staff proved just the combination to bring home the bacon for private owner Rob Walker and to give Cooper's a flying start to the season. And what's more, it was no fluke but a fully merited win. The full result was: first S. Moss (Cooper-Climax 1·9); second, L. Musso (Ferrari); third, M. Hawthorn (Ferrari); fourth, J. Fangio (Maserati); fifth, J. Behra (Maserati); and sixth, H. Schell (Maserati).

To disprove the old theory that lightning does not strike twice in the same place, the Rob Walker–Alf Francis set-up walked away with a second grande épreuve when they won the Monaco G.P., this time from Vanwall, Ferrari, B.R.M., Maserati, and Lotus.

The sixteen starters in the Monaco G.P., on 18th May, were: front line and pole position, Brooks (Vanwall), partnered by Behra (B.R.M.) and Brabham (Cooper). Second row, Salvadori (Cooper) and Trintignant (Cooper). Third row, the first red car, Hawthorn (Ferrari) joined by Lewis-Evans (Vanwall) and Moss (Vanwall). Fourth, fifth, sixth, and seventh rows were occupied by Collins (Ferrari), Musso (Ferrari), von Trips (Ferrari), Schell (B.R.M.), Allison (Lotus), Scarlatti (Maserati), Hill (Lotus) and Bonnier (Maserati), in that order.

Just before the start, Prince Rainier and Princess Grace arrived in a sleek Ford Fairlane and took their seats in the Royal Box. Then down went the flag, and sixteen cars were there, and then they were not. Salvadori got to Gasometer Corner first, then wished that he had not, as going in too fast, he went wide, obstructing all the other machinery—whack, bang, whack—and it was Behra out first, with Brooks, Brabham, and Moss on his tail. Salvadori had paid the penalty of impetuosity, for he drew into the pit after one lap with a detached track rod. All three Vanwalls bore marks of impact, as also did Hawthorn's Ferrari, but a few bumps are expected at Monaco and nobody seemed perturbed.

Behra led after one lap, having done the required distance in a fabulous 1 minute 51·8 seconds from a standing start. Soon the race began to settle down, with the order on lap three, Behra still leading, followed by Brooks, Moss, Hawthorn, and then a small gap and a blue and green Cooper almost side by side, with Trintignant and Brabham both looking very comfortable. All the Ferraris were suffering from understeer tendencies with Collins's car by far the worst. Meanwhile Salvadori rejoined the race two laps in arrears. On lap eight Behra still led from Brooks, but Hawthorn had overhauled Moss and now held third place; Brabham was now in trouble with his front suspension which was slowing him; Lewis-Evans retired on lap ten with defective steering. Hawthorn was sitting on second place man Brooks's tail and driving magnificently. On lap fifteen, after some pseudo fist-waving, Hawthorn took Brooks, with Behra still first in the B.R.M. and going like a bomb.

Trintignant now began to step on it and pushed past Brabham who was definitely slowing and began to close up on the leaders. Musso also moved up and took Brabham's Cooper for sixth place; Brooks chased Hawthorn's Ferrari hard for three laps and then fell out of the race out on the course when a plug worked out of its socket and as repairs can only be carried out at the pit, Brooks could not replace the plug himself without disqualification. This left Hawthorn in second place.

On lap twenty-one Brabham pulled into his pit for repairs to his front anti-roll bar, losing three minutes, and considerably weakening the Cooper works' chances. At this stage the B.R.M. bogey seemed to have been laid as neither Hawthorn (second) nor Moss (third) could reduce the gap, which varied between three and four seconds. Schell, in the other B.R.M., was well back in the field due to a sticking float needle which was causing flooding in one cylinder. The order at twenty-five laps was Behra, Hawthorn, Moss, Trintignant, Musso, Collins, with von Trips seventh; both the works Coopers were well behind and likewise the two works Lotus of Allison and Hill were not nearly fast enough, occupying eighth and tenth places.

Then after leading the race for twenty-seven glorious laps, Behra's brakes began to fail and the B.R.M.'s race was all over bar the shouting. Hawthorn now shot into the lead as Behra slowed to come into his pit for a check, hurriedly charging back into the race, but he retired for good three laps later. Now Scarlatti's Maserati blew up with a loud bang just past the Press Tribune. At thirty laps the position was Hawthorn, Moss, Trintignant, Musso, Collins, and von Trips—two surviving British cars beset by four red cars. Moss, who up to now had played rather a waiting game for him, moved up on the leading Ferrari and passed it on lap thirty-two, raising Vanwall hopes up high, only to drop them with a wallop when Stirling came in to retire with a dropped valve six laps later. The fantastically strong green challenge had all but evaporated before our eyes, for now only Trintignant's Cooper stood between a Ferrari 1–2–3–4, but the dapper little Frenchman was far from dismayed and plugged along barely 13 seconds behind the leading Ferrari lap after lap, and well in front of the pursuing bunch of Ferraris.

Coming up to the half-way stage, Hawthorn's luck deserted him and he came to rest on the circuit with a broken fuel pump. Once again in a grande épreuve Rob Walker's car led the opposition and the stop watch showed Trintignant to be over forty-five seconds ahead of his nearest challenger, Musso. From the Ferrari pit came Tavoni's signal for more speed, and Musso, Collins and von Trips took up the chase. Strangely enough, although the roar of the Ferrari engines gave the impression of much greater speeds, the very much quieter Climax-engined Cooper lapped as quick, if not quicker with seemingly no fuss or bother at all. Alf Francis signalled to Maurice to preserve the engine as much as he could, but 'Trint' had done this sort of thing before and in spite of sterling efforts by Musso and Collins, he was untouchable.

As the race ran its course, the field began to thin. Salvadori retired on lap fifty-six with gearbox trouble; Hill broke a half-shaft on his Lotus on lap sixty-nine; Bonnier (Maserati) crashed on lap seventy-two and von Trips retired on lap ninety-one with a seized engine. This left but six cars out of sixteen starters and Brabham was able to move up to fourth place behind Trintignant, Musso and Collins. During the closing stages of the race, Trintignant had allowed Musso to close up to about 18 seconds behind, but on the last lap or so he actually widened the gap, finally winning by a shade over 20 seconds, with Collins about the same distance away, third. The result was: first, M. Trintignant (Cooper-Climax 1·9); second, L. Musso (Ferrari); third, P. Collins (Ferrari); fourth, J. Brabham (Cooper-Climax 2·2); fifth, H. Schell (B.R.M.); and sixth, C. Allison (Lotus-Climax 1·9).

The position in the Manufacturers' Section of the World Championship was: Coopers—16 points, Ferrari—12 points, Maserati—3 points, B.R.M.—2 points, Lotus—1 point.

But now the G.P. season was at its height, so off went the circus to Holland for the Dutch G.P. held on 26th May at Zandvoort.

With the entry list very much the same as at Monaco, for once in its life, the Cooper was not being looked on as the sporting little outsider, but rather as the big bogey-man to the other marques.

The entry list comprised Trintignant with the Walker Cooper, assisted by Brabham and Salvadori in works Coopers, Moss, Brooks and Lewis-Evans in Vanwalls, Hawthorn, Collins and Musso in Ferraris, Behra and Schell in B.R.M.s, Hill and Allison, Lotus, Bonnier, Gregory, and Scarlatti in Maseratis, and de Beaufort in a Porsche. The three Vanwalls were fastest in practice and occupied the front row of the grid. Less than one second covered the next ten fastest cars, led by Behra and Brabham; the three Maseratis, and the Porsche appeared to have little chance.

As it proved, this was a Moss-Vanwall benefit, the combination leading from start to finish. The Ferraris and Trintignant's Cooper were most definitely not *au point*, and the only real opposition came from the B.R.M.s, particularly Schell's, which driver and car gave their best performance to date. Nevertheless Tony Vandervell must have had his heart in his mouth when Brooks retired on lap thirteen with rear axle bothers and then Lewis-Evans retired on lap forty-six with a broken valve-spring cotter, leaving Vanwall hopes pinned on Moss, who was in top form and was never troubled.

As to the Coopers, Salvadori drove his finest G.P. to date and finished fourth; both Trintignant and Brabham did not show to advantage, although they both finished, Brabham eighth, and the Frenchman ninth. It is quite possible that Rob Walker's car was being driven to finish rather than to blow up his only engine in what might have been a hopeless task. Allison and Hill drove their Lotus with zest, but neither proved fast enough to trouble the leaders, although Allison finished sixth.

The result was: first, S. Moss (Vanwall); second, H. Schell (B.R.M.); third, J. Behra (B.R.M.); fourth, R. Salvadori (Cooper-Climax 2·2); fifth, M. Hawthorn (Ferrari); and sixth, C. Allison (Lotus-Climax 2·2).

The position in the World Championship for Manufacturers was opening out: Coopers—19 points; Ferrari—14 points; Vanwall and B.R.M.—8 points each; Maserati—3 points; Lotus—2 points.

Three weeks later, Ferrari, realizing the challenge to their erstwhile superiority, fielded their strongest team of four cars in the G.P. of Europe at Spa, Belgium, on 15th June.

The entry was: Moss, Brooks, and Lewis-Evans—Vanwall; Hawthorn, Collins, Musso, and Gendebien—Ferrari; Salvadori and Brabham—Cooper; Behra and Schell—B.R.M.; Hill and Allison—Lotus; Trintignant, Bonnier, Seidel, Godia, Gregory, and Miss de Filippis—Maserati.

John Cooper did not rate his chances very high. Having to give away at least 500-c.c.s to all the other G.P. machinery was bound to tell on this course where cars reached their very maximum in several places. In this case, although Salvadori held a rather unexpected fourth place for a major part of the race, a badly slipping clutch put an end to his challenge.

Brabham retired on the sixteenth lap with a blown cylinder head gasket.

The result was: first, T. Brooks (Vanwall); second, M. Hawthorn (Ferrari); third, S. Lewis-Evans (Vanwall); fourth, C. Allison (Lotus-Climax 2·2); fifth, H. Schell (B.R.M.); sixth, O. Gendebien (Ferrari).

Now the position in the World Championship for Manufacturers was: Ferrari—20 points, Cooper—19 points, Vanwall—16 points, B.R.M.—10 points, Lotus—5 points, Maserati—3 points.

Off moved the G.P. circus with an appointment at Rheims, for the French G.P. on 6th July.

With Mike Hawthorn on peak form fighting it out with Fangio, Musso and Moss, this was easily the most exciting G.P. of the 1958 season. Sadly, Musso, the great Italian driver, crashed at high speed receiving fatal injuries.

Salvadori and Brabham were down to run with the works Coopers, in this case Jack with the 2·2-litre engine and Roy with the 1·9-litre. They were joined on the starting line by Hawthorn, Musso, Collins, and von Trips—Ferraris; Behra, Schell, and Trintignant—B.R.M.s; Brooks, Moss, and Lewis-Evans—Vanwalls; Allison and Hill—Lotus; and Ruttman, Bonnier, Gerini, Hill, and Godia—Maseratis, plus World Champion Fangio driving a brand new Maserati. One of the Lotus cars was an entirely new Chapman brain-child, and looked very much like a scaled down Vanwall, to my mind fast but brittle.

Schell and Brooks got away first, with Hawthorn on their tails, but after one very fast lap the Anglo-Italian combination held the lead, closely followed by Schell, Brooks, Musso, Moss, Fangio, and Collins. Then came a second batch comprising Behra, Lewis-Evans, and Brabham.

With three laps behind them three Ferraris led the field, in order Hawthorn, Musso, and Collins, and it was already clear that the severe modifications that had taken place on the Dino 246's had resulted in much better handling qualities. However, on lap four, going into Muizon Corner, Collins went straight up the escape road and rejoined the race in the rear of the field. This let Brooks into third place with Fangio and Schell fighting for fourth spot. So far Moss had been content to let the others make the pace, but now he stepped on it and soon got into the dog-fight between the 'Champ' and 'Arree', who was certainly giving the Argentine driver something to think about.

Then up came Behra's B.R.M. to join the fray and all four cars engaged in a grim battle for fourth position, with Hawthorn going like fury—only his team-mate Musso could keep him in his sights, with Brooks holding a steady third place. Then tragedy, as Musso attempted to pass Hawthorn just past the Dunlop Bridge and lost control as his car touched the verge. The car somersaulted and threw the unfortunate driver out, with fatal results.

Brooks now occupied second place, but two laps later, he was out with a seized gearbox. Fangio, having temporarily mastered the little mob buzzing round him, took second place with Moss and Behra doing their best to oust him. Hawthorn was secure in front and driving a fabulous race, but all attention was focused on Moss, Fangio and Behra. On lap sixteen, the Frenchman shot through to take second place, and with Schell sixth and Trintignant seventh the Mays-Berthon set-up sat up with a jerk. Lewis-Evans was called in for Brooks to take over, a silly move which lost the Vanwall four places.

Around the half-way mark, Fangio made a brief pit stop to check his sticking gear change which was time enough on this circuit to put him into seventh place behind Hawthorn, Behra, Moss, von Trips, Schell, and Collins, the last named having worked his way back from seventeenth to sixth place. Trintignant retired his B.R.M. with a defective fuel pump and Godia spun off and was out of the race. Brabham's Cooper was going like a dream and he was lapping in 2 minutes 27 seconds, against 2 minutes 25 seconds by Hawthorn. Poor Salvadori was not having an easy ride at all as he was beset by shocking clutch slip. The Hornsey challenge had dissolved, both cars having retired without showing to advantage.

By lap forty, Behra and Schell had both retired with engine trouble leaving a saddened B.R.M. équipe wondering why fate could be so unkind after raising their hopes so high. Brooks had likewise retired, and Hawthorn was well in the lead from Moss with von Trips and Collins third and fourth, a not too happy Fangio fifth and Brabham now sixth and very much in the picture: not so Salvadori, who with his race run had parked his car near the finishing line ready to push it over when the race was run and qualify as a finisher. Stirling piled on the pressure in an all-out effort to cut down the 'Farnham Flyer's' lead, but Mike had no desire to be caught, and on lap forty-five turned in a time of 2 minutes 24·9 seconds (128·18 m.p.h.), giving him the course record. Fangio's off-side brake was grabbing and throwing up smoke under heavy pressure, but the 'Master' was able to hold on to fifth place behind Collins, who had driven magnificently to catch up after his early lapse. Brabham clung to Fangio, and John Cooper was very pleased to see one of his cars on the leader board. Very soon, over the finishing line went Mike, to register his second success in a French G.P.; second, and only 23 seconds behind, came Moss in the Vanwall, then von Trips, and then a surprise—Fangio, who had passed Collins on the course when the latter had run out of fuel on the very last lap. Peter was able to secure fifth place with a bit of heavy pushing, with Jack Brabham a very good sixth.

The Manufacturers' World Championship now stood as follows: Ferrari—28 points, Vanwall—22 points, Cooper—20 points, B.R.M.—10 points, Maserati—6 points, Lotus—5 points.

The British G.P. at Silverstone on 19th July was a crucial race, both for the manufacturers and leading drivers. There was nothing to choose between Cooper, Vanwall and Ferrari. Equally close was the fight for the drivers' World Championship between Moss and Hawthorn. Therefore the winning car and driver here could stand a wonderful chance of a clear breakthrough.

Practice did nothing to indicate the eventual winner as the four fastest times were put up by four different cars. Entries for the race were Salvadori, Brabham, Burgess, and Trintignant—Coopers, the last-named being a Rob Walker entry; Hawthorn, Collins, and von Trips—Ferraris; Moss, Lewis-Evans, and Brooks—Vanwalls; Behra and Schell—B.R.M.s; Allison, Hill, and Stacey—Lotus; Bonnier, Shelby, and Gerini—Maserati; Bueb—Dart Connaught; and Fairman—Connaught.

The sensation of the practice was Salvadori's time of 1 minute 40 seconds with the 2·2-litre Cooper. This was third fastest time and only beaten by Moss (1 minute 39·4 seconds), and Schell (1 minute 39·8 seconds). These three were joined on the front row by Hawthorn with 1 minute 40·4 seconds, which was equalled by Allison in the 'Van Lotus'. Consequently, if five cars had been allowed on the front grid, they would have been: Vanwall, B.R.M., Cooper, Ferrari, and Lotus, and in addition, only three seconds separated the fastest twelve cars. Both Burgess (works Cooper) and Stacey (works Lotus), were making their debut in G.P. racing.

The G.P. was due to start at two o'clock, and as the time passed I made the following notes.

1.06 p.m.: Excitement mounting; drivers getting prepared, adjusting helmets, etc.

1.10: Literally thousands of people milling round paddock; suddenly a Vanwall with mechanic aboard roars up paddock and the crowd scatters rather like Mille Miglia.

1.20: Walk round to B.R.M. van which seems to be full of eggs; hope 'Arree' and 'Jean' do not get eggbound.

1.30: Stands beginning to fill up again with people coming back from lunch and visiting paddock.

1.32: Tannoy announcement that Moss is No. 7 not No. 6, from preference, I believe.

1.35: Cars being wheeled onto track.

1.36: Moss and Schell walk onto track together.

1.37: Behra, in usual rigout, red pullover and light blue trousers, walks along confidently beside B.R.M.

1.38: See Collins in Ferrari pit having picture taken; Hawthorn is there as well.

1.40: Moss on front line with Vanwall looks slightly worried; brightens up when Charles Cooper talks to him.

1.42: See John Cooper looking quite smug about having Roy's Cooper on front row of grid; notice preponderance of green in front line.

1.46: Cars begin to take off for circuit lap, which brings them back ready for the start of race.

1.48: Bueb off with 'Dart', has previously told me that he does not reckon his chances; off goes Collins and the Lewis-Evans Vanwall is last away.

1.50: Stands are now choc-a-bloc.

1.51: All cars on grid and revving up.

1.52: Try to get behind starting line, but turned back by J. Eason Gibson for not wearing my pass; dodge J.E.G. and get behind starting line.

1.53: All cars switched off; see John Bolster with B.B.C. box of tricks walking around; Tony Vandervell passes wearing enormous straw hat.

1.55: Buzzer goes for five minutes; Brooks seems calm enough beside his Vanwall and just behind him, dapper little Trintignant climbs into his Cooper.

1.56: Buzzer goes for four minutes; Fairman in back row looks very grim, dressed in black overalls.

1.57: That buzzer again; Moss sits in the Vanwall chewing gum for all he's worth.

1.58: Two minutes to go—cars start up. What a blare!

1.59: Buzzer for one minute. Collins adjusts goggles. Moss looks at watch.

2.00: A deafening roar and they are off!

Going into Copse, Moss had a very slight lead over Schell and Hawthorn, Salvadori made rather a bad start. The crowd expected the first news to come through that either Moss or Hawthorn led, but to everybody's surprise, the leader was not Hawthorn but Collins, who had overhauled Moss and was tearing round the track. Now every head peered to see who would come charging round Woodcote and it was Collins, a good forty yards in front of Moss, with Hawthorn third. Collins had done the standing lap at a fantastic 94 m.p.h.! Coopers were—Salvadori fifth, Brabham eighth, and Trintignant tenth. Last man to come past was Fairman.

Round they came again and it was Collins from Moss, Hawthorn, Schell, Brooks, and Salvadori, and rookie Burgess was trying to take Gerini's Maserati. Laps, 3–4–5. . . . Collins, going like a bomb, had opened up a sizeable gap on Moss, who in turn was well ahead of Hawthorn. Lap seven, Lewis-Evans took Salvadori, putting Vanwalls in a menacing order— second, fifth, and sixth. Coopers had slipped back to seventh, tenth, and eleventh. No. 14 Fairman, pulled into the pit for a check. Lap seven, Collins came round Woodcote in a won- derfully controlled slide way ahead of Moss and about the same distance behind Moss came Hawthorn tucked well down in his Ferrari and obviously playing a waiting game. Bueb circulated steadily, but not fast and on lap eight came the first retirement —Fairman with a sick engine. Hill carved his way through the field and tailed Salvadori; Burgess drove steadily without taking any risks. On lap nine Collins broke the lap record at a speed of 103 m.p.h. Brabham began to close up on Salvadori and Hill and these three had a private dice which caused their lap times to come lower and lower.

On the tenth tour Collins lapped Bueb, and now the enor- mous crowd was strangely quiet as the drama unfolded. On lap twelve Collins led Moss by 5·4 seconds, and never had I seen him drive better. Schell seemed to be having some trouble with the B.R.M. and Lewis-Evans took Brooks and Schell in quick succession to occupy fourth spot. The two works Coopers were close together and Hill could not get by. After fifteen laps, Collins still led from Moss and Hawthorn, and Brooks in the Vanwall was losing ground to Salvadori in the Cooper. Then both Salvadori and Brabham lapped Burgess's

Cooper. Hill had shot his bolt and was suffering with severe overheating on his rear end (his, not the car's!), due to a very hot gearbox and retired on lap eighteen. On this lap the position was Collins, Moss, Hawthorn, with Lewis-Evans fourth; 35 seconds behind Collins Schell's B.R.M. was trailing somewhat with lack of oil pressure. As Brooks slowed, Salvadori and Brabham shot through to take fifth and sixth positions.

On lap twenty the position had not changed, but Behra came flying into his pit for a check-up on his suspension; strangely enough, the trouble was diagnosed as being caused by an obviously mad hare committing *hari-kari* inside the B.R.M.'s front wheel, its bones piercing the tyre causing a flat and deranging sundry parts, putting the unfortunate Behra out of the race. On the same lap Stacey retired due to overheating and two laps later Allison capitulated with the same trouble, exiting the Lotus works team. Trintignant shot into his pit with a miss that cured itself before Alf Francis could get to it and he was away still lying tenth.

As the laps were ticked off, it became obvious that Moss could not do anything about Collins's lead, which, on lap twenty-four, was about 6 seconds. Similarly, Hawthorn, 9 seconds behind Moss, drove calmly, still waiting for something to happen; he did not have long to wait, because there was high drama on lap twenty-five. Moss came round Woodcote and drove right into the pits, past his flabbergasted mechanics and round into the paddock to retire with a blown-up engine. With two red bombs way out in front, British hard-won supremacy was receiving a severe jolt. Now Salvadori and Brabham were fourth and fifth, although the latter's car sounded a bit woolley; not so Salvadori's, and he managed to take Lewis-Evans on the next lap and came round past the pits in third place.

At this stage a large straw hat with Vandervell under it marched past the Cooper pit, and with a significant gesture called out to Charles Cooper: 'That's one down the hole!' Lap thirty, and Collins, driving the race of his life, had a 22-second lead over team-mate Hawthorn, with Salvadori 35 seconds behind, and Lewis-Evans 2 seconds behind Roy with Jack holding on to the Vanwall like grim death. The Ferrari pit, not liking their third man von Trips being beaten by the Coopers, requested him to have a go. Salvadori's lap time on the thirty-first tour was 1 minute 43·4 seconds. With the position out front clearly established, main attention concentrated on the duel for the minor places between Salvadori, Lewis-Evans, Brabham, and von Trips. As the Ferrari driver began to catch Brabham by a second a lap, Jack was signalled but could not increase his pace. On lap thirty-six Salvadori still held off Lewis-Evans, but von Trips was steadily gaining on Brabham. On this lap Collins doubled Brooks. Lap forty, and only the Coopers stood in the way of a runaway Ferrari victory. Hawthorn was taking Woodcote almost without sliding, whereas Collins corrected quite a vicious slide each time. John Cooper noticed what he thought was an oil leak on Hawthorn's car and on lap forty-three Hawthorn waved to his pit that he would pull in next time round. With a shout of 'olio' Mike shot into his pit and all the Cooper équipe held their breath waiting for Salvadori to come round before the Ferrari got away again, but a very slick pit organization got the red car off still in front.

In with a burnt-out clutch came a very disappointed Burgess who had grown to like G.P. racing. With Salvadori only 6 seconds behind Hawthorn, Coopers hoped to challenge Ferrari, but Hawthorn gained a second a lap and Salvadori wisely did not stress his engine too much and contented himself with third place. On lap forty-seven Schell came round sitting on Collins' tail although a lap in arrears, and the B.R.M. suddenly developed a new lease of life, for while slip-streaming Collins, it passed a brakeless von Trips for sixth place. On lap fifty-one Salvadori was 17 seconds in arrears on Hawthorn, and both Gerini and Bonnier (Maserati) were out with gearbox maladies; Schell pressed Collins so hard that Peter waved him through and immediately the B.R.M. driver went in chase of fifth man Brabham. On lap fifty-nine Schell had but 4 seconds to make up on the Cooper driver, and was gaining at the rate of $1\frac{1}{2}$ seconds a lap. The Cooper pit dared not try and speed up their man any more and had to sacrifice Brabham and anxiously work out the position of the flying Schell versus Salvadori which, on lap sixty with fifteen to go, was Roy 23 seconds up and Harry gaining from $1–1\frac{1}{2}$ seconds a lap, so it was touch and go with all watches out.

As Roy came round Woodcote on the sixty-second lap, using all the road, Harry was 19 seconds behind; on lap sixty-four Roy had 17 seconds in hand, but the stop watch showed next time that both Cooper and B.R.M. had lapped in 1 minute 43 seconds and Harry could do no more with his oil temperature rising again. With five laps to go, Collins eased off a little and lapped in 1 minute 44 seconds, but Hawthorn pressed on as before, although about 30 seconds behind. This was going to be a Ferrari benefit, but John Cooper had a new worry as he had an idea that Lewis-Evans was foxing with only about four seconds to catch up on Salvadori. He might have been holding something in reserve, and as it proved he was right, for the Vanwall driver made up nearly 2 seconds on lap seventy-one and was only 2 seconds behind with four laps to go. This was do or die, so out went the board for Roy to step on it. On lap seventy-two the Vanwall was on the Cooper's tail, only half a second separating them. All eyes centred on this last minute duel and when they came round again with only three laps to go, they were neck-and-neck.

Meanwhile Hawthorn chased an easing up Collins as though his life depended on it. Two laps to go, and as the Vanwall and Cooper went past the pits, there was only a hair's breadth in it; Lewis-Evans tried to pass at Copse, but failed; he tried to pass again at Beckett's Corner, but Salvadori beat him to it; he got alongside at Club, but the Cooper was faster through Abbey. And how the crowd loved it! Roy had it really hard on top of having to do the most difficult thing in racing—fight off challengers for the greater part of the race with no respite. The heat in the small cockpit on a very hot day was so intense that in desperation he put his hand up in the air to try and get a draught of air back onto him. He was in a bad state, but the thought of that third place spurred him on and as they came round into the last lap he had a yard or so lead. The crowd went mad as the announcer said that the Vanwall was trying to take the Cooper. Everyone in the Cooper pit held his breath—and the placid Charles Cooper tore my programme to shreds. Then Collins flashed by for a superb victory, followed by Hawthorn. The announcers kept babbling away. Just when it looked odds on the Vanwall coming through first at Abbey Curve, both drivers had to pass a slower car and Roy got through cleanly, but Stuart was ever so slightly impeded, and it was the Cooper which took the chequered flag by a length.

All the limp rags in the Cooper pit could have done with that pint tankard of beer that Hawthorn raised to his lips as he slowly motored to the Ferrari pit. As the drivers climbed out of their cars, both Collins and Hawthorn looked remarkably fresh, but Salvadori looked completely 'shagged' as well he might. While the crowd enveloped the winning drivers, the photographers snapped away from all angles. Hawthorn and

Collins were asked to stand together: 'I'll embrace him if you like!' said Collins, pretending to kiss Hawthorn. 'Smile! I know it's unusual, but you've won, so smile!' said Hawthorn with mock severity. Then up came Collins's father and just to disprove the theory that racing drivers are supermen, Peter kissed his father on the cheek. From underneath the crowd Roy asked for an orange squash and downed it in no time at all. And that was that—we had seen the races. The final result was: first, P. Collins (Ferrari); second, M. Hawthorn (Ferrari); third, R. Salvadori (Cooper-Climax 2·2); fourth, S. Lewis-Evans (Vanwall); fifth, H. Schell (B.R.M.); sixth, J. Brabham (Cooper-Climax 1·9).

Position in the Manufacturers' Championship: Ferrari—36 points; Vanwall—25 points; Cooper—24 points; B.R.M.—12 points; Maserati—6 points; Lotus—5 points.

Two weeks later the fight was renewed in the German G.P., at Nurburgring, on 3rd August. This event was probably best described by *The Autocar* under the heading 'Sunshine and Shadow in Germany', for although British cars and drivers made their finest ever show in Germany, with Vanwall winning the G.P. from two Coopers and in addition, a Formula II Cooper soundly trouncing the invincible Porsche, the price was too high, for we lost Peter Collins, who died on his way to hospital after a heavy crash just after Pflanzgarten. In his passing, we lost one of our greatest drivers and most certainly one of our greatest gentlemen. The result was: first, C. A. S. Brooks (Vanwall); second, R. Salvadori (Cooper-Climax 2·2); third, M. Trintignant (Cooper-Climax 2·2); fourth, W. von Trips (Ferrari); fifth, B. Maclaren (Cooper-Climax 1·5); sixth, E. Barth (Porsche 1·5).

As Formula I and II were run together, the results in the Formula II section were: first, B. Maclaren (Cooper); second, E. Barth (Porsche); third, I. Burgess (Cooper).

Although it was Brabham's turn to drive the larger 2·2 Cooper in the race, the organizers insisted on Salvadori taking the car on the grounds that he was supposedly better-known. This rather upset Jack who showed them during the practice period that even with a 1·5 Cooper, he could do quite fantastic times. When Roy came in after his wonderful drive into second place, John Cooper did one of his special head over heels efforts. This rather amused the Porsche chief 'bod', who had the pit next door to Cooper's. 'What a pity I missed that,' he said. 'I should have liked it on my movie camera.' 'Don't worry,' replied John, 'if Bruce Maclaren wins the Formula II section of the race, I'll do it again for you!' Needless to say, when Bruce came past leading Barth's Porsche, John staged a repeat, but strangely enough, Messrs. Porsche were looking the other way.

Now the position in the Manufacturers' Championship was: Ferrari—39 points; Vanwall—33 points; Cooper—30 points; B.R.M.—12 points; Maserati—6 points; Lotus—5 points. It was still anybody's guess, with Oporto the next port of call.

After practice, the fifteen starters for the Portuguese G.P., on 24th August, were lined up thus: first row—Moss (Vanwall), Hawthorn (Ferrari), Lewis-Evans (Vanwall); second row—Behra (B.R.M.), Brooks (Vanwall); third row—von Trips (Ferrari), Schell (B.R.M.), Brabham (Cooper); fourth row—Trintignant (Cooper), Shelby (Maserati); fifth row—Salvadori (Cooper), Hill (Lotus), Allison (Lotus); sixth row—Bonnier (Maserati), de Filippis (Maserati).

Both Brabham and Salvadori thought that this was a very dicey circuit and they asked John Cooper what they should do in the race, for if they pressed on really hard, the chances were very heavy that they could easily write off the cars. John's decision was to take things fairly carefully in the hope that the boys out in front would fade letting the Coopers through. In this connexion, I had had a chat with John a few days before about his plan of campaign in the World Championship and had volunteered an onlooker's opinion that as Coopers were now well in the thick of the G.P. fight, why didn't they engage one of the top three or four drivers to lead the works team, as I thought that just that little extra polish could make the difference between an outright win against perhaps a second or third place. John certainly shocked me with his reply. Firstly, he said that to get one of the really top boys, even if it were possible, would cost many thousands of pounds as a retainer; furthermore, with so much at stake, he would be compelled to make his team go absolutely hell for leather, which might give a result akin to Ferrari, for instance, who in the last three G.P.s had suffered, at the Belgium G.P., Musso's Ferrari a complete write-off and Hawthorn's engine blown-up, at Rheims, Musso's car a complete write-off, and at Nurburgring, Collins' car a complete write-off. If that sort of awful luck happened to Coopers, John said, they just could not stand it and would have to go out of business.

Considering the overall picture, John went on to say that his father and himself had decided that they could only make a limited assault on the G.P. grand prize and therefore their drivers had definite instructions that although their Climax engines would rev over 7,000, on no account were they to go above 6,000. Yet with these disadvantages, Coopers were still well in the fight for the World Championship. It was almost unbelievable.

As it turned out, the Cooper waiting game did not pay off in this event. The Vanwall and Ferrari big guns thundered through the race, led by Moss and Hawthorn, and neither Brabham nor Salvadori were ever in with a chance. Moss showed his absolute virtuosity and led the race from lap eight until the end, on a track made terribly tricky by showers of light rain. He won from Hawthorn, with Lewis-Evans third. Coopers had the satisfaction of a hundred per cent finish with Brabham seventh, Trintignant eighth, and Salvadori ninth. The result was: first, S. Moss (Vanwall); second, M. Hawthorn (Ferrari); third, S. Lewis-Evans (Vanwall); fourth, J. Behra (B.R.M.); fifth, W. von Trips (Ferrari); sixth, H. Schell (B.R.M.).

Position in the World Championship for Manufacturers, with two races to go was: Ferrari—45 points; Vanwall—41 points; Cooper—30 points; B.R.M.—15 points; Maserati—6 points; Lotus—5 points. To win the Championship, Coopers had to win the last two G.P.s with Ferrari pointless and Vanwall with third place in one race or lower, a far from impossible feat as, in fact, Coopers had won the first two grandes épreuves.

The Italian G.P. took place on 7th September on the fast Monza circuit, where every c.c. counted; and Cooper's minus three hundred of same could not keep up with Vanwall and Ferrari. Nevertheless, although Brabham retired on lap one with a bent front suspension after shunting Gendebien's Ferrari at the start, Salvadori drove a most consistent race and climbed up the leader board as several faster cars crashed or retired. He finally finished fifth, the race being won in magnificent style by Brooks (Vanwall), from Hawthorn (Ferrari) and P. Hill (Ferrari). Trintignant in the third Cooper retired on lap twenty-five with a broken top gear.

This race settled the Manufacturers' Championship; under the ruling of taking the six best performances, Vanwall had five firsts and one second, a total of 46 points against the nearest challenger, Ferrari, with three firsts and three seconds—total 40 points. Third was Cooper with two firsts, one second, one third, one fourth and one fifth—total 31 points. B.R.M., Maserati and Lotus were way behind with 15, 9, and 6 points respectively.

Although the Casablanca G.P. had been upgraded to world status, the result of this last G.P. of the year could not alter the Formula I Championship placings, with the result that Tony Vandervell had brought off the first half of the double for Britain, with the certainty that either Moss or Hawthorn would complete the other half by winning the World Championship for drivers.

With Formula I premier honours settled, Cooper's still had a very big say in the Formula II Championship, which up to now they had looked upon as being in the family, but as always, Lotus was the problem child. With a Formula II race run concurrently with the Formula I race at Casablanca to end the Season, Lotus could still win from Brabham and Maclaren, *if* Allison won the Casablanca Formula II race and Brabham drove the Formula I car. Actually, Lewis-Evans headed the Formula II pool, but he was definitely driving a Vanwall, so he was out, therefore Charles and John Cooper decided that Brabham must drive his Formula II car, and they engaged Jack Fairman to drive the larger engined car in company with Salvadori. As it turned out, Allison drove the Formula I Lotus in the race, so Cooper's had won, even before they had started.

The eyes of the motoring world were most definitely on this event. The issue between Hawthorn and Moss as to who would purloin the Championship had everybody on their toes. Moss had a terrific task: he had to win and put up the fastest lap time and in that event, even so Hawthorn must not finish in the first three. The Cooper line-up was Salvadori and Fairman Formula I, and Brabham and Maclaren Formula II, aided by 'Trint' in the Walker F.1.

The race was run at a colossal pace, easily beating the previous year's speed. Moss did all that was expected of him and more—he led from start to finish and murdered the lap record. Unfortunately, his team-mates Brooks and Lewis-Evans could not hold off the Ferrari challenge. Brooks' engine blew up on the thirtieth lap whilst keeping Hawthorn back in fourth place, and poor Lewis-Evans, when in fifth place, crashed after an engine breakage. The car caught fire and the driver sustained serious burns as he scrambled out, and from these later succumbed. Phil Hill drove the race of his life and kept his Ferrari well in sight of Moss until the three-quarter stage, where he was slowed by his pit to enable Hawthorn's Ferrari to get into second place and thus win the Championship. As to the Coopers, both Salvadori and Fairman drove steadily without fireworks and finished seventh and eighth overall, whereas Brabham easily won the Formula II Class from Maclaren, with local driver La Gaze (Cooper) third.

Thus the curtain fell on 1958. For Coopers, Vanwall and Hawthorn, a wonderful year; for British motor racing splendour tinged with sadness. But nothing stands still in motor racing, and as John Cooper and I wandered onto the Climax stand at the Motor Show recently, the conversation veered round to the Cooper power unit for 1959 and the big boys of Coventry-Climax told us that they were hoping to get a brand new 2½-litre engine ready for 1959 which should develop around the 220 b.h.p. mark. I venture to forecast that with that extra 30 b.h.p., Coopers are going to win many more G.P.s and, who knows, perhaps the Manufacturers' Championship, in which case the long threatened retirement of Charles Cooper might become *fait accompli* and he will be safe from 'the bug' at last.

THE RECORD-BREAKING COOPERS

WITH the recognition of Class 'K', there are now 11 International classes for cars, rated as follows:

Class A	Engine capacity over		8,000-c.c.
,, B	,,	,,	5,000–8,000-c.c.
,, C	,,	,,	3,000–5,000-c.c.
,, D	,,	,,	2,000–3,000-c.c.
,, E	,,	,,	1,500–2,000-c.c.
,, F	,,	,,	1,100–1,500-c.c.
,, G	,,	,,	750–1,100-c.c.
,, H	,,	,,	500– 750-c.c.
,, I	,,	,,	350– 500-c.c.
,, J	,,	,,	250– 350-c.c.
,, K	,,	,,	Up to 250-c.c.

Quite apart from their other exploits, Coopers have had quite a hand in setting up World Class Records. During the period 1951–1957, Cooper cars set up fifty-six World Class Records (some still subject to confirmation). Successful record attempts have been made in 1951, 1953, 1955, 1956, and 1957. Only once have these attempts failed, namely in 1952, when it snowed so hard that the track was unusable.

Montlhéry, 8th and 9th October 1951
Drivers: J. N. Cooper and W. S. Aston.
Sponsored by the Cooper Car Company.
Attempt on Class 'J' and Class 'I' Records.

In this, their first venture into the realms of record-breaking, the Cooper Car Company achieved a most spectacular success, everything going according to plan. The team, including Chris Brew, the official J.A.P. mechanic, arrived at Montlhéry on Friday, 5th October. On the Saturday all the details were arranged including booking the timekeepers and the actual attempts were made on the Monday and Tuesday. The car to be used in both Classes was the new, beautifully streamlined Cooper, designed by John himself, which the Company was hoping to put into standard production if sufficient demand was created.

206

THE RECORD-BREAKING COOPERS

Bright and early on the Monday, John Cooper climbed into the little car equipped with a 350-c.c. J.A.P. power unit, and having got the O.K. from the timekeeper's box, was away and on the road for the one-hour record, which was his prime objective. Exactly one hour later, he had four records to his credit, the 50-km., 50-miles, 100-km., and the one hour. Unfortunately, due to the bumping the car experienced, the fuel tank split and John was forced to come in to refuel after breaking the 100-km. record. This dropped his average for the one hour by about 2 m.p.h., but he still managed to put in over ninety miles in the hour. On and on went the car, buzzing round past the timekeepers every sixty-one seconds, and very soon the hundred-mile record was in the bag. John still kept going and captured the 200-km. record, and then came in.

On the following day, Bill Aston climbed into the streamliner, this time 500-c.c. Norton engined, with a hundred miles in the hour as the target. Here again, the car ran faultlessly, and Aston was able to take the 200-km. record in addition to the five up to one hour, but the elusive 'ton' in the hour was not to be, Bill's average being 99·41 m.p.h. A very near miss. Six years later, almost to the day, we attempted the same feat with an engine exactly half the capacity, and similarly only just missed it. Such is progress in motor racing!

Records
Driver—J. N. Cooper; International Class 'J' (Up to 350 c.c.)

50 km.	..	..	..	90·62 m.p.h.
50 miles	..	..	..	92·02 m.p.h.
100 km.	..	..	..	92·13 m.p.h.
1 hour	..	..	..	90·27 m.p.h.
100 miles	..	..	..	91·80 m.p.h.
200 km.	..	..	..	91·98 m.p.h

Driver—W. A. Aston; International Class 'I' (350 c.c. to 500 c.c.)

50 km.	..	..	..	99·30 m.p.h.
50 miles	..	..	..	99·56 m.p.h.
100 km.	..	..	..	99.59 m.p.h.
1 hour	..	..	..	99·41 m.p.h.
100 miles	..	..	..	99·41 m.p.h.
200 km.	..	..	..	99·13 m.p.h.

The above records were highly praised in motor racing circles, as it was realized that it was no mean achievement to keep the highly temperamental Norton and J.A.P. motor-cycle engines going for well over an hour.

THE RACING COOPERS

Montlhéry, 12th October 1952

Snow stopped play.

Records

Five direct hits on Bill Aston's clock by co-driver John Cooper with very stony snowballs: price of Scotch in Fred Payne's Bar, expense account for taxis from Montlhéry to Place Pigalle to see local colour, price of champagne . . . hic . . . in Place Pigalle.

Montlhéry, 5th to 8th October 1953

Drivers: J. N. Cooper and E. Brandon.

Sponsored by Cooper Car Company.

Attempt on Class 'J', 'I' and 'H' Records.

The Coopers had designed an extremely light streamliner for this job in the hope that the decrease in weight would offset the lack of power of the 350-c.c. Norton engine. They were very anxious to push the '350' Record well over the 'ton'. In order to save weight, lighter components were used, such as smaller shock-absorbers; these were not at all successful and gave trouble throughout the records.

Eric Brandon took first crack at Class 'H' records for 200 km. which stood to the credit of R. Bonnet and C. Deutsch in the D.B. (speed 112·94 m.p.h.). Having to beat this by one per cent meant that Brandon had to do over 114 m.p.h., at which speed the rather frail Cooper was taking quite a hammering. Notwithstanding this, Eric lapped steadily at his target figure of forty-nine to fifty seconds, and it looked as though he had the record in the bag, although the shock-absorber brackets were breaking up, making the car one big handful. Alas, Eric was not destined to be a record-breaker, for a chain broke on the back straight and that, dear sirs, was that!

'Ginger' Devlin, Eric's mechanic, and John Cooper, soon had the large Norton engine out and the '500' Norton installed. With replaced shock-absorbers and repaired shock-absorber brackets, the car was ready for the attack on Class 'I' the following day. This time, all went well and John drove into the pits with seven records under his belt from 50 km. up to 200 miles. Eric Brandon just had time to congratulate him before having to push off to fulfil another Continental racing engagement.

Feeling considerably bucked with their success, John and 'Ginger' Devlin set to work to change the '500' over to the Ray Petty tuned 350-c.c. Norton in preparation for the Class 'J' attack on the morrow.

October 6th was another bright day for the Cooper équipe as

John, with the Norton engine ticking over like a dream, captured another seven records and pushed them all well over the magic 'ton'.

Having obtained fourteen records, John might have been forgiven for calling it a day, but having the 600-c.c. Norton still in one piece tempted him to go for the Class 'H' 200 kms. record once again. Allowing one complete day to strip down the car and check all parts, John booked the track again for 8th October. During this attempt, he was beset by many troubles, not the least of which was finding the steering wheel resting (not comfortably)in his lap due to the steering bracket snapping. Together with this, at least two 'shockers' gave up the ghost, but do these sort of things deter a man with fourteen records to his credit? Not on your Nellie; John just pushed on. Just a small while after 'Ginger' had worn his thumb out giving the O.K. sign to a very preoccupied man who passed regularly, but ignored him, the 200-km. record was broken and number fifteen was in the satchel. Then, in the midst of all the joy, down came the chopper in the shape of one Pierro Taruffi who was due to arrive at any moment with his 'Twin Teardrop' and was determined to chuck a hefty spanner in the Class 'I' works. John carefully considered this piece of 'info'. With the 500-c.c. Norton still a 'goer', he decided to go out once again and strive to raise the Class 'I' records up still more. To add to the competition, Daphne Arnott had also decided to gatecrash the record game and was due down at Montlhéry with her team and brand new Streamliner on 20th October.

With these pleasant thoughts in mind, out went John with his well worn Streamliner and sixty glorious minutes later, he had broken six of his own records, pushing up the speeds by four to five m.p.h. In case he heard that Uncle Tom Cobley was also coming out to have a go at records, John thought he had better take-off, and back he came to England.

Records

Driver—J. N. Cooper: International Class 'J' (up to 350 c.c.)

50 km.	..	..	.. 105·71 m.p.h.
50 miles	..	..	.. 104·93 m.p.h.
100 km.	..	..	.. 105·10 m.p.h.
100 miles	..	..	.. 104·39 m.p.h.
200 km.	..	..	.. 103·87 m.p.h.
200 miles	..	..	.. 103·46 m.p.h.
1 hour	..	..	.. 104·32 m.p.h.

THE RACING COOPERS

International Class 'I' (350 c.c. to 500 c.c.)

50 km.	..	..	..	111·14 m.p.h.
50 miles	..	..	..	111·22 m.p.h.
100 km.	..	..	..	111·40 m.p.h.
100 miles	..	..	..	112·35 m.p.h.
200 km.	..	..	..	112·89 m.p.h.
1 hour	..	..	..	112·61 m.p.h.
200 miles	..	..	..	103·62 m.p.h. (Taken on first attempt)

International Class 'H' (500 c.c. to 750 c.c.)

200 kms.	..	..	..	114·08 m.p.h.

A few days after the Cooper team had left, along came Taruffi who made a mess of their records in Class 'I' up to the hour, increasing them by about three m.p.h., and then a few days after Taruffi and 'Twin Teardrop' had departed, along came the Arnott team led by J. K. Brise who in turn made a mess of Taruffi's records up to the hour, beating them by an average of two to three m.p.h. That's life in the record business.

Montlhéry, 17th October, 1955
Drivers—J. Russell, W. D. Knight and A. Owen.
Private attempt with works backing from Cooper Car Company.
Attempt on Class 'G' Records.

Having had a crack at breaking records in the 250 class at Montlhéry in April—a mission not satisfactorily accomplished because the F.I.A. refused to ratify our times, although we did get them to recognize a new class, 'K'—I had developed the record-breaking itch. Consequently, we talked the Coopers into building a special car designed to attack records up to six hours. The car was basically the same as the Cooper Sports 1,100-c.c., but to increase the power the engine was fitted by Coventry-Climax with the prototype high lift camshaft, which raised the b.h.p. from 75 b.h.p. to 83 b.h.p. Many other modifications were carried out on it such as an extra petrol pump, heavier shock absorbers, long-range fuel tanks, specially designed driver's seat (one's tail gets quite a shaking unless it is well upholstered), and heavier gauge tube for the chassis frame.

Arrangements were made for Charles and John Cooper to take the car down to Montlhéry in the Cooper truck, and for

Ivor Bueb or Jim Russell to help us with the driving. As it turned out, Jim was very keen to come. Bill Knight and I would drive down in my Mark VII to Montlhéry and meet the Cooper party there; the 'Jag' could then be used as a hack by all of us.

Everything went according to plan and when Bill and I arrived at the track, the Cooper had already been unloaded and Russell had had quite a few laps' practice. Although we had seen the car being made at Surbiton, neither of us had driven it. However, Jim was quite at home, as he had been driving the similar works car throughout the season. Against this advantage, he had the disadvantage of never having driven on a banked circuit, whereas our tails knew every bump on the track, having sat them out with monotonous regularity some months before. We had a look at Jim Russell's practice times which started around the fifty-five second mark, but soon worked down until finally he lapped in forty-five seconds. (about 126 m.p.h.), which was very good indeed. It was getting rather late, so we decided to knock off for the day, and Bill and I would practice early the following morning. The question of where to stay was soon solved by Charles Cooper, who fixed us up in the wooden shack run by the La Potinière, the track restaurant. As Charles explained, if we slept there, he could get us up early in the mornings and keep his eye on us. We should have preferred to have stayed in Paris, nearer our work, but Charles was wise to us. We popped into Paris for a quick drink at Fred Payne's Bar and picked up 'Jabby' Crombac, *Autosport* foreign correspondent, whom I met for the first time and who is a most delightful character. After having a little chat we drove back to Montlhéry, had a slap-up dinner at La Potinière and went to bed. Unfortunately, I did not get much sleep as all through the night I could hear what seemed to be some sort of animal crawling over the roof; I went outside once or twice, but could not see anything. Consequently, I was first up in the morning, which certainly startled my colleagues. The mysterious noises during the night proved to be acorns falling from overhanging trees and sliding down the roof.

We wheeled the car onto the track and I took over for a few laps. Although this was the first time I had driven it, it handled so well that I felt completely at ease, and after about six or seven laps, I managed one in 47 seconds. Then Bill had a go and likewise got his times down into the forty-sevens. This meant that we were lapping at about 121 m.p.h. On my second try, I knocked a second off and found that I could lap quite consistently at 46 seconds. When Bill had equalled this time, we passed the car over to Jim who wanted to try one or two quick starts. He found that the gear lever was jumping out, so he brought the car in, in case it should over-rev. John and Charles tried to rectify the trouble, but just to make sure, they rigged up a device which looked like a strand from a chest expander, looped it round the gear lever in such a way that once the gear was in position, the strand slipped down and held the gear lever tightly in place. So that overcame that little difficulty.

When Jim had done a standing start to his satisfaction, we retired to the restaurant for grub and to discuss the plan of campaign for the records the following day. It was decided that Jim would go out first and try to break the records up to one hour (six in all). These were held by either 'Goldie' Gardner with the M.G. Special or George Eyston with a similar car. The hardest nut to crack would be the 50-km. which stood at 123·22 m.p.h. and which had to be beaten by at least one per cent. The trouble here was that the standing start would lose Russell at least thirteen or fourteen seconds, which he would have to make up in eighteen laps for his set average. We worked out that he would have to lap consistently between forty-three seconds (132·56 m.p.h.) and forty-four seconds (129·55 m.p.h.) and must not see a forty-five-second lap at all for fifty kilometres; after that he could slow slightly, but must not see a forty-eight-second lap up to the hour. If the car was in one piece after this, Bill and I would take over and we would go for the records from one hour up to six hours, all of which were held by the French D.B.s, driven by Bonnet, Levegh, Moyatt, and Barnett at speeds between 107 and 115 m.p.h. Having settled this, we asked Jim why he looked so miserable. He replied: 'Wouldn't you if you had to lap in forty-three seconds for fifty kilometres?' to which we had no answer. Both Bill and Jim complained about a nasty bump going into the far corner of the back straight which they said, when it was hit fair and square, almost threw the car on one side. By some freak, I had not encountered this (little did I realize I had the pleasure to come).

Having tried without conspicuous success to cheer up our third partner, we retired to our respective boudoirs to get an early night. My sleep was no longer disturbed by falling acorns as this noise was completely drowned by the bellows emanating from the end room denoting that William had fallen asleep. Rather hollow-eyed, I rose with the crowing cocks and woke the others, Bill grumbling like mad that he hadn't had a wink of sleep all night, and after one or two minor adjustments (we had by now been joined by the Lucas representative and two fitters from the French branch of Dunlop), Grim Jim climbed into the cockpit of the Cooper. We got the O.K. from the time-keepers, and at eight fifty-five he was away. To try and get the last ounce out of the car, John Cooper had made up two spats which were bolted onto the body and partially enclosed the front wheels. John reckoned that this would add about $1\frac{1}{2}$ m.p.h. and Jim used these for the one-hour attempt. For the longer distances, as we expected some tyre trouble, they were taken off to save precious time during tyre changes. We had two signal boards and we were set to give Jim a signal each time he came round, knowing from our April attempt how this kept up the driver's morale.

Jim came tearing by and we timed his first lap at 56·2 seconds (101·06 m.p.h.) which was a new standing start record for the Montlhéry track. This meant that he had to make up 13 seconds as we had anticipated. On the next lap, Jim did 43·1 seconds (131·95 m.p.h). Some going with an 1,100-c.c. engine! Next time round, when we gave Jim his time, he must have felt rather relieved that he had attained his target; from then onwards, he lapped steadily between 43 and 44 seconds, his fastest lap being the eighth in 43 seconds dead, and his slowest the fifth in 44·4 seconds, a model of consistency. We gave him his times on every lap and on lap nineteen, he was given the clasped hand sign together with 'Record' on the sign board. On consulting the timekeepers, we found that he had pushed the 50-km. record up to 128·27 m.p.h., higher than we had hoped. Jim circulated as grimly as ever, slightly slower, but not seeing a forty-seven-second lap. We all shook hands and did not feel so worried now that we had one record in the bag. This is always the case; once the team has gained one record, you tell yourself that whatever happens afterwards, you have not made the attempt in vain.

On lap thirty-one, Jim had taken the 50-mile record at 127·43 m.p.h. and eight laps later he had the 100-km. record at 127·36 m.p.h. Wonderful going, but now he was feeling the strain a little and began to lap slower going down from 45 to 46 and then on lap fifty-five, 47·3 seconds. We made no attempt to speed him up knowing that if he kept going these fractions would not stop him taking the other records. On lap sixty-three, he had gained the 100-mile record at 125·86 m.p.h. We gave him every possible encouragement, either John or I giving the thumbs-up sign whilst Bill gave the lap time on the board. All these tactics seemed to help him for he speeded up and lapped regularly in 45–46 seconds, and on lap seventy-eight, he took the 200-km. record at 125·37 m.p.h. We were now becoming rather anxious about his tyres, and John walked towards the banking to see if he could spot if they were showing too much wear. Jim was definitely tiring now, but managed to do the last two laps in 47 seconds and 47·2 seconds respectively, to give him the difficult hour record at 125·34 m.p.h. As John reported that the tyres seemed fairly good, we let him do another nine laps before calling him in, hoping that only one tyre change would be necessary and that I could take over and go on for the longer distance records without losing much time. When a tired Jim came in, we gave the tyres a quick once-over, but at least two needed changing so we decided to stop, make a thorough check and restart later from scratch for the six-hour record. Jim had put up a wonderful show and raised a modest grin in answer to our joint congratulations.

Just before midday, we received the O.K. to restart and I was off with the 200-mile record as the first objective. The weather had deteriorated and a wind was blowing up. Although I normally wear glasses, I did not have a pair to wear under my visor, but I did not think that this would worry me too much. I knew the six-hour records would be a long grind, but had the consolation that I did not have to go so fast as Jim's hour record. The car sounded wonderful and almost before I knew it, I had done the first lap. I thought I had made a fast start, and was a bit disappointed to find next time round that I was 1 minute 1 second, 5 seconds slower than Jim's first lap. The lightest touch was all that was necessary to steer the Cooper and it was practically driving itself round the banking. Next time round, I saw my lap time was 47 seconds which I reduced to 46·2 on the fourth lap. This was plenty quick enough and I was feeling very happy. I had already found that there was little time to relax whilst going round, the only possible place seemed to be the back straight which, at the speed I was doing, gave me about twelve seconds between corners, with about five seconds off this to concentrate a bit less. At this time, I noticed that the top of the banking was merging into the sky. For a moment, I could not make out why this happened, then I took a quick peek and saw that the heavy clouds above were almost identical in colour to the track surface. As I was lapping well above the white line in order to save my tyres as much as possible, I realized that if I was not careful I could easily make a mistake and go over the top, with disastrous results for yours truly. Whilst keeping my eyes glued to the deck, especially coming out of the corners, I did not see that it had begun to rain until my visor got well bespattered then I certainly knew it. With 126 laps to cover for the first record in a high wind and pouring rain, and a visor fast obscuring, and no chance of wiping it, I don't think I have ever been so miserable or frightened in my life. If it got worse, I thought, I would give up.

Meanwhile, I slowed and dropped down the banking on to the white line, clinging to the latter like grim death and in this way I managed to struggle on for three laps when to my joy, the rain stopped and my visor began to clear. Had I been carrying a spare pair of goggles, this trouble might have been avoided. As the track dried out very quickly, I was soon back in my stride, lapping between 47 and 48 seconds as per programme and everything went fine until Bill gave me the 100 kms. sign. By this time I thought that I knew all the vagaries of the track, but I hit that mysterious bump which the boys had told me about fair and square; the car literally jumped right over and frightened me to death. It took me seven laps to get over the shock and during this time, I was lapping at 50 to 51 seconds, which made John almost decide to call me in. Luckily for me he did not, for after this I settled down and put in one or two 46-second laps to make up time. The boys in the pit were backing me up wonderfully and having something to see each time I went by was an enormous help. I seemed to be missing the bump by going a couple of feet nearer the top and I felt much happier. Going round the back straight, it was just possible to catch a glimpse of my watch at odd times, so I had an approximate idea of how long I had been travelling. I also noticed that as the laps wore on I was clutching the steering wheel tighter and tighter and when this got too bad, I allowed my whole body to relax as I motored along the back straight. For some strange reason, I was unable to do this going down the straight past the pits, possibly because I found the bend facing me more difficult to take than the other. This was the bend on which Musy lost his life.

Down the straight, into the corner, out of the corner, down the straight, into the corner, out of the corner, all this in about 47 seconds made it seem as though I was driving from one corner to another. By now, I had passed the 100-mile mark and was looking hopefully for the one hour sign. When this came up, the worst would be over and I felt I was on the way home. Then I had one or two nasty thoughts about the front offside tyre. Was it going to last the 200 miles? Was I going up the banking high enough? I tried to climb higher still, but it seemed more bumpy, so I gave that up. I wondered what it would be like to have a blow-out at this speed and thought about Jim's front tyre; it had been worn through nearly to the canvas in just over an hour, and I had over an hour and a half to do—not a very pleasant thought, which I promptly pushed out of my mind. More tightening, more relaxing . . . time passed and the 200-km. distance had long since gone. Then came the one and a half hour sign, then fifteen more laps; I tried counting, but lost myself around three or four. Fifteen laps seemed a long way; then Bill hung out '9'. And so it went on, nine, seven, six . . . until after 1 hour 41 minutes 9 seconds, I had my first record at 118·35 m.p.h. I remember singing at the top of my voice but the wind soon filled my lungs and made me hoarse. On the hundred and thirtieth lap I was given the signal to come in after the next lap, but after going round at a high speed for so long, I found it difficult to brake at the right time, and rather timidly used the anchors too soon, losing some seconds running into the pit.

Then all hell broke lose. Under the guidance of the Coopers the entire pit worked on the car. John with one Dunlop man, changed the front tyre; Charles with the other, changed the back one; the Esso rep. and a helper each filled a tank with fuel; Jim checked over the engine and filled the gearbox with oil, and the Lucas rep. checked the wiring. I jumped out, Bill jumped in, final checks, the body was screwed down, Bill was patted on the head, and he was away. All this took 2 minutes 1 second. Bill had some trouble getting his gears on his first lap, but then he settled down to lap around 48–49 seconds. It was still very windy, but the Cooper engine sounded magnificent. After about ten laps, Bill began to get a little unsteady and his times jumped from 48 to as much as 53 seconds—no doubt he had frightened himself. (It is funny how this shows on the lap times.) He settled down again and lapped steadily between 47 and 48.

Jim and I gave Bill the sign-board on every lap. Between us, we tried to keep our signals as interesting as possible and on the car's hundred and ninety-sixth tour, we were able to put up the 500-km. record, which must have pleased Bill no end; speed—115·30 m.p.h. Now he was after the three-hour record, but seemed to be having some trouble (later diagnosed as a slipping clutch) which sent the revs up to as much as 8,500, but even this did not stop the Cooper. It went on and on until at the two hundred and seventeenth lap mark, we gave Bill the three-hour record signal; speed—115·26 m.p.h. Very shortly afterwards, we called him in, and after another first class pit stop, I was away again in search of the 500-mile record. The engine sounded nearly as crisp as when we started and I had to lap between 49 and 50 seconds, which was quite comfortable.

Only once during my drive did I have any trouble with the clutch, but it seemed to free itself very quickly. The 'shockers' were standing up very well, although the car was not riding quite so smoothly, being inclined to jump from side to side as it went down the straight, but not too seriously. The temperature gauge had not moved a fraction since we started. Every now and again I tried to put in a faster lap but I seemed to be going quite fast enough for me even at 49 seconds, whereas when I started, I had no difficulty in doing 46 seconds, so I must have been tiring. Lap after lap I plodded on, until on the three hundred and fifteenth I got the 500-mile record signal; time—4 hours 25 minutes (112·88 m.p.h.). Three laps later I handed over to Bill who had the job of running on to six hours, taking the 1,000-km. on the way. With the clutch slip not bothering him excessively, Bill kept going, and the 1,000-km. record came up on the three hundred and ninety-second lap; speed—111·55 m.p.h., and the six hours on the four hundred and twenty-fourth lap; speed—111·63 m.p.h. This made the day's bag twelve records. We were all highly delighted and adjourned to the bar to celebrate.

Records

Driver—J. Russell; International Class 'G' (750-c.c. to 1,100-c.c.)

50 km.	..	..	.. 128·27 m.p.h.
50 miles	..	..	.. 127·43 m.p.h.
100 km.	..	..	.. 127·36 m.p.h.
100 miles	..	..	.. 125·86 m.p.h.
200 km.	..	..	.. 125·37 m.p.h.
1 hour	..	..	.. 125·34 m.p.h.

THE RACING COOPERS

200 miles	..	..	.. 118·35 m.p.h.
500 km.	..	..	.. 115·30 m.p.h.
3 hours	..	..	.. 115·26 m.p.h.
500 miles	..	..	.. 112·88 m.p.h.
1,000 km.	..	..	.. 111·55 m.p.h.
6 hours	..	..	.. 111·63 m.p.h.

New Standing Start Record—J. Russell, 56·2 seconds, 101·06 m.p.h. All the above records achieved with a standard sports car running on ordinary pump fuel, average consumption 35 m.p.g.

Bedford Airfield, 22nd September 1956
Driver—F. Sowrey; Private attempt on Class 'G' Records.

Fred Sowrey had long been preparing for this foray. Strangely enough the secret had not leaked out, and the only intimation that most of us had was when the daily newspapers announced that the first record attempt in Britain since before the war had been successful.

The late Peter Hughes and Sowrey had planned this campaign the year before when they met during the Brighton Speed Trials. However, Sowrey carried on after he lost his partner in a fatal accident driving back from Le Mans. Using his Mark VI Cooper chassis with a fibreglass body made from the mould of the 1953 Streamlined Cooper together with a 'blown' 1,097-c.c. J.A.P. engine, Sowrey had a crack at the standing kilometre and mile records in Class 'G' held by the Appleton Special at 82·16 m.p.h. for the kilometre and 91·30 m.p.h. for the mile. The car had inboard disc brakes at the rear and Beart modified front suspension. After one or two false alarms, Sowrey carried off his two prizes, beating the existing records by well over the necessary one per cent.

Records
Driver—Fred Sowrey

Standing kilometre	..	87·64 m.p.h.
Standing mile	..	..	93·88 m.p.h.

Monza, 15th and 16th October 1956
Drivers—W. D. Knight, R. Salvadori, and A. Owen.
Private attempt with works backing from Cooper Car Company.
Attempt on Class 'G' and Class 'E' Records.

THE RECORD-BREAKING COOPERS

The main idea here was for Bill and I to have a go at Class 'E' (1,500-c.c. to 2,000-c.c.) records up to twelve hours. As a standby, in case this failed, we would take a 1,100-c.c. engine with us and try and improve on our 1955 times up to six hours. The car was to be a standard Cooper-Climax sports car, but with very much heavier gauge chassis tubes and 500 × 15 tyres on the front with 550 × 15 on the rear, as on the modernized Monza track nobody so far had managed any very high speeds for a great length of time. Taruffi had been out several times with his Maserati engined 'Tarf', trying to push up the 2-litre records. Each time he had had chassis or engine mounting trouble until finally he managed to take the one-hour record at 132·052 m.p.h. We had no chance of doing the Class 'F' Records as the speeds were far too high, having been set up at Utah Salt Flats, but our idea was to get one of the 1½-litre s.o.h.c. Climax engines bored out to just over 1,500-c.c. thus taking us into Class 'E'. The attempt was scheduled for May, but Climax had a difficult job on their hands as their 1·1-litre engine had already been bored out almost as far as it could go in making the 1,460-c.c. engine, and with no engine and no co-operation from Cooper's who were heavily committed for the racing season, we decided to go down to Monza in October.

Meanwhile, Colin Chapman was not idle, and after one or two postponements he got Stirling Moss to take out a specially designed record car for an attack on Class 'G' up to one hour at Monza the day after the Monza G.P. Stirling was going very well and had broken our 50-km. record, when he noticed a Lotus back half stacked at the side of the track. Not remembering another Lotus racing around at the same time, he glanced back to see if he was seeing things and he had quite a clear view behind as it was the back end of his own car which had fallen off! As quite a lot of repair work would have to be done in order to restart, Stirling could not wait as he had to leave Monza to fulfil his other engagements.

At home, we breathed a little easier, but Mackay Fraser, who was in Italy at the time, persuaded Chapman to let him have a go at the hour, to which Colin readily agreed, not wishing to be left out of the record breaking act, on the basis that what Coopers could do he could do better. As it turned out, Mac kept trying until he finally took all the Cooper records from 50-km. up to one hour, the latter at a speed of 137·260 m.p.h. which meant that we would have to do nearly 140 miles in the hour to beat it, a formidable proposition.

Whilst this was going on, Climax had managed to cast a meatier block which they had bored out to 1,530-c.c., so that was one problem solved. Coopers were simmering down and they were able to get the new sports car under way, and final arrangements were made for the record attempt to be made in conjunction with the Rome G.P. and the record car and Salvadori's works sports car would be taken down to Monza in the Cooper truck by George, a friend of John's, and Ray Thackwell, who was going to act as mechanic. John, Bill Knight, and I would fly to Milan, hire a car there and meet George and Ray at Monza. Roy Salvadori was also going to fly down, but not with us. John also arranged to take two 1,100-c.c. Climax engines, one of which was to be specially prepared by Climax. The tight schedule meant that we did not have any time to waste at Monza, as we were due in Rome on the Thursday following our attempt, which was to be on the Monday.

Earlier in the summer my wife and I had been on holiday in Italy and I had taken the opportunity to drive to the Monza track to have a look at it. I was very impressed and felt that it looked considerably easier for record attempts than Montlhéry. The Piste de Vitesse, or Speed Track, was 4·25 kilometres long, just over two and a half miles—about a mile longer than Montlhéry. This meant not so many corners to negotiate in, say, a hundred miles, and also longer straights which would allow more time to relax whilst driving.

Whilst I was there I made the acquaintance of Signor Bacciagaluppi the Manager of Monza Autodrome, who spoke excellent English and proved extremely helpful in every way. I asked him whether it was true that the track was terribly bumpy, and he replied that owing to the rush to get it laid, some of the big concrete blocks had not been put down too well, but he assured me that they were working on the worst part and already it was in a very much better state. He also said that Taruffi had tried going each way round with the 'Tarf' and preferred anti-clockwise, which was a useful tip.

All our plans for the records bore fruit, and the whole team, Roy Salvadori excepted, met at Monza on Sunday 14th October. As there was the usual local race meeting in the afternoon, we were allowed to practice when this was over, and both Bill and I had to pass a special ability test which meant doing a certain number of laps at increasing speeds under the surveillance of Signor Bacciagaluppi. Both of us passed through this and put in quite a few fast practice laps. And so the stage was set for the morning, when we would chase up the Class 'E' records. Meanwhile we returned to the Hotel de la Ville to work out our time schedule.

With our main objective the one-hour record, standing at 132·052, we set our sights at 135 miles an hour. We had booked the track for twelve hours just in case, but were not too optimistic about even the stronger chassis standing up to the constant drumming on the concrete blocks. The 1,530-c.c. engine should give about 105 b.h.p. which we calculated would give us a top speed of 149 m.p.h. at 7,000 revs with a 3·64 to 1 final drive ratio. So if we lapped at 140 plus, we would have a little in reserve. We settled the order of driving which was to be myself for the first hour, Bill for the next hour and a half, and then we would take two hour spells until either the car broke down or we did the twelve hours. My aim for the first hour would be to lap between 1 minute 9 seconds and 1 minute 10 seconds. If I saw a 1 minute 11-second lap I should have to do another in 1 minute 9 seconds to make up the time lost. When Bill took over he would have to lap between 1 minute 10 seconds and 1 minute 13 seconds for his hour and a half. Thereafter, we could slow slightly as each two hour stint passed. Having decided to run clockwise, we bade good-night to our colleagues and retired to bed. Next morning the weather was fine, so we felt fine. As we had both lapped at 1 minute 9 seconds the previous day in practice, our morale was high and personally I was looking forward to my drive. We got the hire car out and all piled in and drove down to the Monza Park, having our usual tussle with the Park staff who seemed to delight in passing one from gate to gate until in desperation you return to the original gate where they let you in without protest.

Having wheeled the car out onto the track, we prepared all the pit equipment, fuel, tyres, jacks, oil, pit boards and Vic Barlow's (Dunlop) invaluable time-keeping apparatus. The timekeepers were alerted, we received last-minute instructions from Signor Restelli, assistant manager of the Autodrome, I climbed into the car, Vic made a hurried check on the width of the tyre treads, and at nine twenty-one I was off.

My first lap was done in 1 minute 21·1 seconds, which meant that I had lost only ten seconds from a standing start. From then onwards I settled down, lapping according to plan. The car handled really well and the enlarged cockpit on this model made it very much more comfortable for the driver as did the fact that Coopers had completely cured the hopping about noticeable on the 1955 model.

Keeping the engine revs around 6,200, I was able to lap consistently in 1 minute 9 seconds, with the odd 1 minute 10 seconds thrown in. This meant an average speed of approximately 137 m.p.h., but it did not seem too fast except when coming round the bend into the home straight, when I found it rather tricky as there seemed to be a very nasty bump in this vicinity. For the first forty or so minutes I cannot remember having a more easy ride, and I was feeling on top of the world. The boys were also enjoying themselves and Bill was giving me the thumbs-up sign each time I circulated, but the undulating track began to take its toll of the car, and very gradually it seemed to become bumpier, due, no doubt, to the shock absorbers weakening. On my thirty-seventh lap, Ray Thackwell put out the hundred-mile board. I was still lapping on schedule, and once I pressed the car a little and did a 1 minute 8·4 seconds lap (139 m.p.h.), still without stressing the engine.

With the arrival of the two hundred-kilometre board and only about seven minutes to go for the hour, I was definitely tiring, and now found it difficult to lap in 1 minute 9 seconds, and was dropping to 1 minute 10 seconds. On the last lap of the hour, I very nearly came unstuck. Dunlop's milled the record tyres almost to a point so that the car would balance more on the centre of the tyre and not give so much resistance. Unfortunately, coming round the nasty bend, I hit the bump and unconsciously must have over-corrected the steering wheel, because the car became unbalanced; I realized what had happened and tried to steady it as gently as possible, whilst braking slightly. Luckily for me, although the car swayed from side to side down the straight, I regained enough control to stop it from tipping over. Meanwhile, John and Bill and Co. were all watching aghast at what must have seemed to be a car completely out of control, swaying dangerously in their direction, but by now in the cockpit the crisis was past and I could appreciate that Herb Elliott, Ibbotson, and the rest had nothing on my mob and what's more they could jump as well, witness their exit over the pit counter! This lap was done in 1 minute 16 seconds, but as I completed the hour half way round, I only lost about three seconds off my time for that record. After one more lap, I was called in for Bill to take over, my official speed for the hour being 135·072 m.p.h.

The usual slick pit organization changed a tyre, refuelled, checked oil, etc. and soon got the car rolling again. With Bill having the 200-mile record as his first objective, he did his standing lap in 1 minute 19·4 seconds—very good indeed. Next lap he was down to 1 minute 11·3 seconds, and then 1 minute 10 seconds. He then lapped steadily between 1 minute 10 seconds and 1 minute 11 seconds, slightly faster than we had planned, but John was anxious to push the records up as much as possible, so we did not slow him. The laps soon ticked off, and just a few seconds after one and a half hours we were able to hoist the 200-mile record taken at 131·685 m.p.h. Soon after, we called Bill in for a change of tyres. Vic had given us the O.K. to go on for the 200-miles with only one tyre change, as there was sufficient tread on the other three to last that distance. Now, to be absolutely safe, we changed the others and sent him off to chase up the 500-km. record. Both Bill and I had covetous eyes on the 1,000-mile record if at all possible, and therefore we had previously decided to drive the car well within its limits. Bill very wisely eased off and now lapped between 1 minute 11 seconds and 1 minute 14 seconds—still plenty quick enough. Meanwhile, we kept him occupied with pit signals. And so he went on his merry way, taking the 500-km. record at 127·885 m.p.h. in just over 2 hours 25 minutes. In answer to our pit signal of 'tired', we got the thumbs-up sign, so we let him go on for the 3-hour record, which meant a higher average speed without a pit stop.

Obviously the car was in tip-top condition, for Bill speeded up a shade and just to be devilish on the hundred and twenty-fifth lap, did a 1 minute 9 seconds. Round about this time, Roy Salvadori arrived at the Autodrome having flown from London. He seemed quite impressed with the showing of the Cooper, and as the worst part of the Class 'E' records was over, John thought that it might be better to keep Roy fresh for the 1,100 c.c. records the next day, so he got stuck into the pit organization. The 3-hour record came up at 128·642 m.p.h. and two laps later, Bill was called in. He demonstrated how fresh he was after a two-hour drive by lapping in 1 minute 9·4 seconds on his penultimate lap.

Another first-rate pit stop and I was off on the way to the 500-mile record. The engine seemed as sound as ever, but the ride could not be compared with the first forty minutes when the car had handled like a dream. Now it had to be driven, whereas before it had practically steered itself. Still there was nothing to worry about and I was quite able to keep up the required average and once or twice I tried to put in a faster lap, but the best I could manage was 1 minute 10·3 seconds, and I was not too keen on going as fast as this now. It seemed ages before I got the 500-mile record sign—speed 126·969 m.p.h.—but this cheered me no end. I was due to be called in on the four and a half-hour mark, so would not see any more records during this stint. I had now got into a set pattern aiming to avoid the bumps altogether, but I never succeeded in doing one complete tour without hitting one or the other.

Time wore on and I was a happy man when I saw the '10 laps more' sign. I felt sure that the engine was losing its edge—it sounded as though it was working much more than hitherto. Nine, eight, seven, six. . . . I thought I would put my clog down on the last few laps, but the best I could do was 1 minute 13 seconds, and then I was called in. The day before, we had decided to do two-hour shifts, but an hour and a half was proving plenty for me. Now Bill took over to take the car up to the 6-hour mark, and I thought he was not going to find this spell so easy. I mentioned to John that I believed the engine was getting a bit rough, so he stuck out the 'leaden boot' sign to Bill who did a 1 minute 10·1 seconds lap, followed by a 1 minute 7·2 seconds (141·5 m.p.h.), the fastest lap of the day. I was shattered! I had been telling myself that the reason I could not go faster was because the engine was getting sluggish, but the real reason was *me*. Having put in two more laps at 1 minute 8·4 seconds, Bill dropped back to his normal 1 minute 12 seconds–1 minute 15 seconds. On his two hundred and thirty-fourth lap, we gave him the 1,000-km. record sign at 125·787 m.p.h., and now he could look forward to the 6-hour record and to handing over. On his two hundred and sixty-fifth lap, one of the rear 'shockers' threw in the towel and gave him a frightening moment before he regained control, and from then onwards, he trod very warily, lapping around 1 minute 19 seconds up to the 6-hours, which he took at 125·716 m.p.h.

As we had now done over seven hundred and fifty miles, we had a brief conference and decided that it was worth my going on at a reduced pace in an effort to take the important 1,000-mile record. Even if I could only average 1 minute 22 seconds, I could do the required distance in about two and a quarter hours, so with this calculation in mind, I climbed into the car and got 'mowing'. The car was handling like a pig, but was still controllable, although at times, it felt as though it might want to go its own way, but I plodded on and was able to average between 1 minute 19 seconds and 1 minute 23 seconds most of the time. When the car felt too bad, I slowed a little, quite content to lap in 1 minute 25 seconds. But now the engine was really rough and gradually getting worse as time wore on. After an hour of this caper, I was still going and had a fifty-fifty chance of pulling off the record, and I had become accustomed to the antics of the car, but the unknown factor was the engine, very noisy and rough. Each lap completed was one nearer my goal, but on the three hundred and thirty-eighth, I heard a heavy clonk from somewhere in the back, and on the next lap I was enveloped in clouds of smoke which made me feel very strongly that the time had come to bale out. However, a quick glance at the rear showed no signs of flames, and the engine was still ticking over, so I pressed on in the hope that I could get to the pit for repairs. The engine conked out coming off the banking towards the pits and in spite of the smoke swirling round the cockpit, I was able to coast in, but the attempt was at an end. The dynamo had fallen off, I had lost all the water and the engine had seized, so with only another ninety-odd miles to go, we had to give up.

We wheeled the car into its shed and John, Ray, Roy, and Bill went over it with a fine-tooth comb. The only thing wrong with the chassis was a small crack right at the back in the joint where the body fixed into the frame. John welded this and it was as good as new. Four new shock-absorbers were fitted, together with new tyres. Everything was tightened up and the 1,530-c.c. engine replaced by the 1,100-c.c. one. More checking and re-checking, and by nine thirty the car was ready for the next morning's attempts on Class 'G' records.

Came Tuesday, and before starting on the records, Roy tried the car to see if he had a chance of beating the Mackay Fraser Lotus records up to the hour, but after a few laps, it was quite clear that the car was 8 or 9 m.p.h. slower than required. As a starting point, we were left with the 200-mile record, still held by us with the 1955 Cooper. We could also try and break our own records up to six hours, and this was voted a good idea by one and all.

The line-up of drivers was to be Roy, first two hundred miles, then Bill up to three hours; I would take over from three to four and a half hours, and then Roy from four and a half to six hours. With strict instructions to give him his lap times to the nearest tenth of a second, Roy had the pit staff on its toes each time he came round, and throughout the two hundred miles he consistently lapped at 1 minute 12 seconds, only varying by tenths of a second right through. We had the impression that Roy put his foot on the floorboards when he got into the car and left it there until he got out! He had a trouble-free run, and gained the 200-mile record at 131·890 m.p.h. against our old record of 118·35 m.p.h. at Montlhéry the year before. Both Bill and I were very much against driving the car on its maximum during long distance records, but John was firmly in favour of it, so we gave in gracefully. However, in the light of subsequent events there is a strong possibility that John may have been wrong, because Bill did not succeed in getting up to the five hundred-kilometre mark, as shortly before this point, a fibre timing-wheel broke and the run was finished. Whether, if Roy had aimed at about 125 m.p.h. for the 200-miles, the car would have lasted longer, is, of course, anybody's guess.

Still, we had nothing to be sorry about, our bag for the trip being seven records in Class 'E' and one in Class 'G', so we packed up and hurried to Rome. It is interesting to note that the three people who seemed most pleased with the records were Signors Bacciagaluppi, Restelli, and Meregali, who, to my mind, should have been the most partisan about our breaking Taruffi's recently acquired records, but just the reverse was the case. They were all highly delighted and congratulated us heartily; truly great sportsmen.

Records

Drivers—W. D. Knight and A. Owen, International Class 'E'
(1,500-c.c. to 2,000-c.c.)

1 hour	..	..	.. 135·072 m.p.h.
200 miles	..	..	.. 131·685 m.p.h.
500 km.	..	..	.. 127·885 m.p.h.
3 hours	..	..	.. 128·642 m.p.h.
500 miles	..	..	.. 126·969 m.p.h.
1,000 km.	..	..	.. 125·787 m.p.h.
6 hours	..	..	.. 125·716 m.p.h.

Driver—R. Salvadori, International Class 'G' (750-c.c.–1,100-c.c.)

200 miles	..	..	.. 131·890 m.p.h.

THE RECORD-BREAKING COOPERS

Monza, 7th to 14th October 1957

Drivers—W. D. Knight, R. Searles and A. Owen.

Private attempt on Class 'G', Class 'J' and Class 'K'.

This was our most ambitious project to date. Planned shortly after the 1956 attempts, it had to be revised several times due to the heavy spate of records that took place in 1957. Our prime object was to regain the hour record in Class 'G' and for this we estimated that we needed a 'blower' to fix to the Coventry-Climax 1,100-c.c. engine. Early in 1957 we scouted round, finally getting Marshall Nordec to make one for us. Our second objective was to be the first in the 250-c.c. Class (Class 'K') to do a hundred miles in the hour, and we talked Ray Petty into preparing a 250-c.c. Norton for us to use. Cars to take these engines were the next problem. We still had the 1956 Cooper, so that could be used for the 1,100-c.c. records, but we reckoned that to get the 'ton' out of a '250' we would need a very streamlined car. The only one suitable for the job was the Fred Sowrey Cooper Streamliner which he had already offered us; unfortunately, by the time we had decided that we could use it, he had sold it elsewhere. Then Bill had a brainwave—he would dig out the old Mark IV Cooper chassis we used in 1955, borrow the blueprint of the 1953 Streamliner from Coopers and make the body in Jersey out of fibreglass with the willing help of Eric Bisson, a local lad, and Underhills, the local body-builders. So that solved the '250' problem.

To make the forthcoming attempts still more foolproof, we asked Ray Petty to buy a 350-c.c. J.A.P. engine for us to put into the new Streamliner and go for Class 'J' records (250-c.c. to 350-c.c.) as well as Class 'K'. The ordering of the J.A.P. engine was a grave mistake for which I was to blame, for we should have ordered a 350-c.c. Norton instead. All these plans looked swell on paper, but our first shock was when we learned that Colin Chapman had the same idea and was going to attack the one-hour 'G' record later in the year with a supercharged Climax-engined Lotus, the 'blower' to be prepared by Climax themselves. That immediately made the 1,100-c.c. records a very risky do for us, but we thought we would go on with the preparation and in addition, order another 1,100-c.c. engine from Climax and go for the records up to six hours as well. Now we had two 1,100-c.c. engines, one to be 'blown', one 250-c.c. Norton, together with two spare 250-c.c. J.A.P.s and one 350-c.c. J.A.P. With this lot we should achieve something.

Our next shock was when we learned that the M.G. team was taking EX179, their 1,100-c.c. car to Utah as well as the new EX181 1,500-c.c. for Moss to drive, which we knew about. (Earlier in the year, George Eyston, who supervises the M.G. team at Utah, had told us that although M.G.s were going to the salt flats during the summer, on a new project, they were not doing any 1,100-c.c. records, so they must have changed their minds.) Before we could properly digest this, the news came through that Frere and Thiele had broken our 'G' records from 500-kms. to 6 hours at between 119 and 124 m.p.h. with the Fiat-Arbath at Monza. We were not excessively worried about this, but we were very perturbed about the M.G.

When Nordec's delivered the 'blower', John Cooper arranged with Climax that they would test it on one of our 1,100-c.c. engines and very kindly took it up there in his light van. However, this part of our plan did not work out for Climax could not make the 'blower' work properly as it kept catching fire, so they wished to return it to us. John prevailed on them to have another try. Meanwhile, out went the M.G. team to the States and with their 'blown' 1,100-c.c. car pushed up the 'G' records from 500 kms. to 6 hours to around the 132 m.p.h. mark, which put them out of range for us at Monza with pit stops to add in as well. For some odd reason, they also claimed the 200-mile record at 131·89 m.p.h. which was silly as Roy Salvadori had set up this record in October 1956 at exactly the same speed—131·89 m.p.h.—consequently, theirs could not possibly count. In addition, the M.G. team had taken the 100-mile, 200-km. and 12-hour Class 'G' records at speeds around 118 m.p.h. so this little bag took the wind out of our sails. When Climax told us they had given up our 'blower' as a bad job, both Bill and I seriously considered cancelling our plans for Monza, and just taking the little Streamliner with '250' and '350' engines down to Montlhéry which would be much easier and cheaper. We rang John Cooper to discuss this problem and he agreed that Montlhéry would be the more sensible, but we hated the idea of not using the 1,100-c.c. Cooper at all and had another look at the 'G' Records. Without a 'blower' we had a slim chance of doing the 200-mile record, but a much better one of doing the 1,000-mile, 2,000-km., and 12-hour records. We would need three drivers for this, and Ron Searles, Cooper's works manager, had been nagging us for some time to come along in place of John who was expecting an offspring about the time of the records (or at least his wife was), so he (Ron) could easily be the third driver. It meant taking a long shot, but if we could take the three distance records away from the M.G.s, it would be a feather in our cap as this would be the first time ever that records set up at Utah would have been beaten in Europe. We contacted Ron about the new plan and he was terribly bucked at being offered a drive and promised to arrange everything for us from the England end, such as borrowing a transporter to take the Cooper-Climax down to Monza, getting the '1,100' prepared, including borrowing a pair of Webbers from Coopers, and also finding a spare mechanic, which was a heavy load taken off our shoulders.

Just before we were due to leave for Monza, I happened to be on the phone to Mr. Jeffrey of Dunlop's who had kindly consented to lend us Vic Barlow and Sid West for the records, when he told me that he had just received confirmation that the redoubtable Pierro Taruffi had knocked off five records in Class 'J' from 50 kms. to 1 hour at between 116 and 118 m.p.h., which was certainly some going, and made our chances of beating these times with the 350-c.c. J.A.P. very slim indeed. A recap of the situation showed that our best bet was the 250-c.c. records, next best the three very long records in Class 'G', and, almost hopeless, the Class 'J' records. On the face of it, it looked like lunacy to make this costly expedition at all, but having gone so far, we got cussed about the whole thing and, on reflection, I think we would have gone in the end just for a crack at the 250-c.c. records.

Our travelling arrangements worked out very well. Ron Searles, Mrs. Searles, and Frank Butler, a seventeen-year-old Cooper mechanic, drove Jack Brabham's transporter, which we had borrowed, to Monza. In it, they had the Cooper-Climax, all the tyres (forty in all), the 250-c.c. Norton, the 350-c.c. J.A.P., the spare 1,100-c.c. engine and other spare parts. Bill and I drove my old Mark VII with trailer and Streamliner on the back, and the two spare 250-c.c. J.A.P. engines in the boot. We met, as arranged, at Monza Autodrome on Saturday, 5th October. Having got the cars into their sheds and been greeted enthusiastically by Signor Bacciagaluppi, and of course, the ever smiling and obliging Meregali, we arranged for our fuel supplies, did some checking on the two cars and then took Ron round the track in the Jaguar to accustom him to the banking as this was the first time he had driven on this type of circuit.

The following morning, both Ron and Frank put in some sterling work checking over the '1,100', and Bill and I busied ourselves with the Streamliner. We arranged with the Management that after the local Sunday afternoon sports car meeting, we would be able to practice, and also Ron would be able to do his compulsory test laps under surveillance. During the morning we took the Cooper-Climax round to test it, but for some reason Cooper's had sent the car out with an exhaust pipe with two outlets instead of one. Although Ron thought this system was in order, both Bill and I were of the opinion that the engine would lose some power by not having one exhaust pipe, but as time was short, we decided not to change over for the time being. We were also having trouble with the Webbers and none of us had much idea how to rectify this, so as the Webber agents were near Monza, Signor Restelli got in touch with them and they promised to send some mechanics down to the track to tune them for us.

The 1,100-c.c. Climax engine was not developing anything like its true power, and we were very puzzled. There were three possible reasons, one—the Webbers, two—the exhaust pipe and three—the final drive ratio might be too high, as we could not get the engine to rev. We were using a 3·64 to 1 so on this last point, perhaps a 4·04 to 1 might be the answer. We left Ron and Frank working on the Climax and had a bash round with the Streamliner (250-c.c. Norton engined). To take the longer body Bill had elongated the chassis, which made it very difficult to reach the brake and accelerator pedals; consequently, as the car had to be driven flat out to do the 'ton' (a reversal of our own policy) we had fixed up a hand throttle. Once the car was in top gear, you yanked this out as far as it would go and held on tight. I tried it for the first time that morning for about four or five laps and found it rather hair-raising. There was no problem as to who would do the first hour with this contraption—as far as I was concerned, it was all Bill's.

During the afternoon Ron and Frank removed the gearbox and changed the ratio to 4·04 : 1 and Vic and Sid got the tyres stacked ready for use. No word of praise is too high for the Dunlop team, especially during record attempts, as drivers and team managers can rest assured that whatever else goes wrong, tyres will not be any bother with Dunlop's experience

behind them. In addition, both Vic and Sid busied themselves
with lap timing and helping in the pit organization. It can be
seen that their help in all directions was invaluable. One thing
we had not bargained for on this trip was the daylight problem.
We soon found that it got dark around six twenty, which meant
that if we wanted to get twelve hours in the light, we should
have to start at six twenty in the morning. After the Sunday race
meeting we sent Ron out to try the 1,100-c.c. Climax. We had
very little time before dark, and after he had completed six
laps we called him in and got Signor Bacciagaluppi to time his
compulsory test laps. Ron passed these with flying colours and
and as neither Bill nor I had to do them because we had already
driven at Monza, we let Ron continue to drive for a while.
Eventually he was called in so that Bill and I could have a go.
When my turn came, I soon realized that the engine was not
giving the revs; even with my foot hard on the floor, I was
about 2,000 down on maximum. The car handled very badly
and gave a most unpleasant ride, which we traced to the fact
that by using 525 × 15 tyres on the front instead of the
customary 500 × 15s, we had completely changed the handling characteristics. (Substitution of the smaller front tyres gave
us a perfect ride.) By this time it was getting dark so we called
it a day and occupied ourselves with preparing the 250-c.c.
car for its attempt on Class 'K' records.

Came Monday, and with the track booked rather optimisti-
cally for six hours, away went Bill in search of the one-hour
record at a 'ton', after which he and I would do one and a half-
hour stints up to the six-hours. The little car got away surprisingly quickly, and in no time at all had done its first lap.
The second was a crucial one, as to make up the standing lap,
the car would have to do over 100 m.p.h. which meant a lap
of at least 1 minute 34·5 seconds. As we timed the car it came
flying past in 1 minute 35·5 seconds, just over 99 m.p.h.—very
good, but not quite fast enough. The third lap was timed at
1 minute 35·2 seconds, still a fraction short, but there was no
point in trying to speed up Bill, he was obviously flat out.
There was a slight possibility that the hand throttle would
stand a little more tugging, so we put out a sign to that effect.
The only appreciable difference was that the next lap dropped
to 1 minute 36 seconds, so we left it as it was, content that the
car kept going. On lap twelve, it recorded a time of 1 minute
35 seconds, a shade over 100 m.p.h., and on laps sixteen and
seventeen again clocked the same time.

By now we had taken the 50-km. record at 96·326 m.p.h., 26 m.p.h. faster than the existing record. The 50-mile record came next and the speed was rising, 97·602, very close to the 'ton'. When the hundred kilometre mark was reached at 97·786 m.p.h., Bill still had a chance for the hundred in the hour, but as we clocked him on subsequent laps, his speed began to fall slightly and he took the hour at 97·260 m.p.h., a most respectable speed.

With the car still full of urge, I hastily buttoned up my helmet, and we all prepared for a quick pit stop after the 100-mile record had been taken. When we shoved out the record sign at 97·184 m.p.h. we expected Bill to come in next lap, but as he rounded the banking, we saw a large puff of smoke coming from the car. Trouble, we thought, and all got ready by the pit as we could see the car slowing. Within seconds it was driving towards the pits, by now doing about fifteen m.p.h., but to our amazement it just glided past. He's mistaken his braking point, I thought, and so it seemed for about fifty yards past us, the car began to turn across the track. 'He's coming back' somebody shouted, but the car slowly crossed the track and ran on to the grass verge and then tilted over as the near side front wheel came off. The whole thing looked so funny that we all burst out laughing. Poor Bill just sat in the cockpit looking absolutely bewildered. On examination we found that the ball-race had broken up and seized on the stub axle which had sheered, resulting in the wheel coming off. It could have been quite nasty if the car had been cornering at speed when this happened. Still, with five records from our first attempt we went to lunch very well pleased. Later in the afternoon, the Webber boys came along and had a go at tuning the twin carbs. We all tried the car during the afternoon, but it was certainly not running well so the mechanics told us they would return the next day and try again. As we needed a new stub axle for the 'tiddler' from Milan, we knocked off, having booked our 12-hour record attempt for the Wednesday, and went in search of the necessary part.

On Tuesday morning we were on the track soon after six o'clock in order to do everything possible to make the '1,100' a runner, but the day slipped by and although the Italian mechanics got the carbs working fairly efficiently, we still seemed short of steam. As we were scheduled to start our 12-hours not later than six forty-five the next morning, we wanted to knock off early, but young Frank, the most coldly efficient mechanic of seventeen years I have ever seen, began rooting about and discovered that the heat of the exhaust pipe was ruining the near side rear shock absorber, which meant that a shield would have to be made. To make matters worse, Ron located a leak from the oil seal which meant the whole gearbox coming out to replace it, and with a twelve-hour gruelling drive in front of us, the situation called for desperate measures.

The track was booked for Thursday and Friday by Team Lotus for their attempts on the hour in class 'G' and 'H', and Saturday was reserved for the Abarth trials, so it was Wednesday or nothing. Tired and hungry and just a little dispirited, we returned to the hotel for a Council of War. Ron made the only sensible suggestion—he and Frank would work throughout the night repairing the car, and Bill and I would go to bed and get to the track early next morning to start the records. As soon as R. and F. had finished they would return to the hotel, snatch '40' and, when fit, go back so that Ron could take over as third driver. We worked it out that Bill and I could manage hour-and-three-quarter shifts for at least seven hours, by which time Ron should be fresh again. As it turned out, on top of the other worries, Ron discovered a hefty crack in the chassis on which he made a rough but wonderful welding job, finally finishing at five thirty in the morning.

At six fifteen we were on the track, complete with Vic and Sid, and raring to go. This was the longest drive we had ever contemplated and to bring home the bacon we had to average approximately 125 m.p.h. all the way to make up for pit stops, which we reckoned would cost us at least seventeen minutes. Before we had everything organized and the timekeepers were present, it was seven thirty, which meant, if successful, sixty-odd minutes of darkness, a far from pleasant thought. At seven thirty-one I took off on the first leg.

The engine did not sound crisp, but it was not too difficult to keep around the 125 m.p.h. mark, which meant doing 1 minute 16·5-second laps on average. With the pre-arranged pit signalling shared by Sid, Vic, and Bill, I was kept well occupied and the time slipped past. I thought that when twelve hours had gone by, I would know every inch of the circuit. With one hour behind me, the car was going fairly well, yet as far as I was concerned, the engine was suspect, it just did not sound quite right. Still it could easily be imagination after last year's experience. All went well, and after one hour forty-five minutes I passed the car to Bill. Owing to the shortage of pit staff, the change-over was rather slipshod, and we lost an extra 1 minute and a half; also, the two fuel tanks were not filled up sufficiently. I asked Bill to watch the engine, and when I showed him the 'engine O.K.' sign, he acknowledged it with the thumbs-up, whereupon I kicked myself hard on the leg.

Bill seemed rather erratic with his lap times for quite a while, until he finally got the hang of it and then lapped steadily around 1 minute 16 seconds to 1 minute 17 seconds. Whilst I had been driving I had noticed that the car was running very cold, so when Bill took over I blanked off a bit of the radiator with cardboard, but this did not cure the trouble. The car should be able easily to do 1 minute 12 seconds, or even less with Webbers, but 1 minute 16 seconds seemed to be its maximum now. Just after the three-hour mark had been passed, the car came round the banking towards the pits and cut out completely. We all nearly had heart failure; what could it be? The car coasted to the pits with Bill waving frantically at the fuel tanks. Like clots, we had based our calculations of petrol consumption on our past experience with S.U.'s, not with thirsty Webbers, consequently the car had run out of juice. A quick slosh into both tanks, the engine fired instantly and away again; more time lost—about four minutes in this instance. We had no more trouble from then until the change-over, but now I was quite sure that the engine was ropey. As it hit the slight incline, you could hear it working abnormally hard. I reckoned our only chance of getting to our first record, the 1,000-miles, was to nurse the engine as carefully as possible, so I dropped down to average 1 minute 17 seconds, which would just squeeze home. Even with the cardboard in front, the temperature was still too low. Towards the end of my drive, I saw Frank's smiling face at the pits and next time round Ron, with helmet attached, looking very workmanlike. They had obviously not been hitting the sack for very long. I had now been driving for nearly three and a half hours, and the constant worry about the engine was making me very tired, so I looked with some relief when I saw the '5 laps more' signal thrust out.

When I pulled in, Ron took over, having been warned to spare the engine; the pit stop was better, but by no means perfect. I waited for about thirty minutes, during which time

Ron settled down nicely and lapped very steadily and then went into the restaurant with Vic, Frank, and Mrs. Searles. We could hear the car quite clearly each time it came round and as we waited for our lunch, Mrs. Searles said, 'It looks as though you are going to do the records,' which, to my superstitious mind was fatal. Unfortunately, I was right, the words were hardly out of her mouth when the car came round, the roar changing to a splutter, then silence. The seconds went by, still no sound was heard; we just sat there waiting. I said to Vic, 'We've had it', and forlornly we returned to the track. Bill had gone out with the Jaguar to see what had happened and we were relieved to see him soon return with Ron looking crestfallen but unharmed, which was the main thing. Afterwards we towed the Cooper in and found that a rod had gone through the side, so all the night work and over six hours' driving had gone for naught.

Later in the afternoon, we talked with Signor Bacciagaluppi about continuing our attempts; he was willing to let us use the track on Friday if the Lotus packed up fairly quickly, but for another attempt on the twelve-hour record, we should have to wait until the following Monday. Ron was due back at Cooper's on that day, so after much weighing up of pros and cons, we decided that if he could get the Coopers to agree to him staying over, we would try again. On the telephone John Cooper gave his permission and also asked Ron to give him a full report on the Lotus activities. We were a bit more optimistic about our chances with the other 1,100-c.c. which was fitted with S.U.s, also Ron would have time to braze the single exhaust pipe on to the car. On examination the chassis was holding up well and Ron's welding job had not moved. We had ordered a new stub axle from Switzerland and if we had a chance, we would have a go at the 350-c.c. records with the J.A.P. in the meantime.

On the Thursday, Team Lotus arrived with, as we expected, Cliff Allison and Mike Costin, but who was hidden under that cloth cap? None other than Jabby Crombac who was going to drive the Lotus 'blown' 750-c.c. in its attempts on Class 'H' records. Cliff was going for the 1,100-c.c. records using the same car and 'blower' on a 1·1 Climax engine. We also had a couple of friends visiting us from Jersey; they said they were very keen on this record business and would pop down next year and do a few themselves! It sounded so easy that we wondered why we had encountered so much trouble!

THE RACING COOPERS

During the day, both the Lotus and the Cooper were in pieces spread all over the paddock, and to the casual observer, it must have looked like an impossibility to get the cars back in one piece for some practice before it got dark. Both Cliff and Jabby had to qualify, so just for the fun of it we had a race to see who could get their car ready first. For a solid hour, Ron and Frank worked like Trojans, finally getting me into the cockpit three minutes before the Lotus was ready. I managed several laps with the new engine before I was called in, but it sounded fine. Jabby and Cliff both qualified with the 750-c.c. unit, but they were having plenty of trouble with the 'blower'.

As Friday was a Lotus day, we busied ourselves getting the cars tidied up; the new stub axle had arrived, but it had to be machined to fit and we were stuck. I happened to mention this to Signor Restelli, whereupon he immediately rang up the Gilera factory nearby and arranged for them to do the job for us. While we were in his office, he told us a story about Taruffi, which we all thought highly amusing. Before we arrived at Monza I sent Signor Bacciagaluppi a photograph of the Streamliner giving him details of weight, etc. and mentioned that we would be attacking the 350-c.c. records with it. The Signor must have been quite impressed, for he told Taruffi who was just about to make an attempt on the same records with his 'Tarf', powered by the quite fantastic Gilera engine. So Pierro thought he would be canny and did not go full out when he broke the records around 118 m.p.h. As Restelli explained, Pierro was lurking at the Gilera factory to see what we could do—if he could have seen our J.A.P. Grass Track Motor, quite the ugliest I have seen, he would have laughed his head off. As it was, each time we looked at the monstrosity and visualized in our minds' eyes Taruffi lurking round the corner, well it was just too funny for words. Still, we took the stub axle to Gilera's and although it was just about lunch time the General Manager called in one of the men and he worked during his break and when we called back shortly after two o'clock, it was ready. The bill? Gratis, on the house, and this from the Gilera people whose records we were trying to break! As Bill so aptly put it, after such treatment, it would not be decent to try and beat Taruffi's record for the hour.

On the Friday Lotus blew up their 750 motor completely after only a few minutes, so we wheeled out the Streamliner with 350-c.c. J.A.P. in the vain hope of pulling off the 3-hour record, there being no point in going for the shorter records. Again Bill drove first, and we were rather surprised when he lapped at 112 m.p.h.; we expected trouble, chiefly overheating, but when, after forty-nine kilometres, a valve dropped in, nobody was surprised.

Saturday and Sunday were spent in getting our last hope, the Cooper '1,100', ready for the 12-hours. Lotus were in big trouble and decided to make their attempt on the Class 'G' Hour on the Tuesday, unless we packed up early on Monday. After the race meeting on Sunday, we had another dice with Lotus to see who could get the car in one piece faster. I am glad to record that once again we were the victors, this time by about one minute. Ron, Bill, and I each did some practice and the Lotus motored round at the same time. As it got dark the mist began to rise and I thought that I would like to go round under these conditions and also try the headlights in case we had to drive in the dark the next day. Even though the light was so poor, I had no difficulty in lapping quite fast— the only point to watch was coming off the wide straight onto the narrower banking. The mist thickened and I came in, but Cliff Allison was still out there and going like a bomb. It got mistier and mistier, but still he went flashing round, the blown '1,100' sounding superb. When vision must have been down to twenty or so yards this intrepid driver came in, pulled off his helmet and said, in his northern accent, 'It's fun, I enjoyed that'—which was more than his manager Mike Costin did, I'll bet my boots!

Came Monday, our big day, and with an early start essential, we left a message to be called at half past four. Unfortunately, the porter overslept and we were woken at half past five, losing a precious hour. Whilst having a hasty breakfast, we went over the plan of campaign. This was to be two hour five minute drives for the first five stints, leaving, after deducting time for pit stops, about one hour thirty-five minutes for the last driver. The driver order was to be myself first, then Bill, Ron third, then back to me, Bill and either Ron or I for the last part of the 12-hours. Two hours and five minutes was a long drive in one stretch, but by doing this, we were saving valuable pit stops, and having to average over 120 m.p.h. to beat the M.G. records meant we had no time to waste.

We had some difficulty in getting through the gates of the Park, and arrived at the track at about six fifteen. Vic, Sid, and and I got all the equipment into the pits, and Ron, Frank, and

Bill made their final checks on the Cooper. We had planned our
start for six thirty, but the minutes ticked away and I climbed
into the car and drove to the line at six fifty-seven, finally
getting the O.K. to start at seven o'clock. This late start meant
driving about twenty-five minutes in the dark if we kept going.

With the prospect of over two hours at the wheel, I settled
myself comfortably. Equipped with brand new tyres and a
practically new engine, I had only to keep going around at
1 minute 16 seconds to put the second driver well on his way.
As it turned out, I had no worries of any kind except slight
fatigue towards the end of my drive. We made a very good pit
stop and away went Bill for his 125 minutes-worth. As we
timed his laps, he appeared most inconsistent, varying between
1 minute 13 seconds and 1 minute 18 seconds—a wide margin
for him. By a process of elimination by pit signals, we learnt that
the rev. counter had packed up, making it very difficult to
keep up an even speed. Soon, however, he got the hang of it
and lapped within a much smaller margin.

Just after he had been driving for an hour, he gave a sign
that he was in trouble in the cockpit, but it could not have
been too serious as he pressed on at his set speed. Although we
again tried to pinpoint the trouble on the sign-board, we were
not successful, and I thought how useful some kind of a walkie-
talkie attached to the car would have been. After ninety
minutes' driving Bill again pointed to the cockpit when he
came round, the engine sounded in the pink so we were very,
very puzzled. We stuck out a sign 'Do you want to come in'
after he had been going one hour forty minutes, to which he
replied 'Yes'. We hurriedly prepared the equipment and Ron
got ready to take over. Five minutes later we called him in and
found the floor under the spare seat awash with oil, which
Frank quickly traced to a leak from the oil cleaner, soon cured
by tightening up the nut. We all did our set jobs and got Ron
away sharpish. Then Bill explained his actions, as he noticed
the oil running through into the cockpit, he had wondered
what had happened and as everything was working perfectly,
including the oil gauge, he had assumed that the leak could
not have been serious. Nevertheless, he decided to come in for
inspection when the oil was level with the chassis tube at the
side of him, which, sensibly, he did.

Meanwhile, Ron had mastered driving without a rev.
counter and was lapping very consistently around 1 minute
16 seconds; all being well, we could look forward to him taking

the car over the six-hour mark. We seemed to be over the worst with the oil leak cured and the engine running very freely, we settled down to giving Ron all the encouragement possible with our usual rude signs, some of which he replied to in the true Churchillian manner. He was driving beautifully and soon had his first hour behind him. Including pit stops we were averaging about 122 m.p.h., which gave us a little margin as the 1,000-mile record stood at 117·48 m.p.h. and we only had to beat this by one per cent. Ron's drive was running out and I got ready to take over. We gave him the two-hour sign and then '3 more laps'; he gave us the thumbs-up sign, he soon cleaned these up, and when he pulled into the pits, there was quite a rush to pat him on the shoulder for he was keeping us well in the hunt.

Vic measured the tyre treads and thought I would have enough on the two fronts for another two hours odd, and with all the pit work completed, away I went on the last lap of the 1,000-mile record. Everything went well for me for the first hour and a quarter, during which time I was able to lap quite easily, if desired, in 1 minute 12 seconds, proving that now it was run in, this Climax engine was equally as good as Salvadori's 1956 record engine. As usual, just when I was getting confident, I hit trouble. When travelling above the white line round the bottom corner, although I steered lightly round to complete the long wind, for a fraction of a second the car seemed to go in the opposite direction. I went cold inside, but tugged the wheel round a bit harder and made the straight; there was no trouble in a straight line, but I was certainly watching points going into the next corner. The car handled perfectly; strange, I thought. Round I went and in almost the identical spot, it happened again, but this time the car seemed as though it would go over the banking. I tugged it back and instinctively slowed. I was in a cold sweat, surely this could only mean the steering had gone, or a wheel was almost off. Normally I would have slowed and pulled into the pits (providing I was able to reach it), but the awful thought of *not* doing the 1,000-mile record after all this, made me determined to keep going if humanly possible. I gently tested the steering along the straight and it seemed quite positive, so that was some comfort. Again the car went round the top bend perfectly; I just could not understand it; I had about twenty more laps to do for the record, and a long pit stop might beat us on the post, so I kept on. For self-preservation, I drove just under the white line going round the bad corner thinking, probably foolishly, that if the car went out of control, I would have further to go to the top of the banking.

I was now lapping in the 1 minute 20 seconds region, and the pit was getting worried. They stuck out the 'faster' sign; I cursed them heartily—full of self-pity I said to myself, 'Here I am sticking me neck out and all those silly sods can say is go faster!' As the wander was not improving, I slowed even more, consequently the pit stuck out two boards with 'faster' on them! I pointed frantically to the front of the car and next time round they had removed the 'faster' signs. Again I pointed to the front, they realized that I was in some sort of trouble and left me alone, luckily I had a slight margin in hand, thanks to Ron's superb drive, and the pit had obviously worked out that even at my slower speed, we would still get the record for they put out the O.K. sign, so all I had to do now was keep the car on the track. As the remaining laps went by, the handling did not get any worse and I was able to cope much better at the reduced speed. To make absolutely sure that we had done the distance I was not called in until about two laps after the thousand miles, in case our lap scoring was wrong. I heaved a sigh of relief as I drew in. Bill was ready to take over and I told him what a dicey do he was in for, warning him that if it got any worse, it would be better to come in rather than take any risks. As we were talking, Sid had removed the off-side front tyre, and he shouted to us to look-see. The tyre was worn in patches, parts were worn quite smooth and yet other parts had quite a lot of tread on them! Both Sid and Bill were convinced that with two new tyres on the front, the car would behave perfectly. I asked Bill to be careful first time round; we got him away in chase of the 2,000-km. record.

Ron and I hugged each other with glee that we had finally got the thousand-mile record, and we went over to the time-keeper's hut to get the confirmation slip. He shook his head and Meregali who was with us, said he would wait and get it for us. Bill came round giving the O.K. sign, and on his first flying lap, we timed him at 1 minute 13 seconds, so Sid must have been right—my trouble was the uneven tyre. When Bill returned a 1 minute 12 second lap we were not worried any longer, but up came Meregali with the timekeepers' slip. Ron looked at me in black despair, the figure in kilometres worked out at 118 m.p.h., not sufficient margin to beat the M.G. record, so after all we had failed. I am ashamed to say that I lost my temper with poor old Meregali and shouted that it was impossible and was about to give the timekeepers a mouthful, but the little Italian restrained me and asked me to leave it to him. He went into the timekeepers' box where he engaged in deep conversation with the officials. Meanwhile, I walked up and down outside fuming. Quite unconscious of this drama, Bill went on his way with the comforting thought that we had broken one record. I peered through the glass box and the timekeepers were busy rechecking the lap times, and after what seemed like an eternity, Meregali's face wreathed in smiles and he came rushing out with another slip, which showed that the timekeepers *had* made a mistake and we *had* broken the record! What a relief! Official time—120·55 m.p.h. Now at least we could all relax and leaving the old reliables, Vic and Sid, to give Bill his lap times, I took Ron into the bar for a snorter of black coffee.

When we returned to the pit, all was well. There was Sid sprinting out with the board every lap as he had done all day. At a modest estimate, he must have covered fifteen miles! We urged him to take time out, but not our Sid, he was determined to see the thing through. With Bill picking up time, the situation looked at its brightest; he should get the 2,000-km. just after the car had been going ten and a quarter hours. I had thought of taking the final spell myself as part if it would be in the dark, but on the face of things, if Ron did the final drive, we would each have taken a record, which would be fair and just. I asked Ron what he thought about this and he was all for it. I emphasized to him that if he did not feel too confident at any time during his drive, he should come in and I would take over. He said he would, his only worry about driving in the dark was that he might hit a hare, which was certainly not impossible! Cliff Allison, Mike Costin and Jabby Crombac had all joined us in the pits and as the day drew on, we urged Bill on to his destination. To all intents and purposes, he seemed to be having an easy ride, and notwithstanding the time lost on the last rather long pit stop, he was increasing slightly our overall average. The time passed very quickly and once again, we let Bill do two more laps than necessary before giving him the 2,000-km. record sign; time—120·74 m.p.h.

Bill came in looking remarkably fresh and Ron took over to do the last hour and thirty-five minutes for the 12-hour record. Once again he drove very consistently and the laps soon began to mount. Meregali had asked us earlier whether we would require some extra lighting on the corners when it got dark. When we agreed, he had raked out some very heavy blinking lamps which he said would be useful. As it was now getting towards lighting-up time, he cycled down on his bike and placed them in position. Unfortunately, he placed two of them actually on the track at the junction where one road goes round the Inner Circuit and the other leads to the Outer Circuit. As it gradually began to get darker, the strain of the day began to tell on me and I popped off to the bar for some liquid refreshment. I could hear the car roaring round as sound as a bell, so I took about fifteen minutes off. Then Vic came in with his lap scoring chart and told me that Ron was slowing and he thought he would have to be speeded up if we hoped to pull off the 12-hours. We returned to the pit and started doing sums; on the face of it, it was going to be a very close thing. By now it was quite dark and Ron could not be expected to keep up the same speed as he had been doing in full daylight. The arc lights were switched on above the pits so that Ron could see our signals better, and meanwhile he was lapping slower and slower. When he got down to 1 minute 24 seconds, I thought that I should call him in, but a quick sum showed that with only about twenty minutes to go, a pit stop would lose us the record, it was cut so fine. So the only other alternative was to try and speed him up. Sid put out the 'faster' sign, but it did not help.

With such a short time to go, every second counted, and when we pushed the 'faster' sign out again and Ron did not speed up, I wondered if he was able to see the board coming from the darkness into the glare of the pits, so next time he came round I stood right out in the full glare of the arc lights and made vigorous motions with both hands sweeping him along. As he passed, I walked back to the pit, when to my horror, I heard a most terrific crash, then a flash of light and then in the distance a red glare and smoke. Mike Costin and Meregali got the track tender going and chased down to the wrecked car. Frank and I followed in the Jaguar, but there was nothing any of us could do: the car was a blazing funeral pyre for poor Ron; he had crashed into one of the winking lights, hitting it square with his off-side front tyre. The car had shot into the air and landed thirty yards down the track on its back. Ron did not have a chance, he must have been mercifully killed outright, with only sixteen minutes to go to achieve his greatest ambition.

THE RECORD-BREAKING COOPERS

Records

Driver—W. D. Knight; International Class 'K' (up to 250 c.c.)

50 km.	..	..	.. 96·326 m.p.h.
50 miles	..	..	.. 97·602 m.p.h.
100 km.	..	..	.. 97·786 m.p.h.
1 hour	..	..	.. 97·260 m.p.h.
100 miles	..	..	.. 97·184 m.p.h.

Drivers—W. D. Knight, R. Searles and A. Owen; International Class 'G' (750 c.c.–1,100 c.c.)

1,000 miles..	..	..	120·55 m.p.h.
2,000 km. ..	..	..	120.74 m.p.h.

On the subject of records we have frequently been asked whether they are a good paying proposition; the answer may be found in the following:

1955 First attempt, Montlhéry 250-c.c. Expenses £420, returns nil.

1955 Second attempt, Montlhéry 1,100-c.c. Three drivers shared profit of £81.

1956 Monza attempt on 2-litre and 1,100-c.c.—profit £60.

1957 Monza attempt on 250-c.c. and 1,100-c.c.—excluding car, loss of £1,200.